MAVERICK

MAVERICK

FIFTY YEARS OF INVESTIGATIVE REPORTING

FRED J. COOK

G. P. PUTNAM'S SONS / NEW YORK

Copyright © 1984 by Fred J. Cook
All rights reserved. This book, or parts thereof,
must not be reproduced in any form without permission.
Published simultaneously in Canada by
General Publishing Co. Limited, Toronto.

Designed by Richard Oriolo

THE TEXT OF THIS BOOK IS SET IN CALEDONIA

Library of Congress Cataloging in Publication Data

Cook, Fred J.
Maverick: fifty years of investigative reporting.

1. Cook, Fred J. 2. Journalists—United States—Biography. I. Title.
PN4874.C665A35 1984   070′.92′4 [B]   84–4813
ISBN 0–399–12993–6

Printed in the United States of America

FOR IRENE,
Who Helped Me to Live Again

Contents

Introduction

FRED J. COOK HAS THE LOOK OF A FARMER. NOT ONE OF those big growers, just a hardworking, weatherbeaten farmer, out of Iowa or one of the Dakotas. Even his speech has a rural drawl, slow and reflective. Don't be fooled. He may be the finest investigative journalist in the land, as close to Lincoln Steffens as you'll find.

Look at his record.

He was among the first to challenge John Edgar Hoover. This was at a time when our chief cop was approaching sainthood. It was a time of Joe McCarthy's flowering. It was a time when discreet newspaper people kept their mouths shut and their typewriters clean. Except when they discovered a red or two under the occasional bed. Or if they couldn't find one, they invented one. Oh, as Mahalia Jackson used to say, it was a time, children.

Fortunately for us—though it did *his* fortunes not much good— Fred Cook was not discreet. He was a reporter and he felt that his job was to dig out the truth, to gnaw at the bone of truth like a famished dog, and to report it to you and me. It didn't matter how "hands off" the subject was, Cook, like Kilroy, was there.

He did nothing fancy. He was an old-time craftsman, who had a job to do. At a time of so much brass check journalism, he was naive enough and stubborn enough and skilled enough to come up with some of the most important stories of our epoch. He has yet to be adequately honored.

Sure, he's a four-time winner of the Newspaper Guild Award for Investigative Journalism; and you could name several more. Honored among his peers, yes. Leonard Downie wrote that Cook, in the 1950s and 1960s, "stood out to those who followed his work as a modern Lincoln Steffens, breaking new ground and making it possible for the muckraker to once again be an important force in American journalism." Yet, how Fred Cook came to be the maker of waves has not yet been told. In this fascinating memoir, we find out. It should be mandatory reading for any college journalism class.

For the past 30 or so years, Fred Cook has been on a crusade. He's now in his early seventies. This tells us that a newspaperman in his forties became a born-again investigative journalist. This would never have occurred to Hildy Johnson, who is far more celebrated for having made *The Front Page* by shooting fish in a barrel. Editor Walter Burns (in the flesh, Walter Howey, a Hearst bully and toady), equally celebrated by Hecht and MacArthur, would never have given Fred Cook his watch. He'd have fired him. Cook spelled trouble; his targets were too big.

On the New York *World-Telegram* he was considered one of the fastest and best rewrite men in town. This was in the '40s. Who knows? Had he behaved himself, he might have become a fairly high-salaried editor. It was not to be. He had that worm inside him, eating away: a natural antipathy toward heavyweights ganging up on featherweights, in the name of Americanism. Fred's trouble is he was just old-fashioned. He actually believed the Bill of Rights meant what it said.

Consider his coverage of the William Remington case in the '50s. HUAC was having a high old time. Alger Hiss had been sent up. Domestic scandals had been knocked off the front page by further discoveries of treason among government employees, schoolteachers, dentists, spot welders and neighboring scrubwomen. In this climate, Remington was convicted of being a red and a spy. Cook's chapter-and-verse coverage of the shameful trial and crucifixion (Remington was subsequently killed in prison) is a classic in dogged, truly responsible journalism. Federal Judge Learned Hand declared he was more disturbed by this case than any other in all his years on the bench.

Consider his exposé of the CIA at a time when nobody in his right mind would take on our cloak-and-dagger heroes. Ten years later, the Senatorial committees of Church and Rockefeller looked into the matter. They found things worse than even Fred had reported. At the time, President Eisenhower, in his farewell speech, warned us of the military-industrial complex, Cook had already been looking into it and came up with a devastating book. The misuse of energy, corruption in high office, organized crime, medical malpractice (set off by the tragic, unnecessary death of his wife) were among his other perverse grails. He's still at it. He doesn't know when to quit.

Studs Terkel
Chicago, February 1984

MAVERICK

1

The Nightmare Decade

HAVING REACHED THE AGE OF ELDERLY ASTONISHMENT—amazed to find myself in my seventies, amazed at how I got so far so fast—I sometimes find myself looking back on my younger self almost as I might look at a stranger. Was that younger fellow really me? And how, unless it was destiny, did he ever get himself involved in so many controversial subjects without even trying?

I pick him up, in this backward look, at what was to prove to be the turning point in his career. It was the late 1950s, and the writer I see seems far removed from myself. He had been a newspaperman for more than twenty years; he was in his forties, no longer young except in spirit; and his real career, though he did not know it, was about to be born.

If someone had asked him, he probably would have said that he had seen just about everything and that nothing could surprise him anymore. And, indeed, he had seen and done so much that one might even expect him to have some justification for such a naive belief.

As a young reporter, he had unearthed the manner in which a first-degree murder case had been fixed; had established the size of the payoff, to whom it had been made and where—and he had been frustrated by his inability to do anything about it. He had seen all the machinery of justice used to protect cretins of the mob—and at the same time to indict, pursue, harass to his death the courageous country editor who had tried to stand up for the cause of justice.

In 1953, as a rewrite man for the New York *World-Telegram and Sun,* he had written a series of articles that exposed the way in which Mafia chieftains had set up headquarters in northern New Jersey; how they had controlled the forces of law and justice and had even extended their influence into the State House in Trenton.

His crime reporting had attracted so much attention that when war broke out in the Mafia after Frank Costello was shot and Albert Anastasia murdered, the mob had adopted the unprecedented tactic of telephoning *him* to deliver public warnings to their next potential victim.

Two themes, I think, had run through his career up to this point. He had never become jaded and blasé as some reporters do; he had never lost his capacity for indignation, the almost visceral impulse to become aroused at what he perceived to be either corrupt or unjust. And he had never lost a trait that seemed to have been born in him—an insatiable curiosity, a driven compulsion to strip away surface veils and get to the very bedrock of events.

With all of this, he had remained as he had been all his life, a quiet and uncombative fellow. Throughout his years as a newspaperman (he always preferred that term to the more pretentious "journalist"), what he had wanted most was to get the daily chore done for his newspaper and then get home to his wife and family. He had not gone out of his way to seek out scandal, to cause trouble; but somehow issues that he couldn't ignore always seemed to be rising up out of nowhere and hitting him in the face. And whenever this happened, he had always found that he could not turn his back; he wrote what he found because he just *had* to, because the very essence of his being, his self-respect, wouldn't let him turn his back on corruption or injustice.

Why did that other self of myself that I see get so involved when so many others didn't? One reason probably, given the writer's particular mind-set, was that inequities always nagged at him and compelled him to dig harder, look deeper. Even as a boy, he had always wanted to know the "why" of things. Looking back over all the years that have passed, I can see him now about to enter high school, thirteen years old, a tall, spindly youth all arms and legs like a young colt from having grown too fast. He is sitting with his mother, a former schoolteacher, who is trying to prepare him for the mysteries of algebra. "Now X equals zero," she says. He stops her there. "Why does it equal zero?" "Because it does." "But why does it? Why doesn't it equal 10 or 100?" "Because (exasperated now) it doesn't. You just have to understand that X equals zero. You have to accept that." The boy shakes his head. He doesn't like accepting the dictum that X must equal zero, and he and algebra, though they declare a mutual truce, never got on what you might call familiar terms.

Anyone can see the lad's problem. If one is born with a brain that can accept the accepted without question, one may slide through life avoiding a lot of trouble. But what is one going to say about the kind of mind that wants to know the "how" and "why" of everything before it is satisfied about anything? That kind of mind can be troublesome, even dangerous to some. As a renegade police chief once said when the young man was just starting out as a reporter, green and untested, "He can cause more trouble with that typewriter of his than any ten men in town."

A maverick intellect of this nature was at particular hazard in that period of the 1950s, where I pick up the writer's story. It was the era he would later label *The Nightmare Decade* in a book he wrote trying to describe it. It was the period when a demagogic junior senator from Wisconsin, Joseph R. McCarthy, rampaged up and down across the land, inventing a domestic Communist menace as the flail to drive the Democrats from the throne rooms of government. Irresponsible with facts and figures, reveling only in the headlines he created, McCarthy convinced a large proportion of the American public that there was a Communist lurking under every other bed—especially in official Washington—and in the process he imposed on the nation an entire decade of terrorized conformity.

Past associations, past beliefs—however brief, however tenuous, however innocent at the time—became the standards by which a person could be labeled, much as a postal clerk files an envelope in a given pigeonhole. If one had had the mischance to attend a "wrong" cocktail party in the 1930s—worse, heaven forbid, if one had had the misfortune to shake hands with a "wrong" man—one was automatically a "pinko" or a "fellow traveler," terms that could put one's livelihood in jeopardy. In such an atmosphere, dissent of any kind became suspect; only "eggheads" used their brains, and they were derided as some kind of unnatural species for having the temerity to do so.

The writer's newspaper was committed to the propagation of this Communist-menace hysteria. Its publisher, Roy W. Howard, had originally supported the presidency of Franklin D. Roosevelt; but after Roosevelt's landslide re-election victory in 1936, the paper's policy had done a 180-degree turn. Some said it was because Roy Howard was miffed at not being named Ambassador to the Court of St. James's; others suggested that the New Deal's encouragement of unions (why, there was even a Newspaper Guild with which publishers had to bargain) was the cause of the rift. Whatever the reason, there could be no doubt about the fact. The paper was almost virulently anti-Democrat, and its favorite tactic was to tie the supposed Communist menace to Democratic Party coattails.

Frederick Woltman was the paper's chief Red-baiter, backed by imitators like Victor Lasky and Nelson Frank. Woltman's assigned task was to discover daily, if possible, some horrifying example of Commies or "fellow travelers" undermining our society from within; and these disclosures were regularly featured on page one.

The writer was disgusted by the performance, but he was not personally involved in it. He concentrated on writing about another menace that he considered more fascinating and more real: the underworld of the Mafia and its pervasively corrupting political ties. Since he never made any secret of his true feelings (an unfortunate characteristic of his), his superiors were usually happy to let him do his thing, an activity that kept him isolated from their more serious endeavor of brainwashing the American public.

However, from his rewrite desk cheek-by-jowl alongside the city desk, the writer got an insider's view of the paper's favorite propaganda ploy, and so he came to know Fred Woltman fairly well. Woltman was a chubby man, balding, with rather thick, rubbery-looking lips that could either twist into a skeptical smile or flap almost faster than he could get the words out when he was excited by some discovery.

The writer had handled some exposés on which Woltman had done much of the reporting, and a kind of mutual respect had developed between the two. It was the respect of one professional for another. Woltman had won many honors for the paper, capped by the Pulitzer Prize in 1948 for distinguished reporting in a series of 1946–47 articles exposing Communist influence in key labor unions and some lesser branches of city government. Those were the immediate postwar years, when Communist influence was at its height; but even after the party's strength faded, as it quickly did, our paper kept up a drumfire about the supposed Communist menace. Woltman was assigned the task of finding Communists or fellow travelers everywhere he could, and his handling of this pet project had given him a close personal relationship with the front office. It had not, however, made him a hypocrite. Unlike some of his fellow Red-baiters, he did not manufacture Communist horror tales out of whole cloth, and he frankly admitted in private conversations that the Red scare was wildly exaggerated.

Communists had labeled Woltman "Freddie the Fink." In their view, an old comrade had turned against them. The writer thought it was a nasty, unfair term. He never knew, nor much cared, whether Woltman had ever belonged to the party, for he respected the Woltman whom he knew. This was a many-sided newsman, too capable to be denigrated by a term like "Freddie the Fink." Unlike some of his fellow Red-baiters, Woltman could handle any story that came along. The task of a rewrite man on a big afternoon paper was one of the most difficult in the business. When major stories broke during the day, often almost at deadline, he had to transform a flood of chaotic incoming notes into readable, vigorous copy with a copyboy standing at his elbow to snatch the story out of his typewriter a paragraph at a time. Feature writers, accustomed to taking hours toiling over their prose, simply went to pieces under this kind of pressure. But not Woltman. On days when all the rewrite men were pounding away furiously—and still another story broke—the city editor would simply say, "Get Woltman up here." And Woltman would leave his desk in the feature section at the back of the newsroom and fill the void as capably as anyone could.

This association with Woltman, both as a reporter working a story and as a rewrite man, developed in the writer a respect for

Woltman's ability and his basic integrity. A couple of incidents are illustrative. One involved a major speech, at the start of the 1952 presidential campaign by Adlai Stevenson, at the time an unknown quantity, the dark horse on whom President Harry S Truman had bestowed the Democratic Party's nomination during the maneuvering at the national convention. Shortly afterward, when Stevenson came to New York to address a veterans' convention, Woltman was assigned to cover the event and assess the new candidate. He came back almost babbling in his excitement.

"This guy is fantastic—just fantastic," he said, waving his hands about. "He was speaking before a hostile audience, and you should have heard him. He stood there and faced them down. He was brilliant, absolutely brilliant. I tell you I think he gained their respect. He is really *something*." He paused, rolled his eyes in the direction of the front office. "You know," he said, "he just might pull it off. Wouldn't *that* be something?" He giggled at the prospect of the nation's press lords' possible discomfiture.

The reaction was typical of that in many a newsroom during the Roosevelt-Truman years. Every four years, front-office moguls would build up their hopes that a Landon or Wilkie or Dewey would tumble "that man" or his successor, Truman; and on election nights, when the votes had been counted, the high and mighty would slink away in disgust, and their working stiffs would enjoy a brief high of quiet triumph. Woltman, despite his ties to the front office, had enough of the mischievous little boy in him to appreciate that feeling.

The second incident that the writer always remembered resulted from Woltman's aftershock following a night on the town with Howard Rushmore, his counterpart in Red-baiting for the New York *Journal-American*. Rushmore had confided gleefully that he had just written a sensational exposé for a scandal magazine with a huge national circulation. Rushmore's concoction fantasized a Communist cell working right in the White House during Franklin D. Roosevelt's administration. Imagine, right in the White House! To achieve this picture, Rushmore had linked together three prominent New Dealers who had been targets of Red-baiting Congressional committees: Lauchlin Currie, a Presidential adviser; Alger Hiss, the bright State Department official who had been convicted of perjury and sent to prison; and Harry Dexter White, a Treasury Department official.

Woltman, who knew intimately all the details of Congressional hearings, had protested. "You can't do that," he told Rushmore. "They never worked together anywhere in government, and two of them never worked in the White House. White was in Treasury and Hiss in State." "Oh, I know that," Rushmore had answered airily, "but it makes a good story. Besides, Hiss has been convicted, and dead men [both Currie and White had died by this time] can't sue, can they?"

As he told the story, Woltman's hands fluttered and his rubbery lips flapped up and down. "Can you imagine *that?*" he asked. "Can you believe it?" His voice rose in incredulity.

This and similar incidents convinced the writer that Woltman in his private moments was dead on the level, and so he stopped Woltman one day as Woltman was passing his rewrite desk. The paper was flaunting another spy scare in a huge eight-column headline. Hadn't the story been blown all out of proportion? he asked Woltman.

Though Woltman had written the story, he made no attempt to defend its treatment. "Oh, sure, it's exaggerated," he said. "It's a story all right, but it's not all that important. Nothing much will ever come of it."

Wasn't the paper's whole emphasis on the Communist menace phony? the writer asked.

Woltman lowered his voice so that the nearby city desk wouldn't hear. "Look at it this way," he said. "Even J. Edgar Hoover's highest figure at the height of the movement put the party's membership in the entire nation at only 80,000. What is that in a nation of more than 120 million people? Oh, sure, there were places where they were strong enough to cause trouble. In New York, at its peak, the party probably had some 8000 to 10,000 members, and some of these were in key positions in important unions. But most of the unions cleaned up their own houses long ago. Sure, it's blown all out of proportion, but [with a shrug] that's what they want."

I recall that conversation as best I can these many years later because it was in its way the prelude to an event, completely unanticipated, that was to change the crime writer's life and plunge him into the world of political controversy.

2

Witch-Hunters:
The Remington Case

IT WAS MIDAFTERNOON ON A WINTER DAY EARLY IN 1957.
We had met the last big deadline, and all that remained was
the minor chore of updating a few stories for the final edition.
I was sitting at my rewrite desk, idle for the moment, waiting for
four o'clock and the chance to catch my commuter train home.
Joe Janoff, who monitored our city desk telephones, turned to
me and said in a low voice, "Fred, pick up on two."

I put on the headphones, flipped up the switch on my rewrite
desk and passed the word to our telephone operator. It was Ed
Fitzgerald, then the editor of *Saga*, a men's magazine for which
I had written occasional articles.

"Fred," he said, "we've been wondering whether you could
do a good, in-depth piece for us on William Remington. We'd
like to answer the question why a man like Remington from a
good family background, a choirboy in his youth, later became a
Communist and a spy. It's like the Alger Hiss case. What moti-
vates such men? We'd like to get some insight into what changes
men from such good, solid, conservative backgrounds into Communists and traitors to their country. Do you think you could do
that for us?"

The Republicans in 1948 had made the issue of Communists-
in-government the cornerstone of their campaign to install Gov-

ernor Thomas E. Dewey in the White House, with the Hiss and Remington cases held up as proof of the charges. Both were, in fact, prosecutions with political purposes; and both have much to tell us about the quality of justice our judicial system administers when it becomes subservient to a paranoia that sweeps the land.

Alger Hiss, who had held several key State Department posts, had been accused by Whittaker Chambers, a former Communist and editor of *Time* magazine, of having been a Communist in the 1930s and having been a spy who passed secret documents to Chambers. When Hiss denied both charges under oath, he was indicted for perjury, tried twice, convicted and sent to prison. This all happened after he had sued Chambers for libel and after Chambers, in self-defense, had produced copies of State Department documents that he testified had been passed to him by Hiss.

Remington's case, though less sensational, had helped to foster in the public mind the impression that Communists were lurking everywhere under the New Deal umbrella. Elizabeth Bentley, a prominent informer, accused Remington, a government economist, of having been a party member and a spy. Like Hiss, Remington fought the charges. He was tried and convicted twice. The first conviction had been set aside on legal grounds, but the second was upheld. Remington was sent to a federal penitentiary, where he was murdered by criminal inmates.

Even though I was aware that much of the press (including my own newspaper) had overplayed the political drama of the Communist menace, I had never had any doubts about the validity of the Hiss and Remington cases. In Remington's case, Nelson Frank had written an article about Bentley's disclosures in advance; and we had the story ready to run with an eight-column headline the instant she took the stand before a Senate investigating committee. If I had had any tendency to be suspicious of this setup, the Hiss case had poisoned and closed my mind. When Chambers produced those secret *documents*, I was convinced of Hiss's guilt and, by a not wholly logical extension of reasoning, of Remington's.

So I told Fitzgerald that I knew a little about the Remington case and I would see what I could do. As I hung up, I saw Fred Woltman coming toward my desk. I told him about the assignment I had just accepted—and got my first shock.

"W-e-l-l," Fred said, puckering his lips and drawing the word out, "I don't know whether you can do that or not."

"Why not?" I asked. "Remington was tried twice and convicted both times, wasn't he?"

"Y-yes," Fred said hesitantly, "but largely on the testimony of his ex-wife, and you know how ex-wives are."

Fred had had some marital difficulties himself, and he obviously had little faith in an ex-wife's allegiance to the unadulterated truth.

"But it was more than that," I protested. "There was Elizabeth Bentley too."

Fred leaned on the edge of my desk. "W-e-l-l," he said again, this time with a smile, "I never put too much faith in Elizabeth Bentley. Oh, she had belonged to the party all right, and she knew some things. But I never knew how much she embroidered on the information that she had. You know, there was one time during the Remington affair when she went into such a blue funk that they had to take her down to a hideout in Louisiana and dry her out."

Woltman had so distrusted Bentley, he said, that he had ducked writing her story and let Nelson Frank handle it. He shook his head.

"I don't know," he said. "I think you've got a tough one. I'm not sure you'll be able to prove that Remington ever was a Communist, and I'm afraid the best you'll be able to do will be to leave it up in the air. Was he or wasn't he?"

I was stunned. I had counted on getting some good leads from Woltman—and here he was telling me that he had doubts about the entire case. Woltman had presented me with an unexpected problem. Had Remington ever been a Communist? The whole scandal was predicated upon his alleged membership in the Communist Party; if that turned out to be untrue, there never should have been a case.

I began the laborious task of digging through piles of clippings, records of Congressional hearings, trial records and affidavits. The more I probed, the more I found my head in a whirl. William W. Remington was an exceedingly complex character. There were moments when I was convinced that he must have been a Communist; other times he seemed more like the all-American boy.

The only son of well-to-do, talented parents, Remington had been brought up in Ridgewood, New Jersey, an exclusive residential community near New York. His father, Frederick C. Remington, was an insurance company executive; his mother, an art teacher in New York City. A strong religious motif ran through Remington's life from earliest youth. He had been a choirboy at St. Elizabeth's Protestant Episcopal Church; later, he had become fascinated with the Oxford Group, a sect that called for an international renaissance looking to the dictatorship of the spirit of God. Remington later testified that, through this training, "I became more than usually concerned with helping the underdog as part of my religious philosophy."

Still, a hint of incipient radicalism showed in the Ridgewood High School 1934 yearbook, where he was described as a future "Union Square soapboxer" and an active orator whose aspiration was "to die a genius of the first water—unrecognized."

Remington's potential was obvious. He was just sixteen when he entered Dartmouth College, and the events of these years were crucial. Remington himself admitted that, as a freshman, his political philosophy "moved left quite rapidly." He believed in government ownership and control of industry, in splitting up big business and in "highly progressive income taxes." He felt labor unions provided an answer to what was "unchristian" in society.

During the 1936–37 school year, Remington decided to work for a year and save money. He got a job as a laborer and farmhand in the Midwest, then went to work for the Tennessee Valley Authority as a messenger. Next he became an organizer for the Worker's Alliance, a union composed of WPA workers, and he and another Alliance worker were badly beaten up when they tried to organize hosiery factory employees in Cookville, Tennessee. Remington later testified that his year of hard knocks left him "a lot less sure of the notions I'd had when I left college" because some of his ideas had been "exploded in the South."

One witness would describe Remington at this time as a wild-looking young man who flitted about the countryside on a motorcycle, his clothing hanging in rags and his shoes so dilapidated that he had to tie the flapping soles to the tops with pieces of string.

However, on his return to Dartmouth he was the same brilliant student that he had been. He was one of seven seniors who were allowed to bypass the regular curriculum and choose their own course of study; he was one of two seniors in the student government; and he was top man in his graduating class.

The impression I had of Remington then was of an over-intellectual, perhaps erratic, young man. But had he ever been a Communist? Some of his activities and opinions as a youth had certainly been radical, but he later described some of these ideas as half-baked. Though he had advocated his beliefs "extensively and loudly," by his own admission he seemed always to have drawn the line at Communism. He claimed never to have agreed with Marxist theories of the dictatorship of the proletariat, revolution, or the suppression of religion. Remington remained devoted to concepts of racial equality, and he was always passionately anti-Fascist.

I certainly knew that the 1930s were a time of political and intellectual ferment. Actions taken during that period could look far different in the conservative climate of 1948; they could make Remington *look* like a Communist. But had he ever really been one?

I was stewing in indecision and confusion when a friend and colleague took pity on me and told me that he had been a classmate of Remington's at Dartmouth. He gave me this description:

> He was exceptionally brilliant. Some of the letters that he and his mother used to write each other were marvels of English composition; they read like something out of Bertrand Russell.
>
> Remington, although he was younger than the rest of us, was tall, strong and handsome. He had the build of an athlete, but he wasn't interested in trying to make the football team. He was completely wrapped up in intellectual causes. He felt the mentally brilliant had a moral obligation to devote themselves to the cause of the underdog, the underprivileged.
>
> My roommate, who was a Catholic and very conservative, looked askance at Remington and the intellectual crowd he ran with. To him, they were all a bunch of lefties and radicals, if not outright Communists. To me, Remington seemed more like an intellectual snob.
>
> He was active in the American Students Union, which had a number of Commies in it, but that didn't necessarily prove

that Remington himself was a Communist. In fact, I remember very vividly one incident that convinced me he wasn't.

In the middle and late thirties, the Communists were energetically wooing the more intellectual students in our colleges. Once, up at Darmouth, I was with a group that included Remington when a couple of these Communist organizers approached us and gave us their spiel. Remington tore them apart in the most ruthless fashion and made asses of them.

I began to feel that the article I had undertaken to write could never jell the way Ed Fitzgerald had outlined it. Was I going to have to settle for Woltman's non-verdict?

I telephoned Fitzgerald. "I'm not through with my research yet," I told him, "but I've gone far enough to know that I won't be able to show that Remington ever was a Communist. I may have to leave it up in the air as to whether he was or not, or I may come to the conclusion that he never was a Communist and the whole case was a terrible miscarriage of justice."

Fitzgerald didn't hesitate. "That's all right, Fred. You go ahead and call it the way you see it. All we want is an honest piece."

I threw myself into an intensive study of the case that had sent Remington to prison—and to his death.

It all began with a fateful infatuation during Remington's senior year at Dartmouth. He had been a delegate to an intercollegiate conference on foreign policy; from Bennington College in Vermont had come a slender, pretty brunette, Ann Moos. Remington was smitten. In the months that followed, he dated Ann constantly. She and her mother, Elizabeth Moos, a teacher and high-school principal who had a large home in Croton-on-Hudson, north of New York, were both ideological radicals, and Mrs. Moos was soon to become an avowed Communist. But Remington was in love. He and Ann were married in a civil ceremony on November 28, 1938; the following June, they were wed again in a religious service.

Upon his graduation from Dartmouth, Remington was torn between law and economics, chose the latter, enrolled at Columbia University, and received his masters degree in 1940. He went at once into government service, where he rose rapidly, serving in the Office of Price Administration and with the War Production

Board. He served as an ensign in Naval Intelligence during World War II, and after the war worked on the European Recovery Program and became a member of the President's Council of Economic Advisers. In 1948, he was transferred to the Commerce Department and became director of the export programs staff of the Office of International Trade. This last was a sensitive post in determining the allocation of shipments to Russia, and it was at this point that Elizabeth Bentley made her public accusation.

Elizabeth Bentley, thirty-six years old, Connecticut born, a graduate of Vassar, had been the mistress of Joseph Golos, the master Soviet spy in the United States, and she had served as his agent in gathering information from Washington contacts. After his death from a heart ailment, she had handled the espionage work alone for a time, but she became disillusioned with others in the party and had gone to the FBI in 1945 to tell her story.

She had testified before a federal grand jury that in 1948 indicted twelve national leaders of the Communist Party for conspiracy to overthrow the government. In her first disclosures, she had named Remington; her charges had been investigated but no action had been taken. Federal agents had questioned Remington in April 1947, and he testified before a grand jury in September. The evidence against him seemed insufficient, for the jury had failed to return an indictment.

The article Nelson Frank had written about "a beautiful, blond spy queen" who claimed to have had contacts in all major government departments touched off a furor. Senator Homer Ferguson, Michigan Republican and chairman of an investigating committee soon to become known as the Senate Internal Securities Committee, and William P. Rogers, the committee counsel, put Miss Bentley on the stand in a public hearing in Washington.

Now in the spotlight as a witness before Ferguson's committee, Miss Bentley was reviving her charges. She testified that she had met Remington at a dinner in New York, where Golos had told her that Remington was a Communist. Subsequently, she said, in Washington, she collected party dues from Remington for both himself and his wife.

Nearly a dozen times in 1942 and 1943, when Remington was with the War Production Board, she had "furtive" meetings with him on street corners, park benches and in secluded restaurants, she testified, and he had given her confidential information written out on slips of paper—never government documents. Some of the information, she said, related to American airplane production, and once he had given her a secret formula for making synthetic rubber out of garbage.

Remington appeared before the committee the next day, July 31, 1948. In his testimony then, in subsequent newspaper interviews, and at two trials, he told the same, unvarying story. His version confirmed the surface details of their relationship, but contradicted Miss Bentley emphatically about the specifics.

According to Remington, Joseph North, editor of the Communist publication, *New Masses*, was an old friend of his mother-in-law's, and he and Ann often met North on weekend visits to Croton-on-Hudson. The two men argued: North suspected American big business was not doing its utmost to aid the war effort; Remington tried to convince him otherwise. On one occasion North invited Remington to lunch in New York for a further discussion, and it was then, at a Schrafft's on Fourth Avenue near 31st Street, that North introduced Remington to Golos as a writer working on a book about war mobilization. Remington described Golos as about fifty years old, short, stocky and "acid in his remarks and outlook on life"; he said he felt "flattered that a writer of books should need my help," and he agreed to see Golos again when he was in New York.

At this second meeting, again at that Schrafft's, in March 1942, Remington was accompanied by his wife, and Golos brought along a woman he identified as "Helen Johnson," a researcher helping him on his book. She also did research for other writers, including some columnists on Marshall Field's experimental newspaper, *PM*. Only years later did Remington learn that "Helen Johnson" was Elizabeth Bentley.

As this second meeting broke up, Golos remarked casually that "Miss Johnson" might contact Remington when she was in Washington, and Golos hoped that Remington would see her. "Oh, sure," Remington remembered telling him offhandedly.

Not long afterward, "Helen Johnson" telephoned his office and asked him to have lunch with her—the first of their series of fateful meetings. According to Remington, the woman he knew only as "Helen Johnson" would telephone him when she was in Washington and ask to meet him, always outside the office. Remington insisted that he had suggested a couple of times that she come to his office, but she always had an excuse for not doing so.

Remington denied that he had ever paid Communist Party dues to Miss Bentley for himself or his wife, although once he gave her $30 as a donation to the Joint Anti-Fascist Refugee Committee, an organization that years later would be labeled a Communist front.

He testified that he had never given her secret information; everything he had passed to her was data publicly available to any writer willing to research government releases closely enough. On occasion, he testified, she showed him articles from Communist publications and asked him to verify certain facts.

In 1943, Remington told the Senate committee, he had become suspicious of "Helen Johnson" when he learned that she had no contact with writers at *PM*, as Golos had claimed, and he had terminated his association with her.

A noteworthy feature of both Remington's and Miss Bentley's testimony was one undisputed item: they had always met alone. There had never been any possible corroboration of Miss Bentley's charges. This explained to me why no action had been taken by federal grand juries: there was no case that would stand up in court—it was simply her word against his. How then had everything changed years later?

Remington had hardly left the Senate witness stand when he had to face a second ordeal—a hearing before the Loyalty Board to determine whether he could still hold a government job. Under suspension until this could be settled, separated from his wife and family, Remington holed up in a rented room in Alexandria, Virginia, and prepared his defense.

He soon realized that he was a marked man, living in a hostile atmosphere in which terror supplanted friendship and conscience. Fearful of wiretaps, friends in government service refused to talk to him except from pay telephone booths; many supporters faded away at the first whisper of accusations. But an impressive number stood firm, making two points: first, Remington's character was such that he would never have acted in the "furtive" manner that Miss Bentley described; second, his whole record in government service had been one that showed a strong anti-Communist bias.

The issue of character was emphasized by Remington's high-school teacher, the former president of Dartmouth, and Dean Lloyd K. Neidlinger of Dartmouth, who wrote in an affidavit: "If he believed in Communism, he might go out and preach it from a soapbox and risk being stoned by an unfriendly audience"— echoes of Remington's high-school yearbook.

Even more persuasive were the *facts* about Remington's conduct in office supplied by a number of respected and loyal officials: David K. Bruce, former assistant secretary of commerce and ambassador to France, declared that Remington had been "in favor of a tougher policy" toward Russia and that "his bias was so strongly against shipments" to Russia "that I questioned the reasonableness of his judgment in this regard on more than one occasion." Richard M. Bissell, Jr., who had been Remington's boss on the Harriman European Recovery Committee, asserted that Remington had been so enthusiastic about giving aid to Western Europe to counter Communist aggression that some of his suggestions had to be toned down.* A State Department official deposed that Remington had been much tougher-minded about Russia than State. A high military spokesman asserted that from the military's standpoint, Remington's thinking in regard to Russia had been right on the beam.

Through affidavits and personal testimony, Remington demonstrated that he had opposed the Communist Party line on at least ten major issues, including the Nazi-Soviet Pact at the outbreak of World War II and the Soviet invasion of Finland. He had supported American aid to Britain and the curtailment of postwar exports to Russia and her satellites. He had helped to draft the Marshall Plan to rebuild the war-racked economies of Western Europe and thwart Russian aggression.

It seemed incredible to me that he could ever have been prosecuted. If a man's actions counted for anything—and *actions* were *all* that should count—surely Remington should have been exonerated. But in fact he never had a chance. The atmosphere in the hearing room—an impalpable but almost overwhelming force that Remington was to encounter again and again—clearly forecast the verdict.

---

*With the passage of years, Bissell's support of Remington seems even more significant. Bissell later became deputy director for plans of the Central Intelligence Agency (in reality the chief of all covert operations). He was second in power to CIA Director Allen Dulles, and he was the principal architect of the ill-fated 1961 Bay of Pigs invasion of Cuba. Could a hard-liner of Bissell's stamp ever have been deceived about Remington's loyalty? It seems impossible.

Remington afterward described his reactions in a *New Yorker* interview:

> The whole atmosphere of the hearing made you kick yourself for everything you had ever done. Why had I ever lectured to CIO workers in Tennessee? Why had I ever made donations to help the Loyalists in Spain? Why had I ever been on peace committees at Dartmouth in 1937? What ever made me attend an American Youth Congress meeting, where I clumsily tripped over the feet of Mrs. Roosevelt? What a pity I couldn't point to a model marriage! What made me blurt out to these strangers that I believed in God, that I had been a choirboy and an acolyte in the Episcopal Church? The Board seemed to be comparing me with their ideal of a loyal American—a composite character, a perfect mediocrity who never existed. If such a man did exist, I wouldn't care to meet him, because he wouldn't have a thought in his head or a beat in his heart. I don't think any of the Board members could have filled the bill themselves.

On September 20, 1948, the Loyalty Board handed down its decision: "Reasonable grounds exist for the belief that you are disloyal to the Government of the United States."

Remington was crushed. He had an impulse, he later said, "to throw in the towel." Instead, he decided to fight for vindication, and he acquired an attorney for the first time.

Joseph L. Rauh, Jr., was chairman of the executive committee of Americans for Democratic Action, a liberal organization that rightists had tried to brand pro-Communist. Actually, ADA leaders had leaned over backward to avoid such branding, and official inquiries concluded that ADA was free of any Red taint. Even so, Remington's case was an especially controversial one for an ADA leader to handle. Rauh realized the damage that could be done if he defended Remington and Remington turned out to have been a Communist after all. So, when the two men met, Rauh cross-examined his client in his toughest courtroom style from six one evening until two the next morning. Remington's answers sounded convincing, but Rauh wanted to be certain. He spent another week investigating every aspect of Remington's life. Then he took the case.

Rauh filed an appeal with the Loyalty Review Board, and he

summoned Miss Bentley to testify. The board had no powers of subpoena, but it "invited" Miss Bentley to appear. She didn't, despite the fact that she had already gone on NBC's "Meet the Press" and repeated her charges against Remington. Since in her television appearance she was no longer in a privileged forum, Remington filed a $100,000 libel suit against Miss Bentley, NBC, and General Foods, the sponsor of the program. But she remained so elusive that Rauh found it impossible to serve her with papers in the libel suit. Several times, the Loyalty Review Board "requested" her appearance, but she always found an excuse for not showing.

Finally, on January 10, 1949, the New York *Post* caught up with her, and Miss Bentley said she had never been asked to testify. The review board promptly contradicted her—and, when she still didn't appear, it announced on February 10 that it had cleared Remington and ordered him reinstated in his government job.

Vindication! And a second triumph quickly followed. Over the protest of Miss Bentley, NBC and General Foods settled the suit for $10,000. One might have thought that Miss Bentley would now be discredited and that Remington would be left in peace. But it was not to be.

The fierce Republican campaign to drive the Democrats from the White House, Rauh would contend, was reason enough for the pursuit of Remington to continue—after all, his vindication alone posed a threat to the entire demagogic battle plan. If Remington was right, then no faith could be placed in Bentley and her tales—and possibly in the tales of other informers also—about Communist infiltration and subversion of Democratic administrations. Bentley had to be rehabilitated—which meant that Remington had to be destroyed.

In April and May 1950, the House Un-American Activities Committee reopened the case, producing evidence designed to show that Remington had been a Communist in Knoxville in 1936–37, when he worked for the Tennessee Valley Authority. Senator McCarthy, then in the early stages of his witch-hunt, thundered at Remington: Remington testified before the House committee. Another federal grand jury was impaneled in Washington; again Remington testified. And again the jury refused to indict. In a relentless prosecution that was turning into a persecution, the government called *yet another* grand jury into session in New York.

Meanwhile, behind the scenes, a significant development had taken place: Remington and his wife had been divorced, and he was soon to marry his secretary. This was to change the entire basis of the case. It all happened with the connivance of the Justice Department and a star-chamber grand jury.

The setup at the New York session was enough to make one shudder. The grand jury foreman, John Brunini, had a contract with Miss Bentley to help her prepare a book of her spy-ring adventures for the Devin-Adair Company. This book named Remington a Communist and a spy, and it could not possibly be published unless Remington was indicted and convicted. The prosecutor, Thomas F. Donegan, was a former FBI man under J. Edgar Hoover, and a lawyer who had represented Miss Bentley in a legal action that resulted in a $7500 award to her.

Once more, Remington testified before the jury and refused the safe way out: he did not plead the Fifth Amendment against possible self-incrimination. Instead, for five days, he testified to what he had always insisted—that he had never been a Communist.

On June 8, 1950, he was indicted for perjury. The indictment was based on this question-and-answer sequence on March 25:

> Q. At any time have you ever been a member of the Communist Party?
> A. I never have been.

The day the indictment was voted, Remington resigned from his government job. Now he needed a new trial counsel, and he chose a veteran New York lawyer, William C. Chanler, an independent Democrat who had served as city Corporation Counsel in the Fusion administration of Fiorello H. LaGuardia and as a corporation lawyer with offices at 40 Wall Street.

One aspect of the grand jury proceedings worried Chanler: Remington's ex-wife. He knew that Ann Remington had testified for hours before the grand jury that indicted her husband, and he wondered what had happened. In preparing his case, he went to Washington and talked to the two lawyers who had represented Mrs. Remington during the divorce action.

"They didn't like Remington because he had given them a hard time," Chanler said. "After the marriage broke up, there was a great deal of bitterness, and Remington hadn't wanted to give his wife a penny; they felt he had been a penny-pincher and had behaved very badly. Nevertheless, they both assured me that it was perfectly clear to them that he had never been a Communist."

Chanler asked them how they knew this and they explained that when Ann Remington was called to testify before the grand jury, she had consulted them, and they, of course, had her tell them her story. "It was a perfectly innocent story, and they told her to go ahead and testify to it. When she came back to Washington, she refused to tell them what had happened before the grand jury."

Chanler went to trial determined to get access to the grand jury minutes, which was the only way he could find out what testimony she might give in court; but he was blocked by a prosecution team and a judge who seemed to be acting in concert.

The prosecution was headed by U.S. Attorney Irving S. Saypol, who was aided by Bentley's former lawyer, Donegan, and a brilliant young assistant, Roy H. Cohn, who was soon to spring into page-one prominence as Joe McCarthy's legal adviser. The judge was Gregory F. Noonan, whose rulings were consistently prejudicial to the defense (a view that would indeed be confirmed later, when the entire case would be thrown out on appeal).

The trial had been billed as "a second Hiss case," and the courtroom was packed with spectators hungering for sensation. The jury was selected on December 20, 1950.

Almost immediately Chanler and Judge Noonan clashed. Chanler argued that the indictment did not spell out the crime of which Remington stood accused. What constituted proof of Communist Party membership? The government was accusing his client of lying in denying the existence of a certain status—and at the same time it was either unwilling or unable to define "what constitutes that status."

"Your argument is ingenious but without merit," Judge Noonan snapped. He added that it was "not incumbent on the government in a perjury trial to define terms relating to Communism." The defendant could say whether he was a Communist or not "and what that means," Judge Noonan ruled, saying that "the double-talk that goes on about Communism defies definition."

It was a ruling that seemed to rewrite the basic American law that considers a defendant innocent until proven guilty; here the burden of definition and therefore of proof was being shifted from the prosecution to the defendant.

After this opening exchange, the trial was adjourned until after Christmas. When it resumed, the prosecution led off with its secret weapon—Ann Moos Remington. Suddenly Elizabeth Bentley, for years the only accuser, faded into the background as the trial plunged into its most critical phase. Those tête-à-têtes to which Elizabeth Bentley and Remington had both testified repeatedly under oath became tête-à-têtes no longer. A third person, apparently invisible to both at the time, had sat in on their discussions—Remington's wife.

Chanler knew from his talks with Ann's lawyers that her original "perfectly innocent" story had been that she and Remington had never been actual members of the Communist Party; that they had met many party members through her mother, and had been well-acquainted with Joseph North, with whom Remington often argued heatedly; that Remington, indeed, had never been as far left in his philosophy as Ann herself; that, as the years passed, they had had less and less to do with her mother's Communist friends; and that, as for "Helen Johnson," they had known her only as a magazine researcher.

Now, on the witness stand, head bent, large bright eyes downcast under sharply etched brows, Ann Moos Remington, thirty-four, a slim, heart-faced brunette, told an exactly opposite story: she said Remington had always been a Communist. She had been "reluctant to marry" him until he assured her that he would "always be a Communist." At one time, she testified, Remington had been "very excited" because he wanted to give a Soviet spy some top-secret formula. She had understood that it was to make explosives out of garbage, but it may have been to make gasoline or synthetic rubber. She wasn't certain about the details, but she was positive about the incident. As for those one-on-one meetings with Elizabeth Bentley, it hadn't happened that way at all, Ann testified. They had met in the Remington family car with Ann herself present, and she had seen Remington give Miss Bentley "some pieces of paper." Arrangements had been made at the restaurant meeting with Golos in New York for "Helen Johnson" to visit them in Washington every two weeks to collect their party dues and bring them party literature.

On and on she went, damning her ex-husband with every word she spoke—and every word at variance with everything she had previously told her own lawyers. To test her account, Chanler launched a furious courtroom battle with Judge Noonan. He insisted that he had a right to inspect the grand jury minutes covering the five hours of grilling to which Ann Remington had been subjected before she agreed to testify against her husband. The law states that the defense is entitled to any exculpatory material in the possession of the prosecution. Remington's defense raised the issue time and time again, but Judge Noonan turned down every request.

Years later, when I talked to him, Chanler was still seething at Judge Noonan's rulings. "I had a right to those minutes, and I still say he had no right to refuse me—but he did. If I had had access to them at the time, if I had had them when it was vital to the defense to have them, when I should have had them, the whole outcome would have been different. I would have blown this case right out of court."

The record does show a trace of the attorney's righteous ire. After being denied the right to inspect the minutes, Chanler moved that the jury transcript be impounded (presumably, so it couldn't be tampered with). The imputation was unmistakable, and Saypol, flushed with anger, leaped to his feet. "I never heard anything so preposterous!" he stormed. "Perhaps counsel would like to take the grand jury and impound that, too."

Rauh, who was assisting Chanler, countered that this might not be a bad idea. In a sensational charge that the government was using the grand jury "for the sole purpose of intimidating" potential defense witnesses, Rauh declared that fifteen witnesses needed by the defense had been grilled before the grand jury *after* Remington's indictment. That very morning, Rauh said, two of his witnesses had been subpoenaed to appear before the grand jury. One woman was so badly frightened, he said, that she planned to plead her Fifth Amendment privilege against possible self-incrimination not only before the jury "but as a witness for us."

Saypol, furious, roared that the intimidation charge was "baseless and made up out of whole cloth." Judge Noonan upheld the prosecution, refused to curb the questioning of defense witnesses before the grand jury and refused to vacate the subpoena against the terrified woman.

In this prejudicial courtroom atmosphere, the case for the defense went steadily downhill. Chanler scored some points in cross-examining Mrs. Remington, but she stuck by the essentials of her testimony. "It was," Chanler later told me, "like trying to question a zombie."

After Ann Remington left the stand, the prosecution brought forward its one-time star witness, Elizabeth Bentley, who now appeared in the drastically altered role of corroborating Ann Remington. Had justice ever been stood so completely on its head? I had to wonder. And the process was only beginning.

When Remington took the stand, Saypol slipped in an innocuous-sounding question that, even with the verdict of this trial still undetermined, was evidently designed to lay the groundwork for future use and another upside-down contortion of the law.

"Now do you deny," he demanded, "that you had any knowledge of the Young Communist League at Dartmouth?"

"Yes," Remington replied. "With emphasis on the *knowledge*."

Chanler, years later, shook his head ruefully at the memory. "It slipped by me," he acknowledged. "I didn't attach any importance to it at the time—nor did he."

The trial closed with one final, bitter flareup between the defense and Judge Noonan. Rauh called on the government to "concede" that reports "of undercover agents and informers of the FBI inside the Communist Party" contained no mention of Remington's ever having been a member.

Saypol objected angrily, and Judge Noonan declared that "these things are entirely inappropriate at the time."

"I think if Your Honor is going to make a statement, we should be heard," Rauh insisted. "There is a basic principle that when the prosecution has evidence which will help the defendant, it is up to the prosecution to produce it, and that principle has not been properly preserved in this case."

"Are you accusing me, Mr. Rauh?" Judge Noonan demanded.

"I am not accusing anybody. I am stating—"

"From this point on, Mr. Rauh, any motions will be made by counsel in chief. You may sit down."

Red-faced, Rauh started to protest. "Your Honor, I wish to say—"

"We will take a recess," the judge snapped, rising and turning his back on the lawyer whose lips he had just sealed.

And so the case went to the jury. The panel deliberated for four hours and twenty-five minutes. At 10:12 P.M., February 7, 1951, it returned its verdict: guilty.

Judge Noonan sentenced Remington to five years in prison and wanted to rush him off to a jail cell immediately. But defense lawyers filed a protest with the Federal Court of Appeals and secured his release within twenty-four hours. They also pressed their appeal to overturn the conviction, and in so doing they at last got a look at those grand jury minutes that the prosecution and Judge Noonan in tandem had refused to show them while the trial was on—when it mattered. Even then, the court refused to let them quote directly from the minutes.

Rauh in his final brief was permitted only to summarize and refer to specific pages in the grand jury transcript at which cited testimony occurred. Even without the impact of direct quotes, the summary was devastating. Rauh wrote:

> The minutes of Ann Remington's testimony show that she told the . . . grand jury substantially the same story concerning her own and her husband's activities and beliefs that petitioner [Remington] has consistently maintained through six years of questioning. She testified that she and petitioner started off as persons interested in the American Student Union, Loyalist Spain, and labor unions who were sympathetic to Communism. She steadfastly maintained that they had never been members of the Communist Party . . . and even related that they had had the usual disillusioning experience of persons sympathetic to Communism in the 1930s when the Nazi–Soviet Pact and the Russo–Finnish War came along—two years, incidentally, before they met Bentley. Foreman Brunini's efforts to get Mrs. Remington to change her testimony by poisoning her mind with alleged lies Remington had told about her and her mother . . . and by implication that he was spending his money on a libel suit against Bentley instead of supporting her . . . were unsuccessful and Mrs. Remington stuck to her earlier answers through continuous grilling . . . , flattery . . . and threats of perjury . . . After hours of grilling—it was now about three o'clock in the afternoon—Mrs. Remington stated that she was getting fuzzy and incoherent because she hadn't eaten

for such a long time, apparently having flown up from Washington in an airplane early that morning. She repeatedly referred to her hunger and need for something to eat . . . at this stage, fuzzy and denied food, she asked whether hunger was being used on her as a third-degree weapon . . . Foreman Brunini's response to this was that the grand jury hadn't shown its teeth yet . . . Foreman Brunini's guilty conscience became evident later in the day when he asked the witness if she felt they had tried to starve her out . . . Despite the fact that Mrs. Remington at this time was "cooperating" fully with Brunini and Donegan, she indicated clearly that the answer she had given at their urging had been the result of hunger. . . .

If the facts already related could leave any possible doubt that Brunini was representing Bentley in the grand jury room, the Court's attention is respectfully invited to pages 7806 through 7809 of the grand jury minutes. There Brunini says that it is not Remington himself who is important; that he is a very minor figure in Bentley's story of her espionage activities, but he had become extraordinarily important because he had chosen to talk and fight back at Bentley. There, too, Brunini lectures Mrs. Remington (and the other grand jurors) that it is extremely important for the American people to be awakened to the dangers that have been related by the ex-Communists, such as Bentley, who have come forward and told their stories, but who have been smeared by persons such as Remington.

An even more graphic account of this star-chamber browbeating of Mrs. Remington was later supplied by Judge Learned Hand of the U.S. Court of Appeals. Judge Hand, a conservative jurist, was shocked at what he found in those grand jury minutes that Rauh had cited. He quoted directly from the record:

Pages on pages of lecturing repeatedly preceded a question; statements of what the prosecution already knew, and of how idle it was for the witness to hold back what she could contribute; occasional reminders that she could be punished for perjury; all were scattered throughout. Still she withstood the examiners, until, being much tired and worn, she said: "I am getting fuzzy. I haven't eaten since a long time ago and I don't think I'm going to be very coherent from now on. I would like to postpone the hearings . . . I want to consult my lawyers and see how deep I am getting in." This was denied, and the questioning kept on until she finally refused to answer, excusing herself because she was "tired," and "would like to get something to eat . . . Is this the third-degree, waiting until I get hungry, now?" Still the examiners persisted, disregarding this further protest: "I would like to get something to eat. But couldn't we continue another day? Or do I have to come back?"

At this point, Brunini, Miss Bentley's collaborator, took over. "Mrs. Remington, I think we have been very kind and considerate," he said. "We haven't raised our voices or shown our teeth, have we? Maybe you don't know about our teeth. A witness before the Grand Jury hasn't the privilege of refusing to answer a question." [Here he painted a picture of the manner in which a judge could send a witness to jail for refusing to answer a grand jury question.] "I said, 'Showing teeth.' I don't want them to bite you. But I do want you to . . ."

Actually, as Judge Hand pointed out, Mrs. Remington did have the privilege, which extended to all confidential communications between her and Remington while she was his wife, and a lot of her testimony dealt with just such confidences. Again, as Judge Hand emphasized, this must have been clear to Donegan, a lawyer, but he stood idly by and did nothing to correct the impression the blustering Brunini had implanted in the mind of the witness.

Innocent of her rights, threatened with jail, hungry and worn out by the unremitting ordeal of the hours of questioning, Mrs. Remington began to give the testimony Brunini and Donegan wanted from her, the testimony that would doom her former husband and the father of her two children.

Though Judge Noonan had barred Chanler from bringing any of this vital evidence before the trial jury, the U.S. Court of Appeals, in a unanimous verdict, threw out the conviction. Among its reasons, it cited the point Chanler had raised in his first clash with the judge—the refusal of the prosecution to spell out what it considered proof of Communist Party membership. Remington, its ruling stated, "did not even know at the end of the government's case what he had to meet" to properly defend himself.

But the appeals court did not throw out the entire case. It merely set aside the guilty verdict and left it up to the government to try Remington again if it wished. The government was definitely determined to do so, and once more shifted the entire basis of its case. It dropped the tainted Brunini-Donegan indictment like a grenade with the pin pulled and *then* it brought an entirely new indictment against Remington for perjury, charging that he had lied in defending himself at the first trial.

I had seen it before in a county court. After the defense exposes a fraudulent indictment, the prosecution drops *that* indictment and hounds the object of its vendetta by bringing a new charge on different grounds. It is a naked revelation of a prosecution turned into a persecution; but that is not of much help to the defendant, who still has to go to the trouble and expense of defending himself against the new charges.

This new indictment of Remington brought a lone cry of protest from the American Civil Liberties Union, which was "gravely disturbed": "It may not be a matter of double-jeopardy technically, but it is morally."

The second trial was almost perfunctory. Remington had exhausted his resources, and Chanler, who had sacrificed his law business during the long first trial, simply could not afford to represent Remington again. Remington's new lawyer was John McKim Minton, a noted New York criminal-trial attorney; a new U.S. Attorney, Myles J. Lane, represented the government; and a new judge, Vincent J. Leibell, heard the case. The trial took place in a small, tucked-away courtroom.

The government's case was basically Bentley and Ann Remington against Remington. Most spectators had little doubt about the outcome, yet the jurors had more difficulty reaching a verdict than the first jury had. They deliberated for thirteen hours before, at 3:30 A.M., January 27, 1953, they convicted Remington on two counts: lying when he denied passing secret documents to Miss Bentley and lying about *knowledge* of the Young Communist League at Dartmouth—that apparently trivial question Saypol had slipped into cross-examination at the earlier trial.

But the jury disagreed on the fundamental issue on which all else depended—whether Remington had ever been a Communist. It had not been able to decide whether he had attended a Communist meeting in Knoxville or ever paid Communist Party dues. It acquitted him on a fifth charge, ruling that he had never induced anyone to join the Communist Party.

The conviction came just as Remington's second wife, Jane, whom he had married between the two trials, was about to give birth to their child. Sentencing was postponed until after the delivery. Then, on April 15, 1953, Remington was sentenced to three years in federal prison.

Pale and a little gaunt, he made one final statement: "I have tried to tell the truth during six long years of questioning. I repeat that I was never a member of the Communist Party; I never gave secret information to anyone; and I never knowingly made a false statement."

His attorneys began the battle to free him on appeal, but the U.S. Court of Appeals, on November 24, 1953, upheld the verdict by a 2-1 vote. Judge Hand wrote a Brandeis-like dissent, arguing not only that the guilty verdict should be overturned, but also that the entire case against Remington should be thrown out because it was so badly tainted.

The second prosecution, he wrote, fell "within the implied ambit of the doctrine of 'entrapment' as well as it is within that of the doctrine against using evidence unlawfully obtained." He spelled out in detail the grand jury proceedings that had forced the turn-around testimony of Ann Remington, comparing it to star-chamber proceedings of the past and the Spanish Inquisition. The second case, in Judge Hand's view, had been manufactured on the fraudulent basis of the first—and so the entire prosecution of Remington was invalid. Afterward, he told Chanler that one of his greatest disappointments had been his inability to persuade his nephew, Judge Augustus N. Hand, also on the Appeals Court, to join him in his dissent.

Rauh, quoting Judge Hand copiously, carried an appeal to the U.S. Supreme Court; but this conservative Truman court refused even to listen. Judge Hand later confided to Chanler that he thought the Supreme Court had made a great mistake. The Remington case, he said, had disturbed him more than any case that had come before him during his long career on the bench.

It was in this Kafka-like atmosphere that Remington began serving his sentence in the Lewisburg, Pennsylvania, federal penitentiary. There, on the morning of November 22, 1954, he was found unconscious on the floor of his cell. Apparently, three hard-

ened convicts who had been looting prison cells had tried to rob
him, and when he resisted, they beat him over the head with a
cloth-wrapped brick, fracturing his skull in several places. Remington was rushed to the prison hospital and died on the operating table without regaining consciousness.

This tragedy still haunted Remington's second trial counsel,
John McKim Minton, when I talked to him three years later.
"That man was *never* a Communist," Minton said. "I *know* that.
He was too intellectually arrogant, too intellectually independent.
He would never have submitted to ironbound Communist Party
discipline. The whole thing was a tragedy."

Here I must add one shocking and horrifying footnote. When
I dug through the clippings in our newspaper morgue, I discovered a little-reported item that had appeared in the press less
than two months after Remington's murder. On January 5, 1955,
Attorney General Louis G. Wyman, of New Hampshire, filed a
289-page report on the results of his eighteen-month-long investigation of Communist activities at Dartmouth. One witness, the
attorney general said, had testified that the Communists at Dartmouth had wanted no part of Remington "because he was considered too erratic as to timing and sense of responsibility"; he
had never been a Communist in his college days.

Chanler told me that this was the very evidence that he and
Rauh had tried to produce at the first trial, the evidence that had
led to Rauh's bitter clash with Judge Noonan and to the judge's
muzzling of the defense attorney. "We had gone up to New Hampshire," Chanler said, "and we had located two witnesses, both
Communists, who knew the makeup and membership of the Communist Party and the Young Communist League in the state. One,
a woman, was a party official with access to all the membership
records. She had checked them and told us that Remington's name
definitely did not appear anywhere.

"We told them that we would call them when we needed them.
Then, I suppose, I made a mistake. I telephoned them from my
office, using my regular phone, and told them to come to New
York. The next morning when they arrived, two FBI agents were
waiting on the station platform with subpoenas for them to appear
before the grand jury. They were so frightened that they notified
us they would claim their constitutional privilege and refuse to

testify. And so we had to let them go back to New Hampshire unheard."

Unless the FBI possessed magical powers of mental telepathy, it must have gained its knowledge of the arrival time of the two essential witnesses by wiretapping Chanler's phone. The implications call the whole system of justice into question. How could any man, however innocent, defend himself when even his attorney could not communicate, unspied upon, with the witnesses vital to his defense? How could any man, however innocent, defend himself when a federal grand jury was being used as an instrument of terror to prevent his witnesses from testifying?

The Remington case was a watershed experience for me. Though I had seen the same system at work in some of our lower courts, though it had made me a skeptic about many official verdicts, nothing had prepared me for this betrayal of justice at the highest levels; nothing had prepared me for the high judicial connivance that had sent an innocent man to prison—and as it turned out, to his death. In my crime reporting, I had admired the efficiency of the FBI; I had even written cops-and-robbers dramas glorifying the agency. In the future, I would look at Hoover's FBI with a much more critical and analytical eye.

It was quite a change for a noncombative, often conservative fellow who had begun life in a quiet seacoast town on the New Jersey shore and had grown up without any idea that he would wind up writing about the most controversial issues of his day.

3

An American Idyll

I WAS BORN ABOUT 2:30 ON THE SNOWY AFTERNOON OF March 8, 1911, in the upper bedroom of the old house in Point Pleasant, New Jersey, that my grandfather had started to build in the 1870s. My mother later told me that I almost didn't make it. The cord was wrapped around my throat, strangling me; but I was disentangled, whacked on the bottom—and began squalling, often to the discomfiture of the powers that be.

The world into which I was born was centuries closer to that of our colonial and Revolutionary ancestors than the world of today. The town of Point Pleasant, a seashore resort, had only some 1500 to 2000 year-round residents. The roads were gravel and, in many places, mere sand tracks that led through stands of beach plum and bayberry bushes, interspersed with a few stunted pines. Deliveries of milk, ice, coal and other necessities were made by horse and wagon. Hardly anyone in our area had electric lights or indoor plumbing. Kerosene lamps, whose wicks often smoked, provided illumination; and for other needs, there was always the outhouse, located at the end of a boardwalk behind our house and bowered with climbing roses in the summertime.

My grandfather, William J. Cook, who preferred to be called "Jim," was an offshore fisherman. He and others launched their New England-type dories from the beach and rowed through the surf until they passed over the sandbar that runs along our coast. There they would step a mast bearing a small sail to carry them out to the "first ridge" of rocks about five miles offshore or, in good weather, to the "second ridge" some ten miles out. Along these ridges they set their lobster pots and trawl lines and hoped for a catch. It was hardscrabble, hit-and-miss living.

The summer of 1888 my grandfather had taken his boat up to Sea Bright, which was only some twenty miles up the coast from Point Pleasant. But in those days, before boats had motors, this was like what flying to California is today. He could not get home except on weekends and had to stay with his boat as long as the fishing held. On July 4, 1888, he wrote a note to my father, then a ten-year-old boy, addressed to "Freddie P. Cook."

It read: "I did not go of [f] at sea to day there has been lots of boat[s] upset to day the surf is bad and I did not have much bait to go with. So I staid ashore. I didnot sell anything on Monday but yesterday I sold for $17.68 if I could do that for a few days it would help me very much. I don't think that we are going to get any bait to day. I will be home on Saturday if nothing Happens. take care of all the things for you know that I must depend on you to look after all the work."

An old, sketchy account book that my grandfather kept indicates the skimpy rewards of a hard and hazardous life. His banner fishing day, according to the old book, was July 16, 1893, when he caught 436 bluefish, which he sold for $18.24. His total return for the week during which he made this record haul was just $32.94; and, from this, of course, he always had to deduct the costs of maintaining the boat, repairing and replacing lines and nets and securing bait. The old account book gives no indication of those costs.

To eke out a living, my grandfather kept fishing for codfish in the fall until the weather became so bitterly cold that he had to stop. My father later told me: "I have seen him come in with his hands so coated with ice on the oars that his fingers had to be pried loose after he made the beach." One of the sketchy records that he kept shows that for enduring such hardships he sold $47.27 worth of codfish in the month of November, 1899 and $51.42 in December.

When the cold became too severe for even this tough ancestor of mine to pursue the cod, he became one of the original members of the old Life Saving Service, now the Coast Guard. In those days of sailing ships, the Life Saving Service hired out-of-work fishermen to patrol the beaches in all kinds of weather to spot ships in distress. Every winter, howling nor'easters drove some ships on the sandy bars that fringe our Ocean County coast; and in especially tempestuous weather it was not unusual for as many as half-a-dozen wrecks to litter our coastline.

Sometimes the stranded ships would be pounded to pieces by huge waves and their crews and passengers drowned. But some vessels, of course, were more fortunate. If a ship was not too badly damaged, tugs would be sent down from New York to haul her off the bar once the seas had subsided; and my grandfather was often appointed shipmaster in charge of the vessel being towed to safe harbor.

My grandfather was one of those born seamen who could smell the weather. One bright summer day my father went offshore for a day's fishing with him and his fishing partner. The sun was bright; the sea almost glassy smooth. They were fishing the first ridge about five miles offshore and were getting a pretty fair catch when, shortly after noon, my grandfather looked around, sniffed the sea and said abruptly, "Haul in your lines."

"Why?" Dad asked.

"We're heading for the beach," my grandfather said simply.

As far as my father could see, nothing had changed; the sun was still shining, the sea calm. But before they reached shore, huge swells began to surge under their boat. Dad used to describe the outcome this way:

"By the time we hit the beach, the first big waves began to break. We were the first boat in, and we got ashore safely. But huge combers began to crash on the shore, and a couple of boats that hadn't left as soon as we had got caught in the rough surf and overturned. We had to help rescue the men and their boats and gear.

"I tried to find out from my father afterward just what made him tell us to haul in our lines and start for the beach. But he couldn't explain it. All he could say was, 'I just didn't like the look of things.' It was just an instinct he possessed, I guess."

Such were some of the tales I heard in my childhood; such, part of my heritage. My father's family evidently had settled in the area around Toms River, New Jersey, before the Revolutionary War. A Major John Cook was bayoneted to death after the Toms River blockhouse was stormed by Tories and bushwhackers in one of the more famous small skirmishes of the Revolution.

My great-grandfather, Abraham Cook, was born at Cedar Bridge, just outside Toms River. He acquired a farm near the headwaters of the Metedeconk River. He married twice and raised two families. I always got the impression that the offspring of the first marriage considered themselves his legitimate descendants and did not look with favor on the progeny that Abraham produced after he married a fifteen-year-old servant girl. I never heard my father mention his grandfather's name, and I had no idea who he was until, as a grown man, I discovered my great-grandfather's grave in an abandoned cemetery known as "the Gravelly." As far as Dad was concerned, the family line began with his father.

In any event, my grandfather, an offspring of Abraham's first marriage, moved from the earlier-settled inland area to the shore, and sometime in the early 1870s built the first section of the house in which I was born. It was a standard, post-Civil War structure: a porch across the front of the rectangular house facing east; there were two square rooms downstairs and two up. Later, after a fire in 1903, a second four-room section was built on the rear of the house; but, since architecture in those days was crude at best, the two halves never joined each other evenly. The newer section was lower, separated from the old part of the house by a step of several inches.

My father was born in this house on March 28, 1878. He was the last of a family of four children, but his two older sisters and a brother had all died of diphtheria within a week while my grandmother was pregnant with him.

My father had one of the best and most retentive minds of any man I have ever met. I have often wondered what he might have become if he had a chance in life. This, I suppose, is one of the reasons that my sympathies have always been with the underdog, not with the residents of the Waldorf Towers. My father's life and mine overlap just a hundred years, yet no two lives could better illustrate the quantum changes in opportunities.

When my dad was a very young boy in the backwater area around Point Pleasant, there were no public schools. A wandering "professor" would come into the region and establish an "academy." Neighborhood children would be sent to the "academy" to get what education they could, with rulers rapped across their knuckles if they didn't behave; and the "professor" was often recompensed for his instructional efforts by a barter system that supplemented the little cash he was paid.

Before my father was out of his teens, the first public school was established, and he received a few terms of more formal education, including one semester in the winter of 1890 at the Princeton Model School. His mother, Sarah E. Cook, suffered from asthma, and her doctor advised her to spend the winter with distant relatives near Princeton, away from the damp seashore weather. That one term in the Princeton school probably represented the only really good instruction my father ever got, for he had to go to work at fourteen to help pay his mother's doctor's bills and to supplement the family income.

I suppose he received no more than what would be considered today a sixth-grade education, and he often wondered later how he had acquired such a desire for books and learning. His father was clearly not at ease with the English language, and there were no books except the family Bible in the home. Yet my father, from the time he went to work as a young boy, always squirreled away a few cents at a time to buy books to compensate for the education he had missed and for which he hungered.

Some of his earliest purchases reveal the intensity of his longing. He bought a set of the Encyclopaedia Britannica and religiously read a few pages a night until he had gone all the way through it. Always fascinated with history, he purchased the eight-volume Library of Universal History written by Professor Israel Smith Clare, who, long years later (I will never forget my father's shock at reading this), died in a Pennsylvania poorhouse. To this nonfiction collection my father added sets of the writings of Washington Irving, James Fenimore Cooper and Edgar Allan Poe.

Throughout his entire later life, he kept abreast of current events by reading the New York *Times*, to which he had a subscription all the years I can remember. Whatever he read he retained. Once we were listening to one of the radio quiz shows so popular when I was a boy. When he heard a question about the name of the Roman general who abandoned his horses in the field and rode into Rome to rally his army to repel an invasion by the Huns, Dad came up with the answer in a flash. How, we asked him, did he know? "I read it in Clare's Universal History some thirty years ago," he said.

As a young man, Dad had wanted to become a lawyer, possibly
even a judge; but the circumstances of his life thwarted such
ambitions. As a boy he went to work full-time in a local hardware
store, and full-time in those days meant some sixty hours a week.
Stores opened for business around seven in the morning and
stayed open until nine o'clock at night, the only break in the
unremitting round of work being that half of the store's staff would
work one night and the other half the next.

My mother's early life was as hard in its way as Dad's. Born
Huldah Compton, in Belford, New Jersey, on December 11,
1883, she came from a family with a history stretching back to
earliest colonial times. One of her progenitors had been forced
to flee the Massachusetts Bay Colony for such heresies as opposing
the union of church and state and infant baptism. And one of
Mother's ancestors, she said, once grazed his cows on what is now
Wall Street. In 1665, the Compton family received the grant of
a large tract of land in Middletown Township, in northern Monmouth County, and there they remained for centuries.

Mother was the oldest of eight children (two others died in
infancy), and from early girlhood she helped to care for the younger
ones and worked on the family farm. She picked berries and beans,
helped gather the cut asparagus and harvest corn, doing in general
the backbreaking work of a field hand for a reward of five cents
a day.

Like Dad, Mother had a passion for education. My Aunt Mary,
who was closest to her in age and shared a room with her when
they were growing up, recalled that Mother kept her oil lamp
burning until one or two in the morning while she read and
studied. Since there was no high school in Middletown Township,
she went to live with relatives in Atlantic Highlands so she could
attend high school there. One of her report cards for the years
1900–01, when she would have been a sophomore, shows that
her overall average was 96. Looking at this old card now, I can
understand, as I did not when I was a boy, why she was always
so dissatisfied with me when I came home with mere 88s or 90s.

After graduation, Mother went to what was then called the
Trenton Normal School (now Trenton State College), which offered a two-year curriculum. In 1904 she became a teacher, with
her first job in Point Pleasant at a salary of $45 a month. An
account book that she kept that first year shows her frugal existence: $10 a month to her mother, probably for money she had

borrowed to help pay her way through normal school; $16 a month for board. That left her only $19 a month for all other expenses, and these she listed penny by penny. In those days teachers had to buy their own plan books, and hers cost her $2 that first October; teachers' association dues were 50 cents; other expenditures included soap, 5 cents; stamps, 10 cents; mend shoes, 60 cents. At the end of the month, she showed a "balance" of $3.95.

It was my great good fortune that it was in Point Pleasant that Mother began her teaching career, for it was there, of course, that she met my father. Dad stood about 5 feet 10, slender with a handsome face and a thick shock of black, slightly wavy hair, parted in the middle. Mother, as old pictures show, was also tall and slender, a truly beautiful woman. They fell in love and were married on June 14, 1908. They often looked back and joked about their wedding day. While waiting for a train to take them on their honeymoon, they got on the railroad station scale and each weighed just 117 pounds. They used to recall, too, that Mother's teaching salary, minuscule as it was, still exceeded Dad's $8 a week from the hardware store.

Dad was thirty-two, Mother twenty-five. Given their financial circumstances, I suppose the wedding would have been almost impossible if they had not had the old family house in Point Pleasant to live in. Dad's father had died at sixty-three and Dad had lived with and helped care for his mother, whose health was always precarious. So it was that the young couple set up housekeeping in the old family home.

"Mother Cook was always very good to me," Mother would recall in after years, "but still it was not the same as having your own home." Given my grandmother's failing health (she died in 1914, when I was three, and I have no memory of her), my parents' first years together must have been difficult.

4

The Jersey Shore

OUR HOUSE WAS LOCATED ALMOST AT THE END OF A ROAD that led to nowhere. It was at the extreme southern end of Bay Avenue, one of the two principal north-south thoroughfares through town. The road was graveled past our house for some 500 feet, where it shriveled to a two-wheel cart track through beach sand bordered with scrub growth. At the end of the graveled road, Osborne Avenue—a narrow, muddy, rutted lane—ran to the east some three-quarters of a mile to the beach. Our beach in the days I like best to remember was really ours: wild sand dunes topped with saw grass, a broad white expanse of sand littered with driftwood, and, beyond, a blue, undefiled ocean that gave us fish and sea clams in abundance.

On Sunday afternoons in summer we would pack a hamper with food and drink, take our fishing rods and tackle and trudge down to the beach, swatting at mosquitoes almost every step of the way. Across the dunes, on the beach, we would gather wood for the driftwood fire on which we would later cook our hot dogs and toast marshmallows. Then we would go fishing.

Those were the days when sails had not yet disappeared from the oceans. Two-masted schooners brought lumber north from the Carolinas, and sometimes, in a storm, part of a deck load would come loose and wash ashore. Sailing craft were still familiar

sights off our coast. Dad taught me to distinguish between a
schooner and a full-rigged ship; to know the difference between
a brig and a brigantine; to recognize Gloucester fishing schooners
built along much the same lines as Nova Scotia's famous *Bluenose*.
I am thankful that I was born early enough to experience the last
living days of the dying past.

For the ocean was swept clean of sails in the early 1920s: traw-
lers replaced the fishing schooners; three-masted ships and four-
masted schooners vanished. Even the sea and the beach were
different. The whales we had always seen making their way down
the coast, blowing their great spouts of spray into the air, vanished
along with the age of sail. And our beach was no longer ours.

Wealthy strangers from the city built houses on our dunes and
acquired riparian rights that gave them control of our beaches
down to the waterline. I will never forget the Sunday when, with
our weekly hamper of food, we gathered our driftwood and began
to build our fire. A man came down from the nearest house on
the dunes and told Dad we couldn't have a fire on "his" beach.
He owned it, he said, and we couldn't even visit there. I was too
young to understand. All I knew was that our beach was no longer
ours, that it belonged to this insignificant and arrogant runt of a
stranger who, because he had money, had the authority to order
us off the strand that had always belonged to residents of the
coast. Was this the beginning of my antipathy toward the filthy
rich?

I grew up essentially without worries, free to roam the woods
and beaches, living close to a nature still unspoiled. For my parents, life was always hard—but always good. Theirs was an almost
unremitting round of work except for our Sunday picnics, but
they found compensations in the peacefulness of the home they
established and the security their work gave them.

Dad had become manager of the hardware department of the
largest store of its kind along our section of the coast. In the early
years of my life, he rode a bicycle to work in all kinds of weather.
His working day began at 7:30 A.M., he would come home for
lunch at 11:30, and get home for supper about 6:30. Even then,
for a large part of the year, his long day was only beginning. Every
year, from late spring until frost came in the fall, there was a large
truck garden to be planted, tended, harvested. We owned a lot
some 200 feet deep across the road from our house and another
almost as large on the south side of the house. As soon as Dad

got home from the store, he and Mother, and I, as soon as I was big enough to help, would work the fields until it became too dark to see and then go home to a late supper.

Even then, Dad's work wasn't done. From 1920 until he died in 1947, he earned an extra few hundred dollars a year as tax collector in our borough; and, after he ate, he would go to work on the tax records to keep accounts up to date. This task completed, he would sit down and spend the better part of an hour reading the New York *Times* before, exhausted, he went to bed for the sleep that would enable him to face the same routine the next day.

Mother's life was as hard and work-filled as Dad's. She had to scrub our clothes by hand and hang them out to dry. Every summer morning she spent hours hoeing and weeding in the garden. When our crops came in, she was forever canning. We had fruit trees—apples, pears, peaches and cherries—and a large chicken pen. Mother preserved the fruit, took care of the chickens and gathered the eggs. Sometimes she sold some eggs to the local stores and hoarded the pennies.

When I describe my childhood to my own children, they look at me as if they can't believe that anyone ever lived quite this way. They are especially incredulous when I tell how, with the approach of cold weather, we would move into what we called "winter quarters." The house would be shut off except for two rooms: the kitchen with the big iron cooking range and the "sitting room" dominated by a round, potbellied stove with plates that glowed fiery red as it toasted your near side—and left your back exposed to the chill of the outer room. At night, we would undress downstairs by the fire, put on our nightclothes and then run upstairs and plunge under the covers in the frosty bedrooms.

The result of these rigors was that we had security. We had a sound roof over our heads with no mortgage to pay; we had no debts and no time payments. We always knew that we would have plenty to eat—a chicken in the pot for dinner along with potatoes and vegetables and preserves that Mother had put down during the harvesting season and stored in the cellar. We had a huge coal bin at the side of the house, and Dad always had it filled in summer when the price of coal was lowest. We enjoyed our self-sufficiency; we were not dependent from week to week on the almighty dollar.

This kind of life has largely vanished and many of us would not wish to bring it back. Yet it had great rewards, chief among them being serenity. Mother and Dad created one of the most blissful homes a boy was ever reared in. The very house seemed to exude warmth, peace, contentment and a sense of sanctuary. The security my parents achieved through unremitting labor had much to do with creating this relaxed atmosphere. They were money-poor, yet they had none of those excessive, burdensome money worries that can cause family dissensions. Equally important was their harmonious regard for each other.

Dad, the gentlest of men, literally worshiped his wife, and Mother was the most even-tempered of women. I can not recall a time when there was any deep-seated, disturbing tension between my parents. Harsh words never passed between them; an angry argument was unthinkable. In all those years I can recall only two minor exceptions.

In the early years of Dad's tenure as tax collector, there was no thought of establishing a full-time office, and Dad conducted the business affairs of the borough from our home. Taxpayers came to pay their bills at all hours, sometimes just as we were about to sit down to Sunday dinner. One day, while we were at the table, a taxpayer arrived. Mother and Dad had identical Waterman fountain pens, but Mother thought Dad's wrote more smoothly and was forever borrowing his. Dad went to his rolltop desk in the library to take the man's money and receipt the bill. He couldn't find his fountain pen.

"Mother, what did you do with my pen?" he asked.

"I didn't have it," she said.

"You *must* have," Dad snapped, with rare asperity. "It isn't where I left it."

Grumpily, Dad borrowed her pen and signed the bill. Later on Dad found his pen in the pocket of a smoking jacket that he had taken off when he sat down to dinner. He was contrite, and Mother, vindicated, was quickly mollified.

The second incident involved a contretemps that occurred while Dad and I were fishing. We were extremely close and Dad in his understated way often used these excursions to impress on me what a lucky boy I was to have so remarkable a mother. His consideration where she was concerned was all-encompassing and he had an invariable rule that, no matter how ravenous the fish might be, we had to stop fishing to be home in time for dinner.

"When a good woman slaves over a hot stove to get dinner for a man, the least he can do is to make certain that he gets home in time to eat it," he used to say.

Only once did we ever break the ironclad rule. At a nearby lake on a fall afternoon the white perch were going out of their minds gobbling our worms. Mother always had dinner ready at the dot of six. Dad checked his watch. It said 5:30, and since we were having so much fun catching those perch, Dad allowed, "Well, I guess we can fish for ten minutes longer." A few minutes later, he looked at his watch again. It still said 5:30. Instantly, we recognized the disaster. We gathered up our gear and rushed home, but we were, of course, at least half an hour late. Mother was in a snit.

Dad explained that his watch had stopped. That didn't satisfy her. "Couldn't you tell by looking at the sun how late it was getting?" Mother demanded. Of course, we hadn't been looking at the sun; we had been concentrating on the fish making their swift darts at our lines.

It was an uncomfortable dinner; an icy silence prevailed and the food tended to stick in the throat. Mother wasn't appeased by any of our explanations. Later, while she was washing dishes and I was drying, I said, "Now look, Mother, you know that Dad always insists on our being home in time for dinner. This is the *only* time anything like this has ever happened, and it *wasn't* his fault." She had cooled off a bit by now, and she had to admit that we had never been late before. So peace was restored.

The harmony in our home was such that others sometimes found it hard to believe. During my freshman year in college, to make ends meet, Mother took a young schoolteacher to board with us. An attractive and pleasant girl, she soon came to be considered more a member of the family than a boarder. After several months she could no longer restrain her curiosity. "Mrs. Cook," she said to my mother one day, "I've been wondering about something. When do you and Mr. Cook fight?"

"We don't fight," Mother said, taken aback by the question.

"You mean you *never* fight?"

"No," said Mother.

"Don't you ever argue even?"

"No," said Mother reasonably. "What is there to argue about?"

The quality of my parents' life together and Dad's life-long devotion to Mother were perhaps best illustrated on their thirty-ninth wedding anniversary, just a few weeks before he died. At her place at the breakfast table, Mother found Dad's gift for her, with this note attached: "To the girl who has made the last 39 years seem like so many minutes and for whom I have been grateful all my life."

5

The Depression Years: Making of a Newsman

ONE OF MY FATHER'S FAVORITE SAYINGS WAS, "I MAY NOT have much money, but at least I can look at myself in the mirror in the morning and not be ashamed of what I see." Given his circumstances, Dad might well have been a bitter and frustrated man, but he was not. In a way, I became his surrogate, feeling for him the frustration that he had put aside. I always felt it was a crime of the times that he had never been given a chance to make full use of his exceptional brains and ability. Yet I would never have known that his youthful ambition had been to become a lawyer if Mother hadn't told me. He seemed completely at peace, with a loving wife, a happy home, and his son.

Deprived of a career, Dad found some compensation in lodge work. Lodges used to be much more important in the social fabric of a community than they are today. Dad was a member and later a state officer of the Knights of the Golden Eagle. Eventually he rose to become state commander. Telling me about the incident that brought him to state-wide prominence, Dad read me a moral lesson that I never forgot.

There was one very unpopular member of his local lodge—an obnoxious individual who scraped nerves raw by almost every word and action—and a movement got under way to blackball him and kick him out of the lodge. The offender was not present to defend himself at the meeting when the motion for his expulsion was made. A lynch-style mob swept the lodge hall, with all the members against the unpopular one, and Dad saw that the motion was going to be passed unanimously. He rose to his feet. "I understand the way you all feel. In other circumstances, I might vote with you, but I think it is wrong to take an action like this when the man is not here to defend himself. He has the right to be heard. And I cannot in good conscience support this movement to stab him in the back when he is not here." Dad was shouted down, and the expulsion motion was passed with a whoop and a holler.

"A few days passed," Dad recalled, "and then some members began to come around and admit to me, rather sheepishly, that I had been right and they were ashamed of themselves. That was gratifying, but it just happened that one of the officers of the state lodge had been present at the meeting. The lone stand I had taken had impressed him so much that at the next meeting of the state lodge he nominated me for state office, gave me his full support, and I was chosen Grand Sir Herald, the second highest position in the state organization."

Dad concluded this account with a little homily: "Never be afraid to stand up for what you think is right. It doesn't matter if you are all alone in the crowd; it doesn't matter how unpopular you may make yourself at the moment. You will always know in your heart that you did what you felt was right, and you won't ever have to be ashamed of yourself."

When I was a boy, the Civil War still lived vividly in the minds of the older generation. World War I burst upon us during my boyhood, but mental attitudes and political faith had been formed and inherited from the era of the Civil War. There were still two or three Civil War veterans who marched in the Memorial Day parades when I was young; and to my elders the Republican Party was the party of Abraham Lincoln, the Grand Old Party that had saved the Union. Republicanism in the area was a blind ideology. Democrats had about them the odor of skunks. A classmate of mine in grammar school once sidled up to me and whispered, "Your father is a Democrat, isn't he?" I said he was. Then, in an even lower, almost conspiratorial tone, he said, "My father is, too, but I guess we better not say anything about it."

Dad's political allegiance should have made him the odd-man out in such an atmosphere, but he was re-elected tax collector time and again for twenty-seven years, often without any opposition. He was respected for his integrity and because he ran the tax office so capably that he became an invaluable asset to whatever Republican faction happened to be in control of our borough.

And Dad guarded his reputation for rectitude. Mother was a member of the Board of Education and earned a small salary as district clerk. In this capacity, she was responsible for making out checks and balancing the books. There came a time when an addition had to be built on the public school. The contract, properly advertised, was awarded to the lowest bidder. Mother had no more to do with this than any other member of the board, but as district clerk she was helpful to the contractor in many small ways. He was so appreciative that when the work was finished he offered to modernize Mother's kitchen for her for just the cost of labor and materials.

Mother, naturally, was eager to have her old kitchen cabinets and small built-in cupboard replaced by new cabinets and a modern sink. But Dad shook his head.

"We can't do that, Mother," he said.

"Why not?" Mother wanted to know. "They're not giving it to us. We will be paying them for the work."

"I know," Dad said in his mild way. "But it might not look that way to some people. Our reputation is worth more than a new kitchen, Mother."

And so Mother continued to live with her old kitchen.

It had always been understood that I should go to college, that I should have the opportunity that had been denied to Dad. In a way, I was to make up for him, and recognition of this fact made me worry when I was still quite young about what I was going to do with myself.

Dad had collected a library of some thousand volumes, and books had been my best companions from early boyhood. My growing up had been a lonely process. There were no playmates in our isolated area, and I was like a lanky woods colt, at home in the woods and fields and streams; but awkward, shy and tongue-tied in society. And so, since books had always been my best friends, I decided when I was fifteen that I wanted to become a

writer. But how did one get started in this field? With naive logic
I reasoned that the best way would be to become a reporter
because reporters had to learn to write, didn't they? It did not
occur to me that I was about as temperamentally ill-equipped for
the news trade as anyone could be. Introspective and unsure of
myself, I lacked all trace of the cocky confidence that one usually
associates with the reportorial breed. Only dimly aware of such
a crucial shortcoming, I enrolled in the journalism program at
Rutgers University in New Brunswick, New Jersey. Fortunately
for me, the university had an excellent journalism course; and
during my four years there, I at least learned the rudiments of
the trade and shed some, if not all, of my inhibitions.

It was during these college years that the black shroud of the
Great Depression descended upon our world, and of course my
family felt its devastating impact. During the last years of the
booming 1920s, Dad's salary at the hardware store had been raised
to $45 a week. But soon business collapsed and the owner of the
store began to wring his hands and worry. As manager of the
hardware department, Dad had an insider's look at the books.
He knew precisely what the store's circumstances were—and how
unjustified the boss's concern was.

The business was a privately owned corporation, a device that
gave the owner a delightful buffer, because when books showed
the beginnings of deficits, the owner and his family were protected
against ill effects. Each department—hardware, furniture, elec-
trical shop and storage warehouse—paid monthly rentals to the
corporation. In addition, the owner's salary and those of the son
and daughter who worked there were paid out of corporate funds
and charged against the running expenses of the various departments. Thus, even when Dad's hardware department began to
dip into the red, the boss and his family were still prospering.

But the boss had a Scrooge complex: he looked at that small,
creeping tide of red ink, worried about where it would all end,
and became convinced that disaster was imminent. His remedy
was to cut salaries to the marrow of the bone. Dad's $45-a-week
shrank to $40 and then back to $35. At the same time, the boss
decided that his son needed a vacation in Mexico, the expenses
of which jaunt were charged to the hardware department. As Dad
remarked to the accountant who had suffered similar salary cuts,
"You and I paid for that little trip to Mexico."

This view of the inner workings of the corporate system filled me with a resentment akin to what I had felt as a boy when the wealthy summer stranger had kicked us off "our beach." I knew how hard my father had labored in twenty-odd years at that store, what a struggle he was having to make ends meet and pay my college expenses. I became convinced that the rich and powerful cared only about themselves, that they really didn't give a damn about the working stiffs who kept their businesses running. Self-centered, absorbed with their own financial interests, these "honorable men" were blind to the needs of others. Dad's boss was a church deacon, a pillar of the community—yet he ran a business like a sweatshop. For me, he was the symbol of a class. Then— and later—I always felt much closer to the workers in the pits than I did to the characters in executive suites.

I graduated from Rutgers with Phi Beta Kappa marks in June 1932 and stepped out into the worst depression in American history. The nation's economy was prostrate, with banks failing as fast as leaves flutter off trees in an autumn storm. Editors looked at you as though you were mad even to think of filing an application.

So, I (like many others in my graduating class) latched on to any work available. I went back to the Point Pleasant Post Office, where I had worked during summers and Christmas vacations to help pay my way through college. Another classmate similarly returned to his job as a shoestore clerk.

One experience of that bleak time has remained especially vivid in my memory. Hubert Ede, one of my journalism instructors at Rutgers, had been city editor of the Newark *Evening News*, then one of the best papers in the nation. In the fall of 1932, Ede arranged an interview for me with the editor of the *News*.

I waited for the editor as the first edition was rolling off the press and he was double-checking for flaws. Finally, I was summoned into his office. A copy of that first run was spread out on his desk, and across the top of page one a large headline announced the collapse of another Newark bank.

The editor, a compassionate man, let me down as gently as he could. "Look," he said, pointing to the paper, "I am sorry for you young fellows getting out of college, but this is what is happening. I don't know where it is all going to end. I think we'll pull out of it eventually; I certainly hope so. But right now there is nothing

I can tell you. Hubert Ede has given you the highest recommendation and so has Allen Sinclair Will (a former New York *Times* editor who headed the Rutgers journalism department), but there is really nothing I can do. It would be wrong for me to hold out any hope to you because all I can do is pray that I won't have to cut the staff I have or cut salaries any further."

I walked out feeling doomed. There seemed to be no chance that I ever could get my start as a newpaperman. But a few months later my luck changed. The Asbury Park *Evening Press*, the largest paper in our shore area, had a staff shakeup; a new city editor was named, and there was a vacancy in the newsroom. Since I had contributed a couple of offbeat items to the *Press* during the summer while I was working in the post office, I got the job.

I started work January 1, 1933, and my first day should have been a lesson to me. That first day stretched into a sixteen-hour stint—my salary was $20 a week. But at last I had a *job*; and anyone lucky enough to get a *job* in those desperate times held on to it the way a drowning man clutches a life preserver.

Besides, I was hooked. The job fascinated me. No matter how long the hours, how poor the pay, there was the excitement and adventure of being in on the development of fast-breaking news stories. This was not just work, it was an enchantment.

6

The Cub Reporter

THERE COULD NEVER HAVE BEEN A BETTER TIME AND PLACE for the training of a cub reporter than the Jersey shore in the four years during the 1930s when I was on the street. Disaster followed disaster, one as sensational as the other, all making headlines around the world. Naming them conjures up memories: the *Morro Castle*, the *Mohawk*, the *Hindenburg*. Not in the previous fifty years—nor in the fifty years that followed— had so much tragic and colorful drama been packed into such a brief period along this small sector of the coast.

It began for me with a telephone call early on the morning of September 8, 1934. Tom Tighe, my city editor at the *Press*, told me that the Ward liner *Morro Castle* was burning at sea in full view of the coast. He wanted me to get down to the Manasquan Coast Guard station and then to roam the shore to see what I could find out.

I was at the time a one-man "bureau" covering all of Ocean County from my parents' home in Point Pleasant. The Manasquan Coast Guard station, located on the south side of the Manasquan Inlet in Point Pleasant Beach, was in my territory, and I got into my Model A Ford and drove there as fast as I could. I had expected to find that the Coast Guard cutter had put to sea on its rescue mission, but instead I found it pulled up against the bulkhead on the south side of the inlet, rocking in the swells. The tall, rail-thin boatswain's mate who was its skipper was standing beside the idled cutter. He stammered nervously, protesting that he had tried to get the cutter out to sea but the waves had been so tremendous he'd just had to turn back.

There was then—and there has been subsequently—a tendency to write about the *Morro Castle* disaster as if it happened in a fierce storm with high seas running. Nothing could be further from the truth. I had lived on the coast all my life, and my first look at the ocean told me there was no reason that the Coast Guard cutter shouldn't have been able to get out of the inlet. A northeasterly wind was kicking up an ocean chop, it was true, but the seas were not what any denizen of the coast would call really rough. They were ruffled just enough to make the water ideal for the surf caster going after fluke or bluefish.

Leaving the idled cutter and its agitated skipper, I got back into my car and headed north up the coast to Spring Lake, where I ran up to the boardwalk and got my first look at the drama taking place out at sea. The *Morro Castle*, only a few miles off the coast, was wreathed in a cloud of smoke from the fire raging along her decks. Lifeboats had already been launched and were pulling toward the shore and safety. As they drew near, the sight was enough to stun one who had been reared on tales of heroic rescues with Coast Guardsmen battling spume-flecked seas to launch their lifeboats through raging surf. Here there was no raging surf and the boats that approached the beach were nearly empty.

The first two lifeboats I saw each carried a handful of escaping sailors, most of them Hispanic, who tugged at their oars every which way, with no rhythm at all. Seeing the sand so near, some of them threw down their oars, jumped up in panic and leaped into the shallow water. The boats, powerless, rudderless, unguided, broached sidewise to the seas and bobbled up on the beach without upsetting—the kind of landings that could never have taken place in a storm-racked ocean.

Then a third lifeboat appeared. This one, like the others, contained no passengers, but it did have a different kind of skipper—a towering Scandinavian boatswain's mate who bawled orders to his craven crew. As this boat neared the beach, a couple of Hispanic rowers started to jump up, about to fling down their oars, but he roared and browbeat them into obedience. He dropped an anchor off the stern to steady the lifeboat and keep it from

broaching, all the while keeping up the tongue-lashing so the men
would keep pulling on their oars—and the lifeboat grounded in
true nautical fashion, stem to the beach, without taking on so
much as a cup of water.

I ran to catch up with the only man I had seen that day who
had acted like a man. Spectators were swarming around him, and
first aid men were waiting to whisk him and other survivors to
area hospitals for examination and possible treatment. I had only
a moment to ask him what it was like out at sea. He turned and
looked at the burning ship, then said in his Norwegian accent:
"Oh, it's none so bad. I'd go right out again if I had me a boat."

When I telephoned what I had witnessed into the *Press*, it got
lost in the welter of other details that were pouring like a flood
into the rewrite desk. Perhaps my editors were hesitant so early
in the unfolding drama to give credence to a single account that
conflicted so radically with the stereotype of hardened tars battling
wind and wave that was created by other reporters.

Official investigation later disclosed the slovenliness with which
the *Morro Castle* had been handled. And even on the day of the
disaster the Coast Guard emerged with egg dripping all over its
face. The Coast Guard skipper who hadn't dared take his cutter
through Manasquan Inlet was shown up when John Bogan, owner
of the open-party boat *Paramount*, sailed right out through the
same inlet and began doing the Coast Guard's work of rescuing
survivors. And Bogan, I learned, wasn't the only one to put to
sea through the inlet the Coast Guard had judged impassable.

That evening, the *Morro Castle* herself, after snapping the
towline of a tug trying to haul her to New York, wallowed ashore
and grounded just north of the Asbury Park Convention Hall.
There she lay, still smoking, her plates glowing a fierce, almost
transparent red from the flames that still raged inside her hull—
a tourist attraction that drew the curious by the thousands to the
Asbury Park boardwalk.

And though Bogan had rescued scores of survivors, others had
been less fortunate. As flames had swept aft through the liner,
panicked passengers had leaped into the sea. Some had been
killed in the fall; others had drifted away and drowned before
they could be rescued. Bodies washed ashore day after day all
along the beach until the final death toll was placed at 126.

The full story of those days has never been told. One reason
was that everyone was so busy trying to keep abreast of new and

changing developments that none of us had much time to do any
real investigation. But, also, there was a ghoulish, more sinister
side to the story that no one wanted to acknowledge long after
the event. In my files, however, I have copies that I kept of the
memoranda that I turned into the city desk in the months after
the *Morro Castle* tragedy; and the old, yellowed, flaking copy
paper contains the clues.

Early in my career as a reporter I had learned that every town
has a local hangout that is a sounding board for the life of the
community. In Point Pleasant at that time, it was the Hendrix
Diner, at the main crossroads in the center of town. I had developed the habit of dropping into the diner at one or two o'clock
in the morning after I had finished writing and dispatching the
day's news. I would have a hamburger and a cup of coffee—and
talk and listen. In time, I became friendly with many of the men-
about-town who knew more about what was going on under the
seemingly serene surface of life than would ever appear in official
accounts. One of my contacts—let's call him George—finally filled
me in on the *Morro Castle* disaster.

The Jersey shore, like other sections of barrier islands along
the Atlantic coast, has rooted in its historic past legends of ship-
wreckers who lured vessels to their doom and then looted them.
These scavengers apparently had their modern counterparts.

Late on the morning of the disaster, George said, a flashy mob-
connected character who owned a powerful, speedy craft ideally
suited for rum-running had sensed an opportunity. He hastily
rounded up a skeleton crew (including a personal friend of George's)
and they set out from Brielle, passing through the same inlet the
Coast Guard had found too rough to navigate. Offshore, they had
searched downwind from the *Morro Castle*, came across a dozen
bodies floating in the water, pulled them up, stripped them of
money and valuables, then let them slip back into the sea.

One victim had been wearing a money belt which the owner
of the boat quickly appropriated. Back at the dock in the Manasquan River, he paid George's friend $280 for his services and
offered him a choice of a diamond ring or an expensive watch;
George's friend chose the ring.

Possession of the ring, however, created a problem. George's
friend wanted to have it appraised, but he didn't want to take it
to anyone who might ask embarrassing questions about where he
got it. George, he knew, had a retired relative in Florida who

had been a New York City cop. By the time George got him the name and address of a discreet expert appraiser in New York, the looter had nasty running sores on his hands and arms—handling dead bodies at sea turned out not to be risk-free. George took the ring to New York, where the verdict was that the ring was worth about $800; the diamond had a tiny flaw, or it would have been worth $8000.

George told me about another incident he had witnessed on the beach in Spring Lake one day. A beachcomber dashed into the surf, dragged a man's body ashore, quickly searched it and extracted a wallet from the dead man's pocket. "Oh, well," George heard him say, "I guess this poor fellow won't have any more use for it," as he pocketed the wallet and strolled away.

Some scavengers made out so well, George assured me, that one man he knew lived all the following winter on the proceeds of his beachcombing efforts.

Only a few months after the *Morro Castle*, a second sea tragedy took place off our coast: the sinking of another Ward liner, the *Mohawk*, Havana-bound from New York, on the inhumanly cold night of January 24, 1935.

The day before, I had been covering a court session in Toms River when it started to snow. This was no ordinary snow; from the start, it was a howling blizzard, and it hit so suddenly and savagely that no one was prepared for it. Snow began to pile up in the roads in minutes, and the courts closed early so that jurors and witnesses could get home.

I headed toward Point Pleasant along the shore route that led across the Barnegat Bay bridge to Seaside Heights and then north through Lavallette, Mantoloking and Bay Head. There were two sections to the bridge; in between was Pelican Island. I had crossed the western span and was driving across the island when I found the road blocked. A car carrying two women jurors on their way home had skidded into a drift at the left, partially blocking the road. Another driver had stopped to help, but he hadn't been able to extricate their car—and then his became stuck in the middle of the road. Everything was blocked. Cars and school buses piled up behind us, stalled in the snow.

Firemen from Seaside Heights managed to buck through the drifts and take sixty-five children off a school bus. The other thirty or so of us spent about five hours huddled around a small coal stove in the island's lone shelter, a real estate office, while the blizzard raged outside. At about 8 P.M., Seaside Heights police and firemen managed to get a Greyhound bus across the short bridge on the east side of the island. From there the police chief fought his way through drifts on foot to the real estate office and told us we would have to walk the quarter of a mile to the bus. One man who had been an athlete at Asbury Park High School in his younger days took off at full charge. "Come on! Come on! Let's go!" he shouted, running ahead of everybody.

The drifts were almost waist deep in places and the northeast wind was driving the snow in stinging, blinding sheets against our faces, the fiercer gusts enough to take the breath away. A touch of rheumatic fever when I was a senior in high school had left me with a slight mitral valve impairment that our family physician hoped I would "outgrow." He was right for the most part, but I hadn't "outgrown" it completely. Extreme exertion like this left me gasping. Head down, I plodded along through the snow ever more slowly. In my exhaustion, a memory flashed through my mind: in the Arctic adventure stories I had read as a boy, men at the end of their tether just wanted to lie down in the soft, bedding snow—and die. I knew that if I ever slipped and fell, I would be tempted to seek such comfort. And I knew I would never get up.

As I continued, I became aware of the eager-beaver sprinter, who was now dragging at an even slower pace than I. He was gasping for breath as I overtook him, and he called out, "Help me! Help me!" I felt ashamed as I crept past and abandoned him, but I knew that I couldn't help. I struggled ahead to the bus and somehow found the breath to tell the driver and a policeman that there was a man behind me who needed help. They ran out into the storm, grabbed the man by the arms and lifted him into the bus.

I got a room for the night in an old summer hotel in Seaside Heights. I stretched out, exhausted, and my strained heart was thumping so hard in my chest that the ancient iron bedstead shook as I fell asleep.

The next morning, the sun was shining on a blinding sheet of white across which nothing moved. Twenty-three inches of snow had fallen, the worst blizzard to hit the Jersey coast since the famous one of 1888. Such huge snowdrifts blocked the shore road that even snowplows could not break through. I telephoned the

Press and dictated an eyewitness story about the marooning on Pelican Island. Then I waited.

In midafternoon, I spotted the first vehicle to break a trail along the snow-clogged coastal road at last. It was the Point Pleasant First-Aid ambulance, which was coming to take a heart attack victim to the hospital. I managed to hitch a ride home that way.

I had never been so glad to get back to the warmth and comfort of my parents' house as I was that night, and I made an incautious pronouncement: "*Nothing* is going to get me out of this house tonight." Minutes later, the telephone rang. Tom Tighe was calling to tell me that the *Mohawk* had been in a collision with a Norwegian freighter and was believed to be sinking off the coast. Could I get to the nearest Coast Guard station?

Since my car was still mired in the drifts on Pelican Island, I arranged with Harry Kroh, of Brielle, who was covering the area for the Newark *Evening News*, to pick me up, and we went to the Bay Head Coast Guard station, located on the beachfront in the center of town. It turned out to be a lucky choice. We had practically a grandstand view of the drama being played miles out to sea.

From the boardwalk, we could see lights flashing off to the southeast as searchlights swept the ocean in the area where the two vessels had collided, and the boatswain's mate in charge of the Coast Guard station let us listen in on the private telephone line that connected all the stations from Sandy Hook south along the coast. Thus we learned everything that the Coast Guard knew at the time. Nothing was clear at first, but as the hours passed and the night wore on to early morning, two facts were definitely established: the *Mohawk* had sunk off Mantoloking immediately after the collision, and some—it was not certain yet how many— of her crew and passengers were missing.

Harry Kroh and I made periodic dashes from the Coast Guard station to the boardwalk. It was a sparkling clear night and so bitterly cold, with the thermometer plunging to five below zero, that we could stand exposure for only a few minutes at a time. Rescue vessels had arrived on the scene, and we could see by their constantly playing searchlights that there must be persons still missing.

We supplemented what our eyes told us with the messages we picked up by eavesdropping on the Coast Guard wire. I kept telephoning the details into the *Press*, where our top city reporter, whom I shall call Ace, was to write the lead story for our extra edition. Since I was also covering the story as a stringer for the Philadelphia *Bulletin*, I kept funneling information to that city desk also. Sometime between 2 A.M. and 3 A.M., I had a long talk with the *Bulletin*. I was questioned closely—cross-examined, in effect—about what I was reporting.

"Do you mean you can *still* see lights sweeping the ocean out there?" the *Bulletin* man asked me.

"Yes," I told him. "I just took another look from the boardwalk. There's a cluster of boats in the same position off Mantoloking, and they're still sweeping their searchlights all around, so they must be looking for some missing."

"Well," the *Bulletin* man said, "we've been talking to your office in Asbury Park, and they're giving us a different picture. We're going to go with what you're telling me, but perhaps you'd better talk to your office again. Here, I've got them on the line now. I can hook you two up through our switchboard and you can talk. Wait a minute."

Then I heard him tell Ace that he had me on the line. Ace growled, "No, I don't want to talk to Cook. We've got all we need on the story."

After that rejection, I did not call my office again. Ace said he had the story wrapped up, and I had no way of knowing at the time how he had wrapped it.

I caught a pre-dawn train to Asbury Park and walked into the pressroom as the extra edition was rolling off the press. One look at the eight-column headline set my tired blood boiling. The *Press* proclaimed that the *Mohawk* had been sunk off Spring Lake and that all aboard had been rescued.

I grabbed a paper off the conveyor belt and stormed into the newsroom, waving it in my hand. "This is all wrong!" I shouted. "Where the hell did you get this stuff? The wreck happened off Mantoloking, and they're still searching for missing people."

"Oh, Cook, for Christ's sake, can it," snarled a weary Ace.

No one else at the city desk said anything. I burned my way to a desk, threw the paper into a wastebasket and sat down. About 9 A.M. reality suddenly burst on the newsroom. One of our reporters, making his routine morning check, telephoned the Shark River Coast Guard station. He turned to Tom Tighe: "Shark River is sending out their cutter again."

Tom bounded out of his office. "What are they going out for again?" he asked.

"They're going out to try to find those men I tried to tell you were missing at two o'clock this morning," I snapped in a voice that carried through the newsroom. Tom shot me a look, but he didn't say anything.

Then the scramble to make the paper look less ridiculous began. In the attempt to fudge that erroneous eight-column headline, the *Press* in later editions moved the site of the crash a few miles down the beach to Sea Girt and accounted for the fact that the masts of the sunken ship were visible above the ocean off Mantoloking by theorizing that the *Mohawk* must have drifted there, some ten miles down the coast, before she sank. Even such a rationalization could not wipe all the egg off the newspaper's face. The next concession was that forty-five members of the crew and passengers were still missing and presumed dead.

I was one angry and disgusted reporter. After the two days I just had, fighting a blizzard and subzero cold and going some thirty-six hours without sleep, I was in no mood for the ragging I took when I dragged myself off the train at home in late afternoon. "Hey, Fred," some of my wiseacre friends hanging around the station called, "does the *Press* know yet what happened to the *Mohawk*?"

Unfortunately, a journalistic goof of this magnitude can perpetuate itself in future renditions. Even in 1979, in retelling the story of coastal disasters, the *Press* was still referring to the collision as having taken place off Sea Girt and was still repeating the "drifting" fantasy to account for the undeniable fact that the wreck rests on the bottom off Mantoloking.

How had the paper gone so wrong? Newsroom postmortems pinpointed two flaws. Tom Tighe had sent Ace down the coast at the same time he called me. According to Ace, he had climbed a sand dune near Point Pleasant, had looked out to sea—and hadn't spotted anything. If he had done what he said he did, he should have seen those flashing lights off the coast, it seemed to me. Anyway, Ace had hightailed it back to the office to write the main story; and he apparently assumed that if he hadn't been able to see anything from that mysterious dune of his, I couldn't have been seeing all that I was reporting from my vantage point only a couple of miles farther down the coast. How he could have ignored all the supporting details I had picked up from the Coast

Guard telephone line is something I have never been able to understand. Ace's mind-set, however, had been solidified when someone on the desk at Spring Lake Police Headquarters picked this night of nights to play games. New York newspapers, with the *Morro Castle* fresh in mind, began telephoning Spring Lake police in the belief that the *Mohawk* disaster might have occurred in the same area; and this joker on the police desk decided to give them a good story. Sure, he told them, the accident had happened right off Spring Lake; he could see the whole thing from the beach; the *Mohawk* was drifting ashore right before his eyes.

He was so realistic and persuasive that the New York *Journal-American* outdid the *Press* in journalistic fantasy. In its first edition, it reported that the *Mohawk*, after colliding with the Norwegian freighter *Talisman* off Spring Lake, had "beached, capsized and sunk"—a feat no vessel in all of maritime history has been able to perform.

The third of these headline-making sensations that reverberated around the world could well have left me as embarrassed as Ace and the *Press*. This was the flaming destruction of the great German dirigible *Hindenburg* at the Lakehurst Naval Air Station in the early evening of May 6, 1937.

By this time I had become the editor of a small Toms River weekly, the *New Jersey Courier*. Lakehurst was only a few miles west of Toms River, and since many local men worked at the station or were in the ground crews, the flights of the *Hindenburg* were major news for us.

Today, with jets spanning the oceans in hours and rockets propelling men to the moon, it may be hard to feel the romance and promise of lighter-than-air travel. Heavier-than-air craft had limited ranges, but the two mighty German dirigibles floated serenely across the vast spaces of the ocean, the *Graf Zeppelin* flying to Brazil, the *Hindenburg* to the United States. The two airships kept regular schedules, except in winter weather, and their flights had been so smooth and uneventful that passengers sometimes complained that "nothing ever happens." Dirigibles, it seemed at the time, represented the future of long-distance air travel.

Then came the *Hindenburg*'s inaugural flight of the 1937 tourist season. From the start, the voyage was beset with trouble. The

Hindenburg encountered exceptionally strong west winds over the Atlantic; she was buffeted about and delayed for hours. Since this was the first flight of the year and since the *Hindenburg*'s American terminal was at Lakehurst, this trans-Atlantic crossing was of major interest to us.

Our little country weekly was saddled with a flatbed press of 1880s vintage, and we could print only a limited number of papers in a given period of time. The *Courier* went on the streets on Friday morning, but we had to run off about 1000 copies late Thursday afternoon to have enough to distribute to northern and southern parts of the county.

The *Hindenburg* was scheduled to arrive at Lakehurst on May 6, a Thursday, but with the delays it was uncertain just when she would arrive. I had to write a story that would read up-to-the-minute on Friday morning.

The hours rolled past, and I fretted, keeping in constant touch with the public relations officer at Lakehurst. Finally, in early afternoon, he assured me that the *Hindenburg* was all right; she was coming down the coast, would fly over New York City, cruise slowly, waiting for the wind to die down at dusk, before nosing up to her mooring mast at Lakehurst. Arrangements had been made to refuel her in record time, and she would take off again at midnight, carrying many passengers who were going abroad for the coronation of King George VI of England. Shortly after this scenario had been described to me, we heard the sound of motors—and there was the proud, silvery *Hindenburg* herself coasting along right above our heads in the sky above Main Street in front of the *Courier* office.

With that sight, I was all set. I went to my typewriter and wrote a page-one story for our Friday morning paper, describing what was supposed to happen exactly as if it *had* happened. We closed up the page and began the Thursday run.

Satisfied, I went home to have dinner with my wife, Julia (we had been married in June 1936, about six months after I became editor of the *Courier*). I hadn't planned to go to Lakehurst to watch the arrival of the *Hindenburg* because my story was all written and there was nothing else I could do. But Julia said, "After all, this is her first trip of the year, and I would like to see her land." And so we went.

I had a pass admitting us to the air station, and we parked our

car and walked down to a spot near the mooring mast. There had
been a late-afternoon shower, but the skies were clearing as the
Hindenburg circled slowly, majestically, in the sky. Then she
drifted across the airfield and nosed down toward the mooring
mast. The forward landing lines were dropped into the hands of
the ground crew, the motors were cut—and then, like twin bolts
of lightning, two spurts of fire jetted from her tail. There was a
breathless, half-second pause, and then, with a thunderous roar,
flames shot skyward, the stern section buckled, and the whole
mighty craft came crashing to the ground in a ball of flame. Julia
and I had turned and taken two horrified, running steps—and,
by then, it was all over. The modern marvel was a burning,
smoking skeleton.

One instant, the *Hindenburg* floated across the field, passengers
in her forward cabin waving to friends and relatives on the ground.
The next instant, the volatile hydrogen gas that filled the *Hindenburg's* huge bags and kept her afloat went up in one flaming
woosh. In what I judged to be about thirty seconds (sound tracks
later showed it only a few seconds longer), the pride of the skies
was a twisted heap of rubble.

When the shock and horror wore off, I shuddered at the thought
of the piece I had written that was to appear on the streets the
next morning. If the *Courier* and I weren't to be the laughing-
stock of the day, I would have to retrieve those papers from the
early run and write a new, entirely different story.

I left Julia in the pressroom and ran back to the field. At the
site of the still smoldering wreckage I talked to the first young
Marine I saw. The first assumption of everyone who had seen
that flaming funeral pyre in the sky had been that all aboard must
have been killed, but the Marine told me no, there were a number
of survivors. "Some of them came just walking out like through
a hole in the flames," he said. Others had been dragged out badly
burned, but living. Even as we spoke, ambulances came screaming onto the field—and with them a Marine sergeant. "Get out
of here," he ordered. I showed him my pass and argued that I
was a newspaperman and had to cover the story for my paper.
All he said, in an even angrier, more peremptory tone was, "Get
out of here—now." The young Marine with whom I had been
talking waved his rifle at me—and so I got.

Back in the pressroom, all was bedlam. I sought out Bob Okin, who had been a classmate of mine at Rutgers and who was covering the story for the Associated Press. It was an assignment no one in the AP bureau had wanted, Bob told me, but he had asked for it because he remembered from his high-school chemistry class how volatile hydrogen gas was and he had had a superstitious hunch that something might happen. When I told Bob that there had been survivors, he went into action and flashed a bulletin over the AP wires—the first indication anyone had had that the disaster might not have been as total as everyone had feared.

The rest of the night passed in a blur of activity. I stayed at Lakehurst as long as I could to get additional details. Then Julia and I drove back to the *Courier* office in Toms River. She got on the phone, helping to round up the staff, and I went to work at my typewriter. By the time daylight came, we had retrieved the papers from the Thursday-afternoon run that had been sent across the street to the post office; I had written one of the most graphic stories of my life; we had torn apart page one and splashed across the page the largest eight-column type that we had. And we had the old press rolling.

Thirty-six persons died in the wreck of the *Hindenburg*. Sixty-four others survived, some so badly burned that they were confined to area hospitals for weeks. There was to be infinite speculation about the origin of the wreck. Official inquiries concluded that static electricity had probably caused a spark that had ignited the hydrogen gas; but many believed there had been sabotage, a theory the recent motion picture was built around. Whatever the cause, the age of lighter-than-air travel died in the rubble of the *Hindenburg*'s charred ribs.

The Germans promptly took the *Graf Zeppelin* out of service, not wishing to risk another holocaust in the sky. They applied to the United States for supplies of nonflammable helium gas to replace hydrogen. But with Adolf Hitler in power in Germany, President Roosevelt refused to release the helium which the United States alone possessed. And so the *Graf Zeppelin*, the lone survivor of the lighter-than-air dream, never flew again. World War II was in the offing, and before it was over, heavier-than-air had come into its own, and huge passenger-carrying planes were routinely spanning continents and oceans.

7

"The Worst of the American Political System"

OCEAN COUNTY IN 1933–34 WAS A CASEBOOK STUDY IN microcosm of the worst of the American political system. It was a living illustration of the mechanics of the tyrannical bossism that dominated all phases of political and official life. Prosecutors and judges were puppets jerked on boss-twitched strings. There was a price for everything—even for fixing first-degree murder.

Some of these evils had been exposed three years before I began reporting in Ocean County. In 1930 a runaway grand jury, headed by one of the most remarkable men I have ever met, had launched an explosive probe of the prosecutor's office. The foreman of the grand jury was William H. Fischer, editor of the weekly *New Jersey Courier* and for more than forty years the conscience of the county. Fischer's obstreperous panel, thwarted at every level in the courts, had been stonewalled before it could do much more than lift the lid on the bubbling caldron of corruption. Even so, the odors seeping out under that lifted lid were so rank that the prosecutor and several of his staff had sought sanctuary in hasty retirement.

The departed prosecutor, J. Mercer Davis, a large, blustering man, had begun his career as a minister and had later switched to the law. He was ensconced with boss-blessing as the prosecutor in a county rife with every conceivable form of illegality, from gambling to rum-running, from bootlegging to the manufacturing of illegal hooch in backwoods stills. All these activities were conducted on such a scale that they must have been obvious to everyone but the most obtuse citizen. And all were crimes about which Davis had done nothing.

For a brief, fleeting moment it seemed there might be one exception. About the time that Fischer's grand jury was investigating Prosecutor Davis's derelictions, a murder occurred in the remote pine barrens of southern Ocean County. A small-time bootlegger named Kanove had been killed and his body dumped in a wild, wooded tract outside Tuckerton. Such mob murders are almost never solved, but this time Prosecutor Davis vowed it would be different.

Mounting his white charger in the rackets-busting style that was making Thomas E. Dewey famous, Davis actually made an arrest. He proclaimed—an announcement that brought him gratifyingly large headlines—that he had an "ironclad case" against the killer of Kanove and that he was going to press for an early trial. But in the meantime, Fischer's rackets-busting grand jury was making the prosecutor's seat too hot for longer occupancy, and Davis was compelled to resign under fire. Once Davis was out of office and conveniently out of the public eye, the charges that Fischer's jury had brought against him were waylaid in the courts and died with hardly a whimper. Left in the limbo of unfinished business was the "ironclad case" against Kanove's killer.

It was at this precise juncture, sometime before I began reporting in Ocean County, that strange things began to happen. First-degree murder was not a bailable offense in New Jersey at that time; an accused murderer remained in jail until he or she was tried. But this case suddenly became different. A visiting judge was brought in from outside the county (this, I was to learn, was a favorite tactic when legal skulduggery was afoot); he listened to the defense attorney's plea for bail and set the accused killer free under a mere $5000 bond.

What was to happen next depended in large measure on who would be anointed as Davis's successor, and there was much speculation about that. The Hudson County Democratic machine of Jersey City Mayor Frank (I Am the Law) Hague had installed its own man as governor in the State House. All Ocean County was the private fiefdom of Republican Boss Thomas A. Mathis, who had an intense personal interest in who was to administer

and enforce the laws and who obviously didn't want a gung-ho
Democratic prosecutor poking his nose into the Mathis Republican heaven. So a two-boss tug-of-war developed.

Hague's governor had the power to appoint the new prosecutor;
but Mathis's own retainer in the State Senate, thanks to the practice of a rule known as "senatorial courtesy," could block confirmation by simply announcing to his brethren in the Senate that
the appointee was "personally repugnant" to him. The situation,
it would seem, had the makings of a stalemate, but political bosses,
whatever their party, have ways of accommodating each other.

New Jersey politicians had perfected a method to reconcile such
supposedly inimical interests. It was a device known as "the blank
resignation." Any candidate for prosecutor or county judge caught
in the two-boss bind had to sign two undated letters of resignation,
one to go into the safe of Boss Hague in Jersey City, the other
into that of Tom Mathis in Toms River. Thus, if the appointed
official ever failed to hew to the line of justice prescribed for him
by one boss or the other, the offended kingmaker had merely to
type a date on the blank resignation form and mail it to the
secretary of state in Trenton. The ousted official could read in the
papers the next day how he had resigned—for ill health or family
reasons.

This kind of maneuvering about who was to fill the shoes of the
departed Davis was at its height when I first went into Toms
River. A relatively unknown lawyer from outside the county had
suddenly popped into town and opened an office; organization
circles gave him a huge buildup, and the word was that he was
to be the next prosecutor. But days passed, then weeks—and
nothing happened.

I was palling around with an itinerant Scottish journalist in those
days and one afternoon we accosted the dignitary waiting to be
born as he sat in a wooden chair propped up on the sidewalk
outside his inactive office. Was he going to be the new prosecutor?
we asked.

"I expect so," the candidate said. "I could have been prosecutor
now if I had been willing to sign a document that would have
tied my hands like *that*." He crossed his wrists in front of him as
if they had been bound. We had no doubt about what he meant.
"That's what's holding it up," he said, "but I still expect to get
the appointment."

He didn't. Instead, Leo Robbins, of Lakewood, was installed

as prosecutor, and the once-prospective heir to office, wrists still unbound, faded from the local scene as swiftly as he had appeared upon it.

Robbins was a short, stocky, ineffectual man who had been an assistant to Davis. When he was in a difficult spot—for example, under pressure to carry out orders dictated by the political machine—you could always tell by his nervous, fidgeting manner and the way perspiration would spring out, beading his upper lip.

Though Robbins had been personally untouched during the scandal-tainted Davis regime, he could hardly have been unaware of events taking place under his nose—and now he had inherited the Kanove case. Obviously, he had to clean his slate of this "ironclad" case that Davis had bequeathed him. Those of us covering the courthouse wondered what was going to happen, and it wasn't long before we found out.

Robbins came into the county court one day and rose to address the judge. One look was enough to tell anyone who knew him that he was extremely uneasy. His upper lip was beaded, and he fiddled nervously with some papers in his hands. He said he was asking the court's permission to nol-pros—that is, to drop for the time being—the murder indictment in the Kanove case. He emphasized that he was not the prosecutor at the time the charge was brought. He conveniently refrained from mentioning that he had been the prosecutor's aide and so could hardly have been totally unfamiliar with the evidence. Now, Robbins explained, he had a letter that he wanted to read to the court from ex-Prosecutor J. Mercer Davis. It said, in essence, that though the murder case had appeared "ironclad" at first, "subsequent investigation" had uncovered details that made it extremely doubtful the case could be successfully prosecuted. Therefore, Davis advised, it would be better to nol-pros the case before the defense could make a motion to have it dismissed entirely. Stressing the narrow legal aspects of this action, Robbins assured the court that he was not dropping the case entirely—heavens, no. All he was asking was that the case be put in abeyance for the moment so that it could be kept open in case further evidence were uncovered enabling the state to go ahead with the trial.

After a brief colloquy, the judge granted Robbins's motion, and the indictment was nol-prossed. To me, it all had the appearance of a well-rehearsed charade.

I didn't know what evidence had made up the now-departed

"ironclad" case, but I had learned from detectives who had worked
on it that they considered the evidence solid. The devious retreat
of the case through the court—from "ironclad" to the release on
bail of the unbailable defendant to the final nol-prossing action—
had the reek of a well-oiled fix.

I am not normally an aggressive man, but I resented the transparent deception in the Kanove case. Unless you were an idiot,
you knew that this case was never going to be tried. Granted that
Kanove was not an estimable character, just a small-time hood,
still the implication bothered me. If an "ironclad" murder case
could be killed off in this fashion, was there any lesser crime that
couldn't be "taken care of"? And what then became of our vaunted
American system of justice, the crowning glory of our free democratic system?

So reasoning, I was not prepared, as others apparently were,
just to drop the Kanove case and forget all about it. I discovered
a stubborn streak in my nature, and I felt myself compelled,
despite some trepidation, to badger Prosecutor Robbins whenever
he held a press conference. I would always ask him if his office
had uncovered any new evidence about the Kanove murder. Dots
of perspiration would spring out on his upper lip as he fumbled
through halting explanations about how difficult it was to uncover
new evidence about a case so old. He never failed to mention
that he had not handled the case originally, and I never failed to
remind him that he had been an assistant in in the office when
the "ironclad" case was born.

My persistent needling made me so obnoxious that a veteran
of the press corps read me a lecture on the facts of life. "Listen,
Fred," he said. "Why don't you lay off the Kanove case? You're
only making Robbins mad, and you're only hurting yourself. You're
going to have to work with these people, you know, and they can
help you or hurt you. Why keep sticking your neck out? Do you
think the Asbury Park *Press* cares anything about you? Hell, all
they care about is selling papers and making money. In this game,
you better look out for yourself. Play along and stop making enemies when it isn't necessary."

That was a creed, I found, that many reporters live by, but I
couldn't—and wouldn't. And, somewhat to my surprise, I soon
discovered that independence had its advantages. A reporter finds
his or her best sources among departmental working staffs, and
one who establishes a reputation for independence and integrity

can gain the confidence of workers whose inside knowledge is invaluable. In Prosecutor Robbins's own office, Robbins's chief of county detectives became one of my best sources of information.

Ernest Burdge was a quiet, soft-spoken man of medium height who walked so quietly that he could ghost through a room before you were even aware that he was there. He had a thick plume of gray hair, parted in the middle, and a small, gray mustache above lips that seemed set in a perpetual, cynical smirk. Those lips seemed to say that he had seen it all, that it was one helluva world and there wasn't anything in it that was going to shock or surprise him anymore. Ernest's somewhat jaundiced view of life included, I felt sure, a measure of contempt for Prosecutor Robbins himself, and so my jousts with Robbins did me no harm where he was concerned.

I visited Ernest Burdge whenever I had a spare moment, and I became aware early on that something was stirring in the prosecutor's office. Ernest was having a frequent and unusual visitor, one Frank (Heinie) Miller, a former state trooper whom I had known slightly in high school. I decided to cultivate Heinie Miller.

I knew that Heinie had been cashiered from the State Police for some infraction of regulations, and I sensed in him a man on a secret boil. He stood about 5 feet 10, had a round, florid, basset-hound kind of face, and walked with bouncy little steps that made him move at a pace that caused a companion to trot. His thick, good-natured lips moved so rapidly that they were a verbal counterpart to his swift stride.

In those days I was up till all hours of the night, and after dispatching the day's news, at one or two o'clock in the morning I could always find Heinie at the counter at the Hendrix Diner. I'd have my coffee and hamburger and then we might take a ride along the beach. In this way I quietly pumped Heinie and learned more about the shadow world of life—the killings, the payoffs, the fixes—than I ever could have otherwise. The Kanove fix, I saw, was not unusual except that it had left a vague trail in court records.

The long Monmouth-Ocean County coastline, with its numerous inlets and bays, its isolated creeks and winter-deserted beaches, its thick pine forests concealing stills in the hinterlands, had been ideally fashioned by nature to become a mecca for some of the most powerful underworld figures of the Prohibition era. Swift boats ferried their cargoes from Rum Row into secluded coves, where the liquor was loaded into waiting trucks that trundled across the state to satisfy parched throats in the great metropolises of Philadelphia and New York.

Shortly after Heinie joined the force, a gung-ho recruit who had graduated from the State Police Academy third highest in his class, he was on patrol late one night and stopped a couple of suspicious-looking trucks. He found that they were loaded with liquor, hauled the drivers into the station, and then, he said, "All hell broke loose." The sergeant in charge of his barracks bawled him out; higher-ups in headquarters were enraged. Those were "protected" trucks, he was informed; and they were released with abject apologies to their drivers. Only Heinie got shafted for trying to do his job. After that, whenever he spotted bootleggers running their cargoes across the state, he just let them go.

The superintendent of State Police at the time, H. Norman Schwartzkopf, a graduate of West Point and a veteran of World War I, had been criticized for the manner in which the State Police had handled the investigation of the Lindbergh baby kidnapping. But later he returned to the Army, became a brigadier general in World War II, and afterward was an undercover agent in the plot that overthrew the government of Iran and placed the Shah upon the throne. For his services he received the two highest awards granted by the Shah's regime. On the surface, his was a highly distinguished career. Yet it had been during Schwartzkopf's tenure as head of the State Police that bootleggers' trucks had crisscrossed the state on their protected journeys. Heinie Miller didn't know how the "protection" had been arranged; he only knew that the influence coming from somewhere at the top was so powerful that no trooper in the ranks dared touch the "protected" cargoes.

After Heinie was ejected from the State Police, he returned to Point Pleasant and put all his energy into vindicating himself and gair ng reinstatement. To accomplish this, he knew, he would have to have valuable information to trade. So he put on an act, cursing the State Police, raving about what a dirty deal he had been given, gradually ingratiating himself with a small-time mob headquartered in an old white stucco mansion on the bank of the Manasquan River. Soon he knew so many secrets that he was a walking source book about official payoffs and mob murders, for this riverfront mob, though small, had handy gunmen who were often called in to do a job for more powerful gangsters.

One night in October 1933 Heinie went with the mob boss to the West Creek Yacht Club, in southern Ocean County, where a cargo of liquor was being landed. Heinie and the boss drove around the circle in front of the club and parked on the far side. They hadn't been there long when a sedan pulled up and the county sheriff, who was, as Heinie put it, "so drunk he could hardly stand and blowing bubbles all over himself," got out and came over to them, accompanied by his son-in-law. The sheriff demanded whether they knew who he was, then jerked open the front of his coat and showed them his badge.

"So the sheriff really took money from the bootleggers, did he?" I asked Heinie.

"Sure, I hope to tell you he did. What do you think he was there for that night? He wasn't there to stop them, I can tell you that."

It should be said that Heinie Miller was a highly reliable informant. Before he went to see Ernest Burdge, he had felt out the Monmouth county prosecutor's office because he had information about a number of sensational mob murders in that county and had come away feeling (with good reason, as it turned out) that the office was not to be trusted.

Then he had contacted Burdge and was helping him build a case against three mobsters involved in another southern Ocean County murder. Heinie's testimony was to send all three to prison. During his conferences with Burdge on this case, Heinie gave the county detective information about a murder in the Belmar Moose Club. Burdge, after checking, developed what he thought was a solid case and spelled out all the evidence for a Monmouth County detective one Friday in May 1934. The following Thursday, just six days later, the hit man Burdge had named was himself murdered. Ernest Burdge and his assistant, Bob Gibson, confided to me their feeling that there was "something screwy" with the Monmouth detective staff. But Heinie Miller wasn't surprised: he had told me that the word in underworld circles was that in nineteen of New Jersey's twenty-one counties protection could be purchased for everything—including murder. Ocean County, he said, was one of the two exceptions because Ernest Burdge, though he might have to wink at a lot of things, drew the line at murder.

Such was the view of the subterranean world of the times that

I obtained from Heinie Miller during our nighttime talks. Everything he told me convinced me more than ever that there had been a brazen payoff in the Kanove murder case, but the details continued to elude me.

Then one day I covered a particularly horrible automobile accident. A wealthy Trenton businessman, drunk and driving a high-powered car, went roaring around a curve on a two-lane macadam road at 60 or 70 miles an hour. The car veered over into the opposite lane and smashed head-on into a Model A Ford in which a farmer and his wife were riding. The impact killed both and reduced the Model A to a heap of bloodstained scrap metal. The big shot's car roared right on down the road, still careening on the wrong side, not stopping until it plowed into a tree.

Tommy Forkin, a trooper from the Toms River State Police barracks, investigated the accident. He charged the wealthy businessman with drunken driving and manslaughter. The peculiar providence that looks after drunks had kept the driver of the death car alive, but leg and hip fractures and internal injuries had him hospitalized for weeks. After he was released, the question arose: what was going to happen to the charges that Tommy Forkin had lodged against him?

It was not long before the reek of the man's money began to permeate the case. Rumors circulated among the lower echelons in the courthouse (my best informants) that no indictment would be returned by the grand jury. How, I wondered, was this possible in a case so tragic where the guilt was so obvious? The answer, it developed, was really simple. When Leo Robbins had to "take care of" a case, he employed his favorite tactic: he just never called the key witness to testify. In this instance, he was maneuvering the case through the grand jury without letting the jurors hear the testimony of Tommy Forkin.

This was the situation the night I walked into the Toms River State Police barracks and talked to the sergeant in charge, a well-cultivated source of mine. "Tommy is really wild about this case," my friend said, "and he's served notice on Robbins that if the prosecutor's office won't call him he's going to walk in and demand that the foreman of the grand jury call him as a witness."

My trooper friend was only beginning with his disclosures. Leo Robbins's patent attempt to quash all charges in the secrecy of the grand jury room hadn't endeared him to the state troopers.

The men of the barracks sympathized with Forkin and admired his courage. It was one of those instances when devious official maneuvering becomes so outrageous that those with secret knowledge are bursting to unload it if they know a newsman can be trusted. My earlier obsession with the Kanove case and my clashes with Robbins were well known, so my trooper friend exploded.

"Do you know what *really* happened in the Kanove case?" he asked me out of the blue.

Of course I didn't.

"Well," he said, "understand, if you use this, I never saw you, don't know you, never talked to you. All right? Well, you remember that letter J. Mercer Davis wrote? This is the way it happened: Davis is standing on a street corner in Camden. He's leaning up against a lamppost reading a true detective magazine. A man brushes up against him, and then Davis folds up the magazine, puts it in his pocket and walks away. And what do you think he found when he got home? Why, there was $5000 in his magazine!"

There is a saying in the newspaper business that the best stories are the ones that can never be printed. I finally knew how the murder charge had been fixed in the Kanove case—but I couldn't use it.

A couple of years later I got an unexpected cross-check on the story. Ira F. Smith, the attorney for the accused murderer, was facing bankruptcy and desperately needed money. In this strait, he came to me and repeated, detail for detail, the story of the $5000 payoff, which he had watched from his car on a nearby street. But he wanted the *Press* to pay for his account, and, though I could corroborate it, the *Press* wouldn't pay, unwilling to accept the risks involved in publishing the story.

There remained the case of the wealthy businessman whose drunken driving had killed a farm couple. Tommy Forkin, after his ultimatum to Robbins, had been allowed to testify before the grand jury; and the jury, having no choice, had indicted the businessman for drunken driving and manslaughter. This meant that the case would have to be disposed of in open court. Considering the extreme to which Robbins had gone in his effort to kill the case before the grand jury, there seemed little reason to doubt that this indictment, too, would be fixed somehow.

It was like a replay of an old, familiar script. Once again, a judge was brought in from outside the county, a judge who could do the desired deed and then depart without facing the repercussions. On the appointed day, the defendant hobbled into court on crutches, making the most of his painful injuries. His attorney, after entering a plea of guilty, argued for leniency on the grounds that his client had already suffered terribly and would be haunted all his life by the memory of the tragedy for which he had been responsible.

Prosecutor Robbins then rose. He seemed embarrassed; his hands shook; his lips trembled. He told the court that he had received a number of letters from prominent persons, one a minister, urging that the defendant be dealt with leniently, and he wanted to join in making that recommendation.

The visiting judge remarked ironically that it was highly unusual for a prosecutor to be pleading for a defendant. But then, his task made easier, he imposed a fine that was a mere pinprick to the wealthy man's bankroll and imposed a six-month term in the county jail—suspended, of course.

The case, as we all knew, would have been buried quietly months earlier had it not been for Tommy Forkin's defiance. But even such a remarkable demonstration of principle by a state trooper could not prevail in a boss-ridden county where the fix was a way of life.

The entire double-fix sequence made a long-lasting impression on me. It demonstrated just how the courts could be manipulated and justice distorted. I encountered other and, in some ways, more horrifying examples during my time in Ocean County; and I have reflected often in later life that I was fortunate to begin my reporting career in a rural area where I could see the skeleton of the system exposed and come to understand how it worked. In a large city, where news is more diffuse and close contact with helpful sources less likely, I might have reported routinely what happened, not knowing what lay behind the event.

When I went to New York and dealt with larger issues, I had at least the grounding in how the system worked. When I saw distortions of justice in the Remington case, the Hiss case and many others, I could understand what I saw; I could recognize that what I had seen working on a small scale in Ocean County was just the same at the top.

8

Bill Fischer
and the
New Jersey Courier

B

ILL FISCHER WAS AN ANACHRONISM IN A TIME WHEN
financial pressures had brought the downfall of the great
New York *World* and had subordinated many a newsroom
to the business interests of the front office. His *New Jersey Courier*, just a small weekly paper with a circulation of some 3000 that
existed on the ragged edge of survival, inveighed against corruption and injustice as if it had all the resources of a Hearst or a
Gannett behind it.

Indomitable, unquenchable, William Henry Fischer would not
be deterred when principle was involved: no pressures—and they
were awesome in a county ruled by Boss Mathis—could make
him swerve by as much as a hair when he was embarked on a
crusade. And it was not long before I adopted him as my professional godfather.

The editor was sixty-six and I, the cub reporter, was twenty-
two when we met in the spring of 1933.

There was a distinctly Dickensian flavor about Bill Fischer. A
gnome of a man only a mite over five feet tall, he elevated himself
at his desk by sitting on a couple of fat metropolitan telephone
directories as he punched away in two-fingered fashion at an old
Oliver typewriter with keys arranged in stepladder fashion up the
sides. His attire was a miracle of indifference: a shapeless gray

jacket from the upper pocket of which poked wisps of narrow-cut copy paper on which he jotted notes; baggy pants and scuffed tan shoes; a bow tie that looked as if a drunk might have wrestled with it in his sleep.

The office from which he chronicled the affairs of his town and county was equally Dickensian. The *Courier* was located on the second floor of an old, rickety wooden Main Street building that must at one time have been a private mansion. Its entrance was an inconspicuous wooden door opening on the street. A sign just inside proclaimed: THE PRINCIPAL OFFICE OF THE NEW JERSEY COURIER. It was, of course, the *only* office of the *Courier*, and I never knew whether the sign represented some unfulfilled dream or was simply an uncharacteristic bit of pretense. A flight of some twenty dusty, dingy steps led up to a door with a frosted glass panel in its center, beyond which was a dark hall, another door with frosted panel, and then a final door at the end of the hall opened into the newspaper office. Behind a long counter, piled with recent files of the paper, and across the room, almost hidden behind a high rolltop desk, sat Bill Fischer, pale blue eyes shielded by a battered green eyeshade, punching away on his Oliver on one of his scorching editorials.

He had an acerbic style which coupled with his high principles often irritated many political powers in the county. With a long, straight, sniffish nose and a lifetime of contacts, he caught the scent of political knavery almost before it had a chance to develop; and he never hesitated to expose what he found in the pages of the *Courier*.

Fischer had led a lonely life of dedication. Legend had it that he had once been deeply in love with a beautiful young woman who died suddenly and he had never courted another. In the years I knew him, he lived with two maiden sisters a few blocks from his office; watchers along Main Street could set their clocks by him as he walked to the *Courier* every morning at seven.

When he was young, Fischer had worked as a printer in Philadelphia, coming home to Toms River on weekends. One weekend he learned that the down-at-heels, four-page weekly *Courier* was for sale for $500. He borrowed the money and bought the newspaper, which he wrote and edited for the next forty-five years, only once taking a week's vacation—and that to be a delegate to a Kiwanis International convention.

During the Roaring Twenties, the paper had prospered, and Fischer had become a fairly wealthy man. As such, he was drawn into a real estate deal involving a large tract of ocean-to-bay land on Long Beach Island. But a hurricane struck, bulkheads were washed out—and the real estate market collapsed in the Great Depression. He was wiped out financially, left only with his paper that once more had to struggle to stay afloat.

Still, he always said what he believed needed saying, and once he was convinced an important principle was involved, he'd say it in a vitriolic style that pierced even the walrus hides of the most hardened politicians.

As far back as 1905, he had fought the first of his three great battles. Here again, there is a Dickensian flavor to the story, which takes us back to another age, another world—the world of small-town individualism and town-meeting democracy that was about to be submerged in the tides of mass production, huge concentrations of power and ever-larger governmental projects.

"You'll laugh at this," Fischer told me once, "but graft first came into rural communities in a small way when a law was passed providing for free textbooks in the public schools. At the time, one company had a virtual monopoly on the printing of textbooks. However, another firm entered the business and sent men into New Jersey. A bitter rivalry developed, and it eventually came to the point where book agents had to go into the field and buy up members of local school boards in order to sell their books."

A much juicier source of local graft—one that had led to the indictment of the entire Board of Freeholders—had come with the extension of rural road systems and the building of bridges. Fischer liked to tell how one bridge-building corporation had feted the entire Board of Freeholders by taking them to its plant in Ohio and then on a junket up into Canada.

"I had a very good friend on the board at that time," Fischer told me, "and I argued and argued with him, but I could not make him see that his first duty was to the people—to vote for the firm that would build the best bridges. 'Bill,' he said, 'after all these people have done for us, I simply can't go back on them now.' And he was a man, too, who never did a thing in his life that he thought was dishonest."

On behalf of the taxpayers Fischer mounted a taxpayers campaign in the *Courier* against excessive spending. As a result, the

Supreme Court Justice having jurisdiction over the county appointed a special investigator to examine the freeholders' records. The probe uncovered procedures that have become all too familiar by now. Money appropriated for other purposes had been diverted by the board to build roads and bridges; the cost of this work had often exceeded the contracted price (what we now call overruns); many contracts were mysteriously missing from the files, presumably to cover up chicanery. The prober reported that out of twelve road contracts only three could be found in the official files, and two of these were incomplete. Only four of eight bridge contracts were still in existence.

The indictment based on this evidence accused the entire board of having been derelict in its duties, and all of those indicted pleaded guilty. A year later, Fischer happily reported that whereas the county had been $35,000 in debt before the taxpayers' revolt, the entire debt had been paid off and the county entered the new fiscal year with a $12,500 surplus.

Such figures seem minuscule in the era of multibillion-dollar federal deficits, but in 1905–06 this $35,000 probably represented twenty times what it does today, and in a poor rural county in those days it was certainly a sizable sum.

When I met Bill Fischer, he was about to engage in his final, climactic battle for justice. Fischer had been at one time a political power in the county, although he had never been a boss in the conventional sense of the term, functioning for many years as the brains of a loosely knit coalition of responsible civic leaders. Then Tom Mathis had come on the scene.

A master mariner and one-time skipper of the famous racing yacht *America*, Mathis started with a small state job—which had been secured for him by Bill Fischer. But, it soon emerged, Mathis had more lofty ambitions. In one election he pledged his support to a ticket sponsored by Fischer and his allies, but as primary day drew near (victory in the Republican primary was tantamount to election in Ocean County), Fischer heard a rumor that Mathis was going to double-cross him. When Fischer confronted Mathis, the future boss virtually laughed in his face. "Sure. What did you expect?" he said. When the votes were counted, Mathis had destroyed the Fischer coalition and won for himself the nomination for state senator.

When I began covering Ocean County, Tom Mathis still looked

very much like the sturdy mariner he once had been. His stocky, burly figure seemed to exude physical prowess. He had heavy jowls and steely cold eyes. To attend one of his Thomas A. Mathis Club rallies was to get a lesson in the coarser side of politics. First, a couple of his chosen spellbinders would warm up the crowd with fulsome oratory, praising God, motherhood, our great democratic way of life, our glorious freedom—and somehow equating Tom Mathis with all of these cherished symbols of 100 percent Americanism. Then the beer kegs would be tapped. All the while, Mathis sat at the head of the speakers' table, a square, granite block, and a queue of supplicants for his favor would pass slowly before him, each nearly genuflecting as he made his plea. Mathis would merely nod in acknowledgment, his unblinking eyes revealing nothing.

Such was the man who held the county in his grasp. Every town of any size had its Thomas A. Mathis Club, and anyone who wanted to run for local office had better have a T.A.M. endorsement. Even someone who wanted a job so menial as working on the roads had better have a rabbi in the T.A.M. ranks. Any contractor who wanted to do business with the county was well-advised to walk up to the second-floor office on Washington Street where Mathis's real estate and insurance business profited greatly from the policies it wrote on county property. And it followed that those bent on bending or breaking the law needed some kind of clearance from the boss of the all-powerful machine that controlled law enforcement agencies.

Never were two more opposite protagonists—in physique and principle—pitted against each other. While Mathis's obsession was with power and its prerequisites, Bill Fischer's deepest concern was with what was ethical and what was best for the people, and his taxpayers' success was small change compared to the amounts involved after the Mathis machine acquired complete dominance over the county. Grafting contracts became almost inconsequential compared to the payoffs associated with the rum-running of Prohibition days. It was this type of graft—the corruption of law enforcement and the inevitable perversion of justice—that most incensed Fischer in his later years.

The Mathis machine had always found a way to pack the grand jury with its faithful followers. But when the April 1930 grand jury was selected, something happened that was never supposed

to happen: the names of a number of independents had been
slipped into the drum from which the jurors were drawn. And,
by the luck of the draw, several of these unharnessed souls had
been picked for jury service—Bill Fischer among them.

"I wasn't feeling well at the time," Fischer told me later, "and
I knew the kind of battle I would be getting into. But friends
kept telling me, 'This is our last chance. If we don't do something
now, we never will.' "

So Fischer heeded the call of duty and became foreman of the
grand jury. The customary practice had been for the jury to meet
only at the call of the prosecutor. But Fischer determined to use
the rarely exercised inherent power of the grand jury and announced that the jury would meet every week. Sensing trouble,
Prosecutor Davis dredged up all the cases he could find in his
files, but eventually ran out of them. At that point, Fischer ordered him to leave the grand jury room because, he said, the
jury had some matters it wanted to take up on its own.

The action was unprecedented, incredible. Fischer was heading
a runaway panel that began calling witnesses to testify about one
of the more flagrant sources of corruption in the county: a wide-
open numbers-running and slot-machine racket in Lakewood.
Fischer contended with impeccable logic that such scandalously
blatant violations of the law couldn't be going on unless law enforcement officials were being paid off.

Almost at once, he ran into opposition from judges whose political obligations exceeded their responsibilities to uphold the
law. A Supreme Court Justice, one of the most powerful jurists
in the state, expressed his concern thus: "Who knows where all
this might lead?" Fischer replied that he didn't care, that he was
prepared to follow the trail of evidence wherever it took him.
Fischer asked for a special prosecutor to supersede Davis and
give the jury needed legal advice, and the distinguished Justice
threatened to refuse this request and disband the jury. If the
Justice took such action, Fischer warned, he would expose the
whole judicial roadblock in the *Courier*. He got his special prosecutor, but it did not end his problems with a judicial system
concerned less about crime than about where the trail of crime
might lead.

The grand jury indicted Prosecutor Davis, his chief of detectives, an investigator in his office and a state trooper. A circuit

court judge promptly directed verdicts of acquittal for all four men and the T.A.M.-controlled Board of Freeholders appealed to Supreme Court Justice Joseph L. Bodine to discharge the jury. Bodine obliged, reprimanding the jurors in the process.

Fischer promptly took the war to the front pages of the *Courier* as he had promised, and his editorials about the political-judicial cabal that was jobbing justice attracted so much attention and caused such a public backfire that Bodine, in an almost unheard-of action, publicly reversed himself and reinstated the jury. The jurors once more indicted Davis, charging him with conspiracy to break the law and malfeasance; it also indicted the slot-machine and numbers boss of the county.

Now another fix had to be arranged to keep Fischer from finding out how high the trail of corruption might lead. This called for the machine to use its favorite strategy, one available only to a political boss powerful enough to jerk court assignments around. The ubiquitous visiting judge was brought in from outside the county, and he dismissed the indictment against Davis and imposed a harmless fine on the gambling kingpin. Once this had been done, Davis and all his crew who had been tainted in the investigation resigned.

There the probe stopped. Fischer's grand jury had achieved a partial cleaning out of the prosecutor's office, but the judicial system, instead of permitting the jury to continue to sit, as it could have done, disbanded it at the end of its regular term in September 1930. The cover-up was complete. Fischer never had a chance to show how high the corruption went. But the extreme measures that had been taken to thwart him suggested very strongly that it had gone very high indeed.

9

Showboat

ONE SPARKLING MAY MORNING IN 1934, I STOOD NEAR THE Manasquan Inlet and, as the sun glinted off the blue waters of the Atlantic Ocean, I watched the arrival of a clumsy craft that looked like a scow with a large house on top that was being brought through the inlet to be docked in a nearby channel, where it was to become a floating nightclub. According to the publicity, this strange-looking craft had been the houseboat of Sir Thomas Lipton, the British tea tycoon and yachtsman who had tried so often and so futilely to take the America's Cup back to Britain.

There were two others in the reception party at the inlet that morning—Police Chief Ridgeway T. Lane, of Point Pleasant Beach, and his deputy, Sergeant Russell Archer. Along with this weird house on a scow came a short, dapper, wisecracking advance man who greeted Lane and Archer familiarly. What I remember most vividly about him, aside from his expensive clothes, were his pointed, highly polished, yellow-tan shoes; pointy shoes of that particular shade seemed to be a Mafia badge in those days. He answered my skeptical questions with assurances that the docking craft had indeed been Sir Thomas Lipton's houseboat and that it was now going to be transformed into a showboat with the name S.S. *Club Royale*.

The whole affair had a suspiciously phony taint, but I could only write the story straight, simply reporting the arrival of the once famous Lipton "houseboat."

The proprietors launched their venture with an elaborate party for local and county officials, and the true nature of the *Club Royale* soon became evident. A few days later I began to hear much joshing about the fervor with which some of the guests had tried out the roulette wheels and birdcages.

Bill Fischer too began to hear the stories and found himself right back where he had been four years earlier when he headed the runaway grand jury. The *Club Royale* was obviously an illegal enterprise, and it could not be running wide open, with Sergeant Russell Archer on nightly duty helping to direct cars into its parking lot, without the knowledge and compliance of law enforcement officials. To Fischer, the protection of crime by officials and the resultant corruption of the law was no minor matter. If the law was for sale, there could be no justice; and with justice defiled, no man could consider himself safe.

On July 5, Fischer telephoned Prosecutor Robbins and warned him he understood the *Club Royale* was not just a nightclub but a gambling den. What did the prosecutor plan to do about it? Robbins said he was preoccupied with preparing a murder case for trial and he would look into Fischer's charges about the gambling boat as soon as he had time. In a prominent box on page one of the *Courier,* Fischer notified the public of the warning he had given Robbins, though he did not at that time name the showboat.

When a week passed without action, Fischer began to build a fire under officialdom. In a front-page editorial, he called the attention of the Supreme Court Justice with jurisdiction over the county to the illegal gambling. The Justice subsequently asked the grand jury then in session to take action—a demand Fischer reiterated the following week in an editorial which gave the showboat's name—but the jury was well stacked. It did nothing.

As a result, Fischer himself acted.

Sometime after midnight one night the ringing of my phone jolted me awake. A familiar voice said, "Fred, this is Bill Fischer. We've raided the showboat."

I couldn't put my clothes on fast enough. By the time I got to the showboat, all was confusion. The raiding party was loading a truck with roulette wheels, birdcages, crap tables and other gambling paraphernalia. Fischer was standing to one side, supervising the operation. Just then, an agitated policeman rushed up to Fischer. The arrested employees of the gambling room had slipped through a side door, he said, while all the officers had their backs turned.

Fischer jerked up angrily. "Search the boat," he ordered. "They couldn't have gotten away. You know who they are. Arrest them." The officer began to slink away, pursued by Fischer's angry questions: "How could you have let them get away? How could you have let it happen?"

It was fairly obvious, of course, how it had happened. A lot of palms get greased in the gambling racket, and Fischer's raiders apparently had not been immune to temptation.

In the end, four men were rearrested and taken to Toms River along with the truckload of gambling paraphernalia. They were held under bail to await the action of the grand jury, and then the reassessments started.

The raid had been one of those shocking things that could never happen—but did. Ordinarily, there were just three law enforcement agencies that could pull such a raid: the local police, the county sheriff, and the prosecutor. With all of these potential sources of trouble conveniently blind, the showboat had been enjoying a perfect immunity. Then Fischer had taken advantage of a quirk in the law that everyone else had overlooked.

A constable is the lowest form of badge-toter. He's a part-time, amateur cop, whose principal function usually is to serve legal papers. But the constable has one unique prerogative: his authority is not limited to one town as a local policeman's is; he can go anywhere in the state to serve his summonses.

A week before he pulled the raid, Fischer, accompanied by the pastor of his Methodist church, had visited the showboat. They had no trouble getting into the gambling room and observing the play there. Toms River was then in the control of a local Democratic organization at odds with the Mathis machine, and Fischer easily obtained the loan of town constables and went right over the heads of all the regular law enforcement authorities.

The alibis were feverish; the screams of indignation loud and shrill. Prosecutor Robbins's favorite line was that Fischer's amateurs had blown the chance to make a solid case. Admittedly, they had seized a truckload of gambling paraphernalia—after all, the stuff was right there in the courthouse yard, and he could hardly deny it—but the raiders had let the gamblers get away.

Who could be certain that the four men they had later arrested were the right ones? Now, if he, Robbins, had pulled the raid, it would have been done professionally; the gamblers would never have been allowed to slip out the side door.

Fischer ripped this contention to shreds in a series of sizzling editorials. Operators do not undertake such a costly illegal venture as the showboat unless they have ironclad assurances in advance that they will not be disturbed, he said. And they could get such solid guarantees only from the political machine that controlled the county. Fischer emphasized that, according to the testimony at the preliminary hearing, the first request of the men on the raided showboat was that they be given permission to telephone the sheriff's office. Fischer cited his earlier warning to Robbins, his call for the Supreme Court Justice and the grand jury to act. Nothing had been done, and he held the Mathis Republican machine in the county totally responsible.

It was like puncturing a beehive. The courthouse corridors swarmed with angry buzzings; venom filled the air. "Mad," some called Fischer. "What good does he think he's doing stirring up such a mess? Just gives the county a bad name." Deputy Surrogate Percy Grover (a relation of Fischer's by his eldest sister's marriage into the Grover family) was especially vehement: "He must have a screw loose, that white-haired old son of a bitch," he sputtered to me one day.

No one seemed disturbed that the raid had exposed a breed of underworld vermin who should have been banished from any self-respecting community. One of the four men arrested on the showboat, FBI fingerprint records showed, had been arrested twelve times previously under a number of aliases for offenses that ranged from jostling to grand larceny and robbery with a gun. But the official protestations made it sound as if this poor, wronged innocent ranked with some of our most eminent citizens.

On August 3, the grand jury met to consider the showboat case. That same day, an editorial by Fischer called on the panel to do its duty. He charged that "the almighty dollar" was proving more potent than "the majesty of the law." Arguments advanced in defense of the showboat, he said, boiled down to contentions that "gamblers are making money and spending some of it in Point Pleasant, and they should be permitted to break the law, provided they spend money in Point Pleasant."

He concluded: "The grand jury is in session today. The evidence is not to be questioned—unanswerable. If the State's representatives demand an indictment, how could a grand jury refuse to vote true bills?"

The politically packed grand jury had no trouble in refusing to do its duty. Its task was made easier by Prosecutor Robbins, who adopted his characteristic tactic for preventing an indictment by simply not calling the witnesses essential to the voting of an indictment. For example, neither Fischer nor his Methodist pastor was called. It was as if Robbins had never heard their names. With their damaging testimony blocked out, Robbins fed the jury his favorite line—that the raid had been botched; that Fischer's amateurs hadn't secured "the right kind" of evidence. And so the complaisant jury refused to indict; bail was canceled for the four men who had been arrested and they were released, in effect exonerated.

The following week the flaws in this strategy became glaringly apparent. D. Frederick Burnett, then state alcoholic beverage commissioner, conducted a hearing in Toms River to determine whether the showboat's liquor license should be revoked. In just one day, Burnett uncovered more facts than law enforcement officials had in a month. He called witnesses who mattered. Fischer described his two visits to the gambling sanctum, and a pastor from Ocean Grove testified that he, too, had observed the activities in the room of chance.

Burnett also subpoenaed the officially listed owner of the showboat and the man in whose name the liquor license had been issued. The showboat owner acknowledged that he had leased the gambling room to one of the four men who had been arrested; that he had been aware gambling was going on there; that he "hadn't liked it," but he had just never gotten around to doing anything about it. The liquor licensee was a tall, well-built, brash hood. He was arrogant and contemptuous of the whole proceeding. Sure, he said, he held the liquor license, but he couldn't be expected to know everything that was going on in the showboat. What had he thought was happening in that gambling room? He had no idea. Perhaps some customers were playing cards there. How was he to know? He was too busy.

On the basis of this testimony, Burnett canceled the showboat's liquor license. Prosecutor Robbins, red-faced, upper lip bedewed with perspiration, protested with waving hands that he just hadn't known about all this evidence (not that he'd wanted to know); but now that the evidence had been dumped in his lap, he was going to reconvene the grand jury and go right after those scoundrelly showboat gamblers.

The farce now reached its climax. On this second try, the grand jury ignored the testimony given Burnett by the showboat owner and liquor licensee. It simply indicted the man who, the owner had testified, had held the lease on the gambling room. The only trouble was that the accused gentleman had vanished after his bail had been revoked when the grand jury had previously failed to indict. Authorities weren't even sure they knew his right name; and so, of course, to no one's surprise, he was never heard of again.

The fiasco was made to order for Fischer's biting invective, and all kinds of efforts were made to shut him up. Since the showboat was docked in my hometown, I had come to know some of the employees, including one who had been given the task of buttering up Fischer with some lucrative advertising. A seedy character, he tried to impress me with the oldest saw in the trade: "I used to be a newspaperman myself, worked on the old *World,* you know." He walked into Fischer's drab office and offered the *Courier* a full-page of S.S. *Club Royale* advertising for ten weeks. It was a thousand-dollar deal, no mean inducement in those hard times for a weekly newspaper that was just scraping along. But Fischer didn't hesitate: the *Courier* wouldn't accept a line of *Club Royale* advertising, he said, and he would be obliged if the visitor would just get out of his office.

I encountered the shocked and incredulous emissary as he left Fischer's office. It was obvious that "the old *World,*" if indeed he had ever seen the inside of the *World,* had never prepared him for Bill Fischer. "I never said a thing about his editorial policies," he protested, explaining what had happened. "I wasn't trying to buy him—you *know* I wouldn't do that. How can he turn down a thousand dollars? What is he—crazy?"

Purchase having failed, pressure followed. Fischer described it in his issue of August 10:

> Since the *Courier* first published the opening of a gambling house in Point Pleasant Beach, it has been beset with offers to buy its silence on the one hand, and threats of what would

happen to the editor on the other, if the opposition to gambling was continued.

Its refusal to take advertising of the S.S. *Club Royale* and print no more about the gambling house was followed by approaches among its own advertisers who, on failure to make the *Courier* see the propriety and desirability of such a course as taking gambling money as hush money, have canceled their own advertising.

Business acquaintances have been sent to the *Courier* to plead that they were "getting theirs" out of the showboat, and while they did not condone gambling, still it was a good thing for the boro of Point Pleasant Beach and they pleaded with the *Courier* to say no more about it.

This failing, threats followed. In two issues of a town paper [Mathis's own *Ocean County Sun*], it has been threatened that "the front of a Main Street place of business" might be found blown out by a "pineapple."

This week threats have gone further. It has been told that the grand jury would be called together next Friday and if the *Courier* editor did not call off his opposition to the *Club Royale* . . . he would on the 17th be indicted for criminal libel.

The present grand jury last Friday voted no bill in the *Club Royale* case, with the evidence at its disposal that is given to the *Courier* readers in this issue.

I have no doubt that if the present grand jury wishes, it can find an indictment against the editor of the *Courier*.

Fischer had, in effect, met the threat with a dare. It was the first intimation that the county gang—lambs where the operators of the showboat were concerned—might turn into raging lions of the law to prosecute Fischer. Nothing came of the threat at that time, perhaps because the machine did not want by its actions to confirm the accuracy of Fischer's pronouncement. The showboat, its business ruined, kept open until fall, and it was generally understood that it would not try to open the next year.

In the fall, a new grand jury was selected. Later court proceedings were to demonstrate just how well it was packed. The Republican county chairman was its foreman; fourteen of its twenty-one members were directly affiliated with the T.A.M. organization.

In early November, three weeks before the jury was to meet, I walked into Ernest Burdge's office. Ernest sat in his usual relaxed position with his feet on his desk, and we talked in desultory fashion for a few minutes. Then his lips twisted in that satirical smirk of his and he said, "I can give you a tip on a good story that is going to break. But you must promise me you won't tell anybody. And I mean *anybody*."

I told him, as I had on other occasions, "Of course, I won't tell anybody if you say so. You have my word on it."

Ernest knew, as everyone did, how close I was to Bill Fischer. His face seemed to take on a Machiavellian cast as he said, "The grand jury is going to meet three weeks from today, and they're going to indict Bill Fischer for criminal libel."

I was stunned. Ernest's bland announcement of what the jury was going to do three weeks before the jury even met in itself illustrates the kind of conspiratorial control the Mathis machine exercised over the processes of justice. But why did he tell me? I do not know to this day. Did he expect me to break my word and warn Fischer? Or did he, knowing how I'd always kept my word but also knowing how highly I regarded Fischer, want to put me on the spot and see me squirm?

If the latter was his intention, he certainly succeeded. The promise I had given Ernest, not knowing what was coming, was one of the hardest I've ever had to keep. I never went to Toms River without going to see Bill Fischer. He had become my professional godfather—and now I did not dare to go near him for fear I wouldn't be able to resist the temptation to give him a hint.

Silence became almost intolerable for me as I learned more about the despicable details of the organization's plot. The grand jury would return the indictment but keep it secret until night, after the courts had closed. The sheriff's deputies would then arrest Fischer and throw him into the county jail, where he would have to stay until he could raise bail in the morning. The organization's hatred of Fischer was so intense that the one thing they wanted above all else was to get a picture of him behind bars.

In this, they were foiled. The grand jury met on schedule and, in a perfunctory session that took only twenty or thirty minutes, indicted Fischer and the *Courier* for criminally libeling the sheriff and every member of the Republican county committee. But the second part of the game plan miscarried. What I, Fischer's friend, couldn't do, one of the organization's very own did. The municipal

judge in Toms River, a man with close ties to the Mathis organization, warned Fischer. The little editor got out of town that
afternoon, hid out with friends in Lakewood, and walked into
court with his lawyer the next morning, ready to post bail. The
Mathis gang never did get the picture it wanted.

In writing the story for the *Press* then and in the months that
followed, I never failed to put a burr under Leo Robbins's seat.
I pointed out prominently in every story that only the accuser
was being prosecuted—the accused had all been set free.

The indictment lifted Fischer from the relative obscurity of a
small-town editor to statewide prominence. The daily press unit
of the New Jersey Press Association, composed of the most powerful newspapers in the state, joined the battle and hired counsel
for Fischer's defense. The State Supreme Court granted a defense
motion for hearings to determine whether the indictments were
the product of a conspiracy. This had the effect of turning the
prosecuting authorities into the defendants, and, at this point,
Leo Robbins bowed out.

He announced that he was asking Attorney General David T.
Wilentz—the prosecutor who had acquired national fame for convicting Bruno Richard Hauptmann for the kidnapping of the Lindbergh baby—to name a special assistant to handle the case. As
he made the announcement, Robbins cast a sidelong glance at
me, bluffed a smile and made a washing gesture with his hands.
"I don't want any more of this business that only the accuser gets
indicted and the accused go scot free," he said. "Oh no, no, I've
had enough of that."

Named to pick up Robbins's fallen spear was Assistant Attorney
General Robert Peacock. Shortly before the scheduled Supreme
Court hearings, there was a great stirring of legal cerebellums—
one of those secret sessions that take place when lawyers who are
trying to make a deal deny that they are trying to make a deal.

The day the meeting was held I waited for Fischer to come
back from the conference in his attorney's office just across Main
Street. He entered and stood behind the counter in his editorial
office, the green eyeshade shoved up on his forehead and the
customary strips of copy paper poking upward from his gray jacket.

"Well," he said—the restless tapping of his pencil on the counter
was the only sign of tension—"they offered to drop the whole
thing." His head bobbed in a way he had whenever he gave vent

to a brief, mirthless chuckle. "That is, if I'd just run a little story."
He continued: "They said I could make it as innocuous as I pleased,
just so I run some little thing to say I didn't mean what everybody
knows I meant. Almost anything so that they can save face." Again
he gave that contemptuous chuckle. "And they told me, too, that
if I didn't they'd make it tough for me. Even if these indictments
are thrown out, they said, they'd call a new grand jury and have
me indicted all over again."

He was silent, still tapping the counter.

"What are you going to do?" I asked.

This short, frail, aged man seemed to grow in stature before
my eyes. "What *could* I do?" he said. "I could never look myself
in the face again if I did that. How could I live with myself?"

As he spoke, my mind flashed back to an incident that had
occurred a few months before. A welter of New Deal agencies
had just been created in an effort to prime the economic pump.
Although a Democratic administration was in power in Washington, the Mathis organization had still found ways to manipulate
the spending of Ocean County funds. One of Fischer's trusted
acquaintances had tipped him off to an especially juicy story about
the political misuse of funds intended for work-relief assignments.

Fischer had run the story. But what he hadn't realized at the
time was that only a small circle was privy to this particular bit
of political chicanery and the machine easily traced the source of
Fischer's tip and delivered him an ultimatum: "Tell Fischer to
print a retraction or you lose your job."

When Fischer told me he was going to repudiate the story, I
had protested, "But it was true, wasn't it?"

Fischer just looked at me mildly from behind his rimless glasses.
"Yes," he said, "the story was true. But I know this gang. They'll
do what they say. And this man has a wife and four children."

So Fischer had retracted a story that he knew to be true in
order to save the livelihood of his informant's family. But now,
standing there behind the counter in his newspaper office as night
fell, he made it clear that he wouldn't do the same for himself,
even if he had to go to jail.

The fight went on. Depositions were taken. Eight hundred
pages of testimony were compiled—testimony that showed the
rigged, political complexion of the jury that had indicted Fischer;
testimony that showed how Prosecutor Robbins turned the di-

rection of the jury over to the aggrieved sheriff's private counsel, who had indictments ready in his pocket; testimony that showed the Republican county chairman had run the show in the grand jury room, summoning the political gang's chosen witnesses and reading a prepared list of questions from a paper he held in his hand.

It was all a waste of time, effort and money. When the case came up for argument before the State Supreme Court, the state did not attempt to defend the indictments. It announced it was dropping them. At the same time, it disclosed it had made good on the gun-to-head threat made earlier to Fischer: a new grand jury indicted Fischer and the *Courier* again, this time charging criminal libel just against the sheriff.

Attorney General Wilentz professed to be shocked at this action. But I knew him to be about the slickest operator I have ever seen in action in a courtroom. It's inconceivable to me that he could have been totally ignorant of the threat and subsequent punitive action taken by his own deputy. Indeed, it was so blatantly persecutive an action that it raised a new storm in the state's press, and Wilentz hastily announced that the new charges were to be dropped.

Even Wilentz, however, couldn't get the deed done. At his order, Peacock walked into county court and asked the presiding judge (who held his position thanks to Tom Mathis) to nol-pros (in effect, drop) the charges. The judge refused. He cited as justification the manner in which a predecessor on the bench had been severely reprimanded by the Supreme Court for nol-prossing an indictment; but the case on which he relied had not the slightest resemblance to the issue before him. In that case, the motion had been made by defense attorneys; here, the prosecutor himself was saying in effect that his own case was bad and he wanted to get rid of it. It was almost unheard of for a judge to keep an indictment in force in such circumstances (the judge might have cited the Kanove murder case as a precedent) and Attorney General Wilentz let it be known that the new indictments against Fischer and the *Courier* would never be prosecuted as long as he was in office.

In a sense, Bill Fischer had been vindicated, but technically he was still a man under indictment. And the long struggle had taken its toll. On Monday, December 16, 1935, he walked down

Main Street precisely at 7 A.M. An hour later, one of his printers, coming to work, found him slumped at his desk, dead of a heart attack.

In the printshop, his associates found the last piece of copy he wrote. It was the text for a Christmas card, the type for which he had set himself:

A friend in need
Is a friend indeed;
I have found this to be true . . .
And so I bundle up my thanks
And send them,
Friend, to you.

10

Julia I

I WAS CHOSEN BY BILL FISCHER'S HEIRS TO SUCCEED HIM AS editor of the *Courier*. It was at once an honor and an almost unnerving challenge for a man not yet twenty-five.

The editorship paid $45 a week—a vital sum at this particular juncture in my personal life. I had recently met the woman with whom I was to be in love for the next forty years.

She was Julia Barbara Simpson, a tall, lissome lass from Island Heights, a resort on the Toms River a few miles east of the county seat. Julia was the secretary for the attorney Ira Smith when I met her. Hers had not been an easy life. Her divorced mother had had to struggle to raise her three children without alimony or child support, and Julia had gone to work right out of high school. She gave her mother virtually all her earnings, never had much for herself, but life had not soured her. She was a joyful companion, with a pixielike sense of humor and a breezy optimism that all would turn out right in the end.

We had wanted to get married before, but I was making only $28 a week at the *Press*. Now the higher salary at the *Courier* made marriage possible.

On January 17, 1936, I took over at the *Courier* and found my lead story waiting for me. In preparing for his defense in case the criminal libel charges should ever be brought to trial, Fischer had obtained a number of notarized affidavits attesting to the pervasive crookedness and corruption in the county—the kind of sworn documents newsmen rarely obtain. Only the widespread indignation aroused by the persecution of Fischer had induced witnesses to talk.

Some of these affidavits had been shown to members of the state legislature in the hope of triggering a state investigation of Ocean County officialdom. The Newark *Evening News*, then the largest and most prestigious paper in New Jersey, reported from Trenton that legislators were "seriously considering" such a probe. "Seriously considering" turned out to be all they ever did. I expected nothing more. It was naive to imagine that state legislators would authorize an investigation of one of their own. The legislature would never lift the lid on such a Pandora's Box as Ocean County. Who could tell where such an action might lead? What senator or assemblyman who voted to probe Tom Mathis's private fief today could be certain that it might not be *his* turn tomorrow?

I, however, had no reason to let the truth remain buried in the files. I could not name names; that could be done only in a court of law, but I could at least publish the details.

The information that Bill Fischer had collected dovetailed with everything Heinie Miller had told me earlier on our long night rides. One affidavit signed by a former law enforcement officer was especially significant. This ex-officer had become closely involved with a rum-running ring operating in the southern section of the county. The mastermind and financial angel of the operation, he averred, was the chief of county detectives in a neighboring county—a man who had acquired a national reputation as a wily, cornpone sleuth who had solved the most baffling crimes.

According to the affidavit, this famous detective supplied the money to build the rum-running boats and provided the capital to get the trucks and organize the traffic. Cargoes were landed at an isolated farm bordering on a small creek, and the county sheriff appeared regularly at the landing to supervise the unloading and receive the protective payoff. The signer of the affidavit asserted that he had seen money passed on several occasions and added that, after the trucks left the isolated landing, the corrupted official followed them in his car to make certain of their safe passage through the county. When low tides made it impossible to use the small creek, cargoes were landed at a more public dock. The same corrupt official was always on hand to supervise the operation and get the payoff. The maker of the affidavit estimated that between 20,000 and 25,000 cases of liquor had been landed at the secluded farm in the period of about one year.

A supporting affidavit from a municipal police officer described how he had been ordered to keep his hands off the liquor traffic. He told of conversations he had had with the bootlegging chief and of seeing the same county official named in the previous affidavit on the scene whenever liquor was being landed. He declared that the bootlegger had told him this corrupted official provided his principal protection.

Another affidavit, again from a former law enforcement officer, described an experience that virtually duplicated Heinie Miller's when he had stopped two liquor-laden trucks in the northern part of the state. This former law officer had halted a truck on one of southern Ocean County's main highways. The driver had protested that his cargo had an official OK. While the policeman and driver were arguing, a private car stopped and the same county official named in the other affidavits accosted the interfering officer. He told the officer that the cargo had been cleared with authorities, and the truck was allowed to proceed on its way escorted by the protecting official. After that, the ex-lawman said, he just let the liquor trucks roll on whenever he saw them trundling along county highways. They always had the protecting official escorting them, he declared.

Though this former lawman hadn't been able to touch the bootleggers' trucks, he rebelled at having to ignore flagrant violations of the law right under his nose. On one occasion, he discovered a small still running full blast in the pine woods just over the border in an adjacent municipality. He informed his brother officers in the next town and urged them to take action. They refused, so the officer turned to federal authorities, who came in, raided the still and demolished it. Then there was the devil to pay. According to the affidavit, the zealous officer who had caused the trouble was visited by a prominent law enforcement official who told him that he had made a great mistake. The still had been guaranteed protection, he was told, and by inspiring a raid on it, he had incurred the wrath of very influential parties. He had been warned, the ex-officer said, that he would be jeopardizing his job if he didn't behave himself in the future; and so, when another still went into operation shortly afterward at the same spot, he had had to ignore it.

Such charges prominently displayed in a lead story under a three-column headline in the county seat's most respectable newspaper might have been expected to provoke some official reaction. Perhaps some prosecutor or judge or Supreme Court Justice would say, "Hey, wait a minute. Let *us* see those affidavits. We have to put a stop to this kind of corruption." But nothing of the kind happened, and it seemed to me that the answer to Bill Fischer's question: How high does the corruption go? was: All the way to the top.

I let the matter rest for a few weeks. But when, in early March, a new grand jury was sworn in amid rhetorical flourishes about how it was going to root out gambling and corruption, I thought the time had come to challenge such hollow pretenses by calling for a few indictments.

A new sheriff, the first Democrat elected in the county in more than two decades, had conducted a gambling raid in Lakewood. In the lead editorial in the *Courier,* I tied this raid to Fischer's earlier raid and reminded readers of "the disgraceful farce that made a mockery of justice in the S.S. *Club Royale* case." I wrote:

> The grand jury may be told, if it has not been told so already, that the raid developed from a background of political conflict, that it resulted from an underworld war, and that it was "aimed" at someone. The panel may even be told that the raid did not produce the "proper" evidence. . . . In a word, the panel may be told that while there is no doubt gambling was conducted, there is no evidence that anyone conducted the gambling.
>
> Such reasoning would be no more far-fetched than that which won the official blessing of a previous panel for gamblers of the *Club Royale.* It is to be hoped that the present jury will not be blinded by arguments so asinine, by arguments so obviously intended to create prejudice and to thwart the cause of justice.

Knowing the complete control that Tom Mathis exercised over the life of the county, knowing the way grand juries (with the exception of Fischer's panel) were always packed with his faithful followers, I had no illusions that things would change as a result of my editorial, but I thought the challenge should be issued, the effort made.

The outcome was exactly what I had expected. The grand jury disbanded in June 1936 without taking action. Though it had been well packed, as usual, a few of the unlassoed had been chosen to serve. They thought, as I did, that the record should not be allowed to stand with Bill Fischer as the only person the system had tried to prosecute. An effort was made to indict the showboat gamblers, but the packed majority operated as usual and refused to act.

As it happened, my father was a member of that grand jury. This handicapped me because grand jurors are sworn to secrecy and I knew there was nothing the county gang would have liked better than to haul me into court with proof that I had gotten some forbidden information from Dad. So I had to stay completely away from my own father.

But, knowing Leo Robbins, I didn't have to be told what must have happened in the grand jury room. I knew that Robbins would become, in effect, a defense counsel for the showboat gamblers and would give the jury the only excuse it needed for adhering to the prescribed political line. This was precisely what happened.

Months later, when it was safe to talk, Dad told me that Robbins had used the very lines of argument that I had outlined in my editorial and he was swishing the case through the nodding, indifferent jury when Dad challenged him. Dad said he couldn't see any justification for not voting an indictment against the man who had testified in the Alcoholic Beverage Commission hearing that he owned the showboat, that he knew gambling was going on there, and that he had done nothing to stop it.

Incredibly, Robbins insisted that there had been no such testimony. "Here," he said, offering the transcript of the hearing to Dad. "Take a look and see for yourself." As Dad later told me, "You know I looked through the testimony in that transcript, and he was right. There was no testimony of that nature anywhere. I couldn't understand it because I *knew* the testimony had been given, so I looked through the transcript again—and found a page missing. It had been torn out and stuffed in the back of the book."

Dad had pulled the page of testimony out of its hiding place and held it up for Robbins to see. "Here is the testimony I was talking about," he said. "Somebody must have torn it out."

"He gave me such a look," Dad told me, "that if it could have killed, I would have been dead."

Despite this exposure and the momentary embarrassment it caused Robbins, the trained seals on the grand jury did their political duty and refused to indict. Dad was so disgusted that he said, "I hope I'm never called to serve on a grand jury again."

This was another step in my education: the entire sequence from the first whitewash of the showboat gamblers to the indictment of Fischer to this final brazen tampering with evidence had been an invaluable lesson in the way facts can be twisted in the secrecy of the grand jury room and made to serve political purposes.

The lessons I learned in Ocean County still seem to me to apply. Gambling has become accepted as a way of life; most of it is run by the mob, and the law protects the mobsters. Ignored are the underworld's heavy investment in both illegal rackets and the operation of legal casinos; ignored is the inevitable corollary of protection and corruption.

I wrote about the grand jury's dismal nonperformance in a two-column editorial, boxed at the top of the editorial page and headlined, THE END OF JUSTICE:

> If the action of the present grand jury in failing to indict gamblers of the S.S. *Club Royale* means what it seems to mean—namely, that no one responsible for the open and flagrant gambling on that "showboat" shall ever be brought before the bars of justice—then we are forced to the inescapable conclusion that there is no justice and that none can be obtained through the enforcement of the criminal laws in Ocean County.
>
> If men whom the law explicitly says are guilty of an offense against society are to be allowed the same freedom and the same privileges as the law-abiding citizen who has never offended, then there is no occasion for anyone to obey the law, and all respect for law and order, by which alone civilization may survive, is ended.

11

City Editor
vs. Front Office

I HAD BEEN EDITOR OF THE *COURIER* FOR EIGHTEEN MONTHS when I sensed a growing disinclination among some members of the Grover family, Fischer's heirs, to continue to buck the county establishment. The paper's finances were precarious, and there was a sentiment, most clearly expressed to me by Percy Grover, that we could all prosper if I would only ease up a bit.

The time had come for me to leave Toms River. I had a chance to return to a desk job at the Asbury Park *Press* and decided to take it. My parting pleasure, however, was that within two weeks of my leaving, a federal grand jury in Camden indicted Secretary of State Thomas A. Mathis on charges of "willful attempt to defeat and evade his income taxes for 1930 and 1933." He was accused of defrauding the government of $2450 in 1930 and $3224 in 1933 on a total income for the two years of $67,856.19.

I had known for months that the federal grand jury had been taking testimony about Mathis. Some of the persons who had signed those affidavits that Fischer had collected, those I had summarized in the first issue I edited, had testified before the jury about the rum-running and bootlegging payoffs. Sheriff Walter A. Applegate, the one who conducted the Lakewood gambling raid, had been another witness. I did not know what Applegate had told the grand jury, but he had charged in public speeches that he had obtained "the little black book" in which Eli Newmark, the gambling and racket kingpin of the county, had recorded his protection payoffs, and the book showed that Newmark had paid more than $300,000 for protection, $1000 a week of it to "one man in Ocean County" whom Applegate did not name but about whose identity there could be little doubt.

Still, I had had little faith that the jury would ever act. John Grover, a member of our own board who sat on the panel, kept whispering in my ear that the jury meant business, but I still doubted anything would come of it. No other effort to interest federal authorities in Mathis's affairs had succeeded, regardless of the evidence. But this time I was wrong.

The boss was getting a suntan in Hawaii when the indictment against him was returned on August 27, 1937. When he came back, he refused comment, but it was not long before he exhibited his muscle. He was arraigned before a U.S. Commissioner in Newark on September 7 and released under $10,000 bail—a most peculiar proceeding, foreshadowing the future. Such arraignments had always been held in open court—but not this time. Mathis was taken into the commissioner's private office, the doors were closed and the press barred. The event was to prove what many people have come to suspect over the years—that the politically powerful are above the law. The federal government dragged its feet about bringing the case to trial; time passed, and finally a new U.S. Attorney for the Southern District of New Jersey dropped the prosecution with the consent of the court. Some years later, Mathis, reportedly in poor health, took a shotgun and committed suicide in his Toms River home. The political organization that he had built, however, continued to rule the county under the leadership of his son, W. Steelman Mathis.

Leaving the wars of Ocean County behind, I took up my editorial chores with the *Press*. Tom Tighe, that red-haired, go-getter Irishman, my first city editor and one of the best I ever worked for, had left to buy his own small weekly. I was brought in to fill the desk vacancy his departure created, and in a couple of years I became city editor.

J. Lyle Kinmonth, founder of the *Press*, was a publisher of the old school. Like Fischer, he had borrowed a small sum of money when he was young to acquire a small, struggling rag of a paper.

He had worked long hours throughout the early 1900s, doing every conceivable job in the shop, and he had built the *Press* into a highly respected, principled newspaper.

Though he owned the paper, there were no restrictions on the newsroom, not even in the coverage of stories involving him. In 1933, shortly after I went to work for the paper, the Seacoast Trust Company, one of the major banks in the city, had been about to fail, and a new board of directors, Kinmonth among them, had tried futilely to save it. Some furious stockholders and depositors sought to make Kinmonth the scapegoat, and at one mass meeting, he was excoriated in the harshest terms. Our reporter wrote the story straight, citing all the derogatory statements made about Kinmonth. Tom Tighe decided it was the hottest story of the day and planned to lead the paper with a large headline: KINMONTH ATTACKED. Tom wondered if he was being too daring, but the old man simply said, "Go ahead and use the story just as you would if it involved anyone else."

The *Press*, as long as Kinmonth remained at the helm, was that kind of newspaper. Unfortunately, shortly after I returned to the paper, Kinmonth suffered a stroke that incapacitated him. Though he recovered to a degree, he was no longer capable of running the paper, and control was vested in the hands of Wayne D. McMurray, who had begun as Kinmonth's secretary and had become the publisher's right-hand man. I have often thought that this change symbolized the shifts in power throughout the newspaper world. The rugged founders of many good and even great newspapers were being succeeded by a lesser breed who had risen to power either, like McMurray, as secretaries to their bosses or as front-office accountants whose role in managing finances gave them a special leverage. The effect, as I saw it, was to crimp the independence of the newsroom and to impose front-office policy on the handling of the news. The era in which a city editor could put his publisher's name in a large, unfavorable headline was gone; the new breed, lacking in newsroom experience and not so dedicated to journalistic principles, more wedded to the exigencies of finance, took the attitude that *their* paper must be run *their* way, even if this meant slanting the news.

Soon after I began running the newsroom, one of our reporters wrote a story covering a municipal meeting, and someone involved took umbrage. When the man came storming into Kinmonth's office, demanding a retraction, the boss called me and told me to send in the reporter with his notes. That was the end of it. Kinmonth stood behind his reporters.

Under McMurray, however, if one of his friends complained, the newsroom was convicted out of hand. Once, on a story involving the local ASPCA, I instructed a reporter to telephone for comment; when the ASPCA refused to comment, we ran the story. Someone complained and McMurray came raging into the newsroom and bawled out both the reporter and me for not having checked the story. I told him I *knew* the reporter had checked because he had sat right beside my desk when he made the phone call. But McMurray wouldn't hear any of it; his friends had told him differently—and that was that. He might as well have called me a liar in front of the whole staff as he refused to listen, turned his back on all of us and swept out of the newsroom.

McMurray had a colossal ego and a temper to match. Perhaps if I had been older, more sure of myself, more cocky, I might have found a way to deal with him. Possibly. But for the life of me I don't see how.

World War II intensified the stresses between us. When the Germans launched their all-out blitzkrieg against the Allies in spring 1940, it seemed obvious that they were sweeping all before them and that a major disaster was impending. At such times there is always turmoil in news accounts: one side makes claims of stunning victories; the other insists the claims are false or, at most, insists it is just conducting "strategic withdrawals" to better defensive positions. An editor has to use his or her best judgment and give the play to the version that seems most reliable. On the eve of Dunkirk, I put an eight-column line on the story of the Germans' breakthrough to the sea.

Almost at once one of McMurray's interfering, busybody friends protested to him that the *Press* seemed to be pro-German. I was called on the carpet by McMurray; his blood pressure was boiling. I was taking the German claims as facts, he said; the Germans were putting out false stories, reporting they had achieved what they only hoped to achieve—and I was falling for their propaganda. I pointed out to him that I had backed up the main story with an eyewitness sidebar written by Louis Lochner, the Associated Press war correspondent with the German Army, who described standing on a hill behind the German lines and seeing the English Channel before him.

"Well, who is this Lochner?" McMurray demanded.

He was, I explained, a veteran war correspondent with the Associated Press.

"Well, how do we know he's not a German secret agent?" McMurray demanded. The man was serious; I was speechless. "You're going to have to be more careful about these German claims," he said.

Twenty-four hours later, of course, the reality of the debacle at Dunkirk could no longer be denied. But I got no acknowledgment from McMurray. And when the United States became involved in the war, our relations became even more strained.

One of the last acts of Roosevelt's New Deal before its idealism became submerged in war preparations had been the passage of the 1938 40-Hour Wages and Hours Act. The outrage in business and journalistic circles was unconfined. The idea of having to pay workers overtime wages if they worked more than forty hours a week hit the big moguls of the nation in the area closest to their hearts—their pocketbooks. "A man isn't a man if he can't work at least forty-eight hours a week," was the refrain I kept hearing.

Publishers were especially incensed. From earliest times they had worked the peons in their newsrooms fifty to sixty hours a week, and the thought of having to pay overtime made them shudder. Thus they became partners with big business in one of the most insidious right-wing organizations ever spawned in America. It was first given the cumbersome title The National Committee to Uphold Constitutional Government, but in 1941 this was simplified to The Committee for Constitutional Government.

Frank E. Gannett, of Rochester, New York, publisher of the Gannett chain of newspapers, was the chairman of the committee that welded the interests of newspaper publishers with some of the most powerful industrial interests in America. After the war, a Congressional investigation in 1950 showed that the committee's treasury had been constantly replenished by hefty donations from various du Ponts; J. Howard Pew, of Sun Oil; Texas Oil tycoons; and firms like Armco Steel, Champion Spark Plug, Kennecott Copper, Eli Lilly & Co., and Republic Steel. These forces poured millions of dollars into campaigns to send "strong men" to Congress—men who would save "free enterprise" by lowering taxes on the rich, by making the poor pay, and by passing "legislation with teeth in it" to curb "predatory" labor unions.

Although I did not know the dimensions of this activity at the time, I was caught in the middle of one of the committee's first and most demagogic campaigns. Wayne McMurray, a highly dedicated participant in the enterprise, was constantly checking the newsroom to see whether some scheduled mailing of the committee's literature had arrived. I was under permanent orders to rush any communiqué to him the instant we sorted the mail.

McMurray's all-consuming interest had to do with the nationwide campaign The Committee for Constitutional Government was sparking to force the repeal of the forty-hour week. The committee's pitch was based on simplistic logic: We are at war. How can we win a world war by working only forty hours a week? We must work at least fifty to sixty hours a week. Patriotism demands that the forty-hour week be scuttled, that everybody put shoulder to the wheel and work longer hours.

Day after day the drumbeat of propaganda became louder, and McMurray would come into the newsroom to make certain I gave prominent page-one play to the latest pronouncement of the National Association of Manufacturers, the U.S. Chamber of Commerce, or some equally prestigious business organization, about the need for patriotism and the abolishment of the forty-hour week.

When Roosevelt was absent from Washington for several days on a trip to inspect defenses in the Caribbean, the propaganda campaign, wrapped so neatly in the flag, roared ahead like an avalanche. Wire services turned out almost daily leads on the rising groundswell of support for junking the forty-hour week. I do not know how our readers were affected, but we in the newsroom were certainly convinced that the forty-hour week was doomed. At the height of the campaign, McMurray stopped by my desk one day, rubbing his hands together. "You boys are going to lose your overtime," he told us with unfeigned delight.

Then Roosevelt returned to Washington and held a press conference. McMurray could not wait to find out what "that man" said, and he came hurrying up to my city desk. "What did he say?" he asked. "What did he say?"

I'm afraid I couldn't keep a malicious smile off my face as I told him: "He said we would work forty hours a week, fifty hours a week or sixty hours, whatever is necessary to win the war—but we'll work it at overtime rates with cost-plus contracts for industry."

A red, angry flush suffused McMurray's cheeks, and he whipped around and almost fled from the newsroom. He knew of course that the press lords' industrial allies weren't going to continue the anti-forty-hour week campaign as long as they were guaranteed their own profits through those cost-plus contracts.

As the war intensified, so did my problems with McMurray. One month we had to cover an exceptionally heavy load of fast-breaking news. A German submarine torpedoed a tanker right off our coast; there was a major conflagration in the northern section of the country around Keyport. It seemed that I had to keep dispatching reporters and photographers everywhere. Shortly after the monthly financial figures were compiled, I was summoned to McMurray's office.

"You're going to have to pay more attention to these expense accounts," he said. "We can't afford to let expenses get out of hand the way they are."

I pointed out to him that we had had an exceptionally busy month.

"Well, you'll just have to cut back on some of this coverage," he told me. "These newsroom expenses are getting out of hand."

Desperate, I asked him, "Well, how much higher were the expenses last month than they were the same month last year?"

In all seriousness he said, "Eight dollars."

The final rupture with McMurray came when the Russians had the effrontery to wipe out a whole German army at Stalingrad. I saw the sweeping Russian victories on the eastern front, the disintegration of the seemingly invincible Nazi war machine, as one of the most startling and important developments of the war, and I played the story accordingly.

McMurray went into one of his increasingly intemperate rages. I was using too much wire news in the paper, he said; I should concentrate more on local coverage; and he didn't want me to keep playing up those Russian victories.

"You know as well as I do that we're going to have to fight the Russians when this is all over," he said as he stormed away from my desk.

It was obvious that I was no longer my own man. I had to get out. With the help of friends, I got a job on the rewrite bank of the New York *World-Telegram*.

12

Jersey Rackets, Jersey Justice

I F IT WERE POSSIBLE TO MAP THE OUTLINES OF A POLITICAL system, the Ocean County graph would have been a perfect overlay for the states of New Jersey and New York in 1953. In that year, I wrote two exposé series for the *World-Telegram and Sun* about a system that operated on state-wide bases very much as Boss Mathis's machine had in Ocean County.

The New Jersey scandal involved massive payoffs, a sensational mob murder and an unvarying pattern of state-dictated action best described as firing the rackets-buster whenever he threatened to bust the rackets.

Under pressure from Senator Estes Kefauver, who was conducting his sensational rackets probe, the Republican regime of Governor Alfred E. Driscoll sent Nelson F. Stamler into Bergen County, ostensibly to clean up. The county, just a hop across the George Washington Bridge from New York, had long been known as the graveyard of rackets-busters. But Stamler emitted a roar of outrage that rocked the state. He charged that he had been trying to follow the trail of a $228,000 payoff that had reportedly gone to the governor's office; and he aired his suspicion that wisecracking Willie Moretti, the payoff man for the mob, had been murdered at the order of state politicians, not by the bosses of the underworld.

These sensational charges in late January 1953 compelled the Republican-controlled State Senate to order an investigation of its own state administration. It was at this point that our paper received a tip that the office of District Attorney Frank S. Hogan in Manhattan had a lot of unpublicized information about the Jersey rackets. As the paper's resident expert on organized crime, I was given the task of going to Hogan's office.

What I found out resulted in a copyrighted story that the *World-Telegram and Sun* ran under an eight-column headline on March 30, 1953. It began:

"This is the story of a mob bankroll that corrupted an entire state—the story of the incredible $13,500,000-a-year gross that wealthy suckers dropped into the coffers of gangland's fabulous Joe Adonis in the gambling paradise of Bergen County.

"It is the story that underlies the complete paralysis of law enforcement in New Jersey from the years 1947–50—a period when Joe Adonis, Willie Moretti and their ilk ran with brazen openness the richest gambling preserve possessed by the national syndicate of crime east of the Mississippi."

The information to support that lead came from a long night session I had with two of Hogan's principal aides, assistant district attorneys Vincent A. E. O'Connor and Andrew Seidler. Hogan's suspicions had been aroused by a lavish "charity gambling" party held in a Park Avenue penthouse on July 28, 1948. The gossip columns had been full of the names of the society figures who, in the sweet name of charity, had gambled and lost on roulette, chemin de fer, dice and birdcages. Questioning some of these players, O'Connor and Seidler learned that many of the players made out checks after they had exhausted their supplies of cash. The checks passed through the hands of a check-casher, triple-chinned Max Stark, of Teaneck, New Jersey, and wound up in Stark's bank account in the Merchants Bank of New York.

The check trail led Hogan's deputies into a colossal financial maze. They found that in just twenty-five months Max Stark had banked $6,810,347 in checks; and he had made daily trips to the bank carrying satchels bulging with as much as $50,000 to $90,000— wrinkled, sweat-stained bills from the previous night's gambling that he wanted to exchange for tempting new currency.

Adding cash to checks, O'Connor and Seidler arrived at $13,500,000, a figure they felt was ultraconservative, since what they had learned came from just one Max Stark bank account, and Stark had other accounts in Jersey, beyond their reach. They felt they had stumbled on a mammoth $15-to-$20 million annual operation of the syndicate.

This was only part of the story. Questioning losing players who had signed some of those checks, O'Connor and Seidler pin-pointed Joe Adonis as the syndicate boss of a gambling racket that spangled Bergen County and much of the rest of New Jersey with casinos. The operation was so well organized that fleets of chauf-feured Cadillacs would pick up high rollers at their Park Avenue apartments or swank New York hotels and ferry them over the George Washington Bridge for their nightly shearing. Many of the losing players identified Joe A. as the boss who constantly oversaw the play, sometimes accompanied by Solly Moretti, the somber brother of wiseacre Willie.

Joe Adonis was operating a capital of crime. "General Motors can't run without a headquarters," Seidler said, "and neither can underworld operations of this magnitude." Adonis, born Joseph Doto in Italy, had long been an underworld power. He was the partner of Frank Costello, then known as the prime minister of the underworld, and he was the superior of Albert Anastasia, who commanded the Murder Inc. squads that enforced the syndicate's rule across the nation.

Joe A. was sometimes referred to as "the gentleman of the mob," because he always dressed in the conservative attire of a millionaire businessman and he spoke in a softly modulated voice that was almost a whisper. He was stockily built, swarthily hand-some, with a pair of bright, hard, brown eyes, unblinking and inhumanly cold.

His original base had been in Brooklyn, where he had wedded hijacking, extortion, gambling and murder with a variety of le-gitimate businesses and had become a hidden political boss of the Borough of Churches. When Mayor Fiorello H. LaGuardia began a crusade against the mob in the early 1940s, Adonis moved to the greener pastures of the Garden State.

He had a home in Palisades Park, and Anastasia, the grim enforcer, established himself in a Spanish-style mansion just three blocks away. In a nearby tavern called Duke's, directly opposite the Palisades Amusement Park, Adonis organized the governing council of the underworld.

In a sequestered and guarded conference room in the back of
Duke's, Joe A. met daily with his board of criminal directors.
Anastasia sat at his right hand. The other members of the crime
council were Willie and Solly Moretti, and Anthony (Tony Bender)
Strollo, lord of the Lower Manhattan docks, owner of Greenwich
Village nightclubs and the chief lieutenant of the most bloodthirsty
mobster of all, the temporarily exiled Vito Genovese.

Security at this unique capital of crime was as tight as at Fort
Knox, O'Connor and Seidler said. "You couldn't get an informer
within yards of the place." New York detectives were literally run
out of town by local police. "Sometimes, trying to gain a few
minutes, we would raise the hood of the car and pretend we had
engine trouble," Seidler said, "but the local cops would come
along and say, 'We know you guys. Come on, get moving.' "

As a result, Hogan's staff had to resort to long-distance surveillance through court-ordered legal wiretaps on New York
mobsters who went to Duke's. Both Hogan's office and the Federal Bureau of Narcotics, the only two law enforcement agencies
to exhibit an interest, traced the most powerful mobsters in the
nation going to confer with Adonis's crime council. Frank Costello
came from New York; Abner (Longy) Zwillman from Newark;
Meyer Lansky, the financial wizard of the syndicate, was a regular
consultant; and such powers as Jake Guzik and Tony Accardo,
heirs to the Chicago rackets of Al Capone, would often appear on
Tuesday afternoons, the day scheduled for weekly national conferences.

The interests of these powers spanned the nation: wide-open
casino gambling at Saratoga during the racing season (when Governor Dewey was always on vacation and New York State Police
were given to understand they were not to interfere); hidden
shares in legal Las Vegas casinos, where the skim off the top ran
into millions; casino interests in Florida, Covington, Kentucky,
and Louisiana; racetrack bookmaking, with the huge national layoff operation under the direction of Frank Erickson in Bergen
County.

The bookmaking gross must have rivaled Adonis's astonishing
casino revenues. The mob established a 2500-telephone network
in the safe haven of Bergen County, where homeowners were
paid $50 a week to let bookies use their phones for a few hours
a day while the heavy betting play was phoned in from New York.

In addition to this local racket, Erickson's national layoff headquarters returned millions. One check of three Erickson accounts in a New Jersey bank showed deposits totaling $6,683,362.20 in a little more than four years.

When I blew open the story of the Jersey rackets and their ironclad protection, reaction was swift. I began to have visitors in the newsroom. The first was a tall, excited agent of the Intelligence Unit of the U.S. Bureau of Internal Revenue. He came into the newsroom waving photostats of checks that had cleared through Max Stark's bank account. Furious, he described his trials with corrupted New Jersey law enforcement.

Internal Revenue, he said, had been aware of the tremendous cash flow in the hands of the mob, and he had wanted to shadow some of the racketeers in their spend-free moments in hopes of building a tax case against them. "But that son of a bitch of a police chief in Fort Lee was always on the lookout for us," he said. "He would be on our tails almost the instant we crossed the bridge." The Treasury agents had never been able to shake their police tails and they had been virtually run out of Bergen County.

My next visitor was one of Stamler's predecessors as a rackets-buster, John J. Winberry, a stocky man with a determined face. Winberry gave me a copy of a letter he had sent to Governor Driscoll—a letter in which he laid responsibility for the disgrace of Jersey justice squarely in Driscoll's lap. I took his letter, but did not use it at the time, saving it for an appropriate opportunity. That letter was to spark a chain reaction and become one of the most significant bits of evidence in the State Senate investigation.

Winberry had been appointed a special prosecutor in 1947 after a Middlesex County dice game had become so notorious it was labeled "the largest in the East." Winberry relied on records meticulously ferreted out, and he had spent hours checking telephone calls and cultivating informants. He became quickly aware of the huge bookie operations in the state, and he decided to strike at these first.

"On December 18, 1947," Winberry told me, "I went to Trenton and requested seventeen State Troopers to raid eight horse-rooms my agents had uncovered in Perth Amboy. The State Police referred my request to Governor Driscoll at ten minutes to twelve. . . . At ten minutes after one, one of my undercover men in Perth Amboy telephoned me that he had heard the word being passed: 'Lay off all bets for a few days. The heat's on.' Someone had leaked the news to the mob and the word had gone out within an hour and twenty minutes. The raids could not be pulled."

New Jersey officials could hardly plead ignorance about events in their state, for O'Connor and Seidler in mid-August 1948 had deliberately leaked a bit of the Max Stark story. The Bergen County chief of detectives and Attorney General Walter D. Van Riper immediately beat an anxious path to Hogan's office, where O'Connor and Seidler spelled out the significance of Max Stark's bank transactions; pointed out that more information and other Stark accounts were available in New Jersey; and emphasized that "the New Jersey operation was headed by Joe Adonis."

The Jersey officials thanked Hogan's deputies for the information, went home—and nothing happened.

Such was the wall of inertia that confronted Winberry. He had kept in close touch with Hogan's office, and in early November 1948 he conferred with O'Connor. Officials often foiled investigations by screaming that they were a waste of taxpayers' money. Winberry needed a sensational breakthrough. O'Connor warned him, "If you don't turn up something pretty big, if you don't put up, the first thing you know you're going to find yourself on the spot."

"I guess you're right," Winberry conceded. "I guess I'll have to take the bull by the horns."

Winberry was convinced that the Middlesex dice game was linked to four mob murders. He identified two Brooklyn underlings who had worked in the Middlesex dice game, and on November 12, 1948, accompanied by a New Jersey State Police sergeant and a New York City detective, he surprised the pair with unscheduled visits to their homes. At first, both refused to talk. But Winberry, with a magnificent bluff, roared that he didn't care so much about their gambling involvement, he was interested in just one thing—murder. They'd better spill their guts or they would find themselves right in the middle of a murder case, he told them. Frightened, they both talked and identified Joe Adonis as the boss of the syndicate, giving direct evidence about the number of gambling operations that he ran.

A weekend intervened after Winberry's coup—and, when business resumed on Monday, Van Riper fired Winberry.

"Can you believe it?" O'Connor said to me years later, shaking his head in amazement. "I suppose in a way you could say that I was responsible for getting Winberry fired. Here I was urging him on for fear that if he didn't come up with something really hot he would get fired, and he takes my advice, barges in, gets the most fantastic break and gets the evidence—and we *knew* he got it, no question about that because we had one of our own detectives right there—and almost the minute he accomplishes all of this, he's fired!"

That was Jersey justice under Governor Driscoll, a man who had been hailed as the greatest governor of the state since Woodrow Wilson; a man instrumental in revamping the state's archaic constitution and in reforming the court system and appointing Arthur T. Vanderbilt, former president of the American Bar Association and a jurist of unquestioned integrity, as Chief Justice of the State Supreme Court. Yet nothing had happened to bother the mob.

Three years after Winberry's firing, Governor Driscoll won reelection and made some cosmetic changes in his administration. He shed Van Riper and appointed a new attorney general, Theodore F. Parsons, of Red Bank, a lawyer of superior reputation, a man of religious bent who often served as a lay preacher. It was Parsons who responded to pressure by Kefauver and sent Stamler to clean up Bergen County.

Stamler, appointed on October 30, 1950, obtained indictments against Joe Adonis, Solly Moretti and three lesser hoodlums in just ten days. Hogan, who was preparing criminal informations against the same five in New York at the time, knew he would have difficulty making the action stick, since most of the acts charged were beyond his jurisdiction. He turned over all of his grand jury testimony to Stamler. The repercussions were swift and startling.

On the night of November 12, a gangland delegation appeared at the home of Republican State Chairman John J. Dickerson, the political boss of Bergen County, campaign strategist and political sponsor of Governor Driscoll. Dickerson's was the only version of this weird confrontation to survive. According to his testimony in the state investigation, Willie Moretti was the spokesman for the mobsters. Behind him stood his brother, Solly. And bringing up the rear—silent, grim and watchful—was Joe Adonis. Also, according to Dickerson, Willie said that "he had paid out a lot of money and he didn't intend to take this lying down, and I believe he used the term 'unless something is done about it, he is going to blow the lid off" and language along that type."

Willie said the mob had paid $228,000 for protection to Harold John Adonis (no relation to Joe A.), a clerk in Governor Driscoll's office. The payments had been made at the rate of $12,000 a month for nineteen months, Willie said. Adonis was to keep $2000 of each installment and pass the rest to the governor.

Dickerson said he told Willie, "No one can ever sell me on the idea that the Governor ever got a dime," and added, "I think you have just been sold down the river."

Willie Moretti was adamant. He had paid, and he expected protection. He would return to Dickerson's home the next night for a final answer.

Dickerson telephoned Attorney General Parsons and told him it was urgent that they meet. Parsons said he was driving to Hackensack, the county seat of Bergen County, the next morning and he was picking up Stamler on the way. No, no, Dickerson said, he did not want Stamler present; and so, the following morning, the two met outside the Pennsylvania Railroad station in Newark and walked around a couple of blocks while Dickerson briefed Parsons.

In his later testimony in the state inquiry, Dickerson insisted that he had told Parsons "everything," including the vital detail that the mobsters were going to pay him a second visit. Dickerson's "everything" turned out to be questionable. Both Parsons and Governor Driscoll insisted that Dickerson had not mentioned the return visit, and that was why, when Willie Moretti showed up again, there were no detectives waiting in the shrubbery, no recording devices installed to catch his words. The only word about what had happened was Dickerson's. He testified that both Parsons and Driscoll had been shocked when he told them about the alleged payoff; both denied they knew anything about it— and so, when Willie Moretti returned, Dickerson told him that the investigation would proceed.

It did, but in the oddest fashion. Stamler, who was supposed to be in charge, was the odd-man out. First, he had been blocked out of information about the $228,000 payoff; next, he was kept in the dark about the handling of the indictments he had obtained against Joe Adonis and his cohorts.

Parsons negotiated behind Stamler's back. Testimony at the state inquiry showed that John Selser, attorney for the mobsters, conferred a dozen times with Parsons with the mutual understanding that Stamler was to be told nothing. "There was definitely a deal made," Selser testified. The gangsters would plead guilty and get mere eighteen-month-to-two-year sentences; they were to be fined $50,000; and they were not to be placed under probation when they were released from prison. With no probation, they would be free to carry on as they wished.

But the carefully arranged deal fell apart, apparently because stern Chief Justice Vanderbilt had interceded. The Bergen County judge sentenced the mobsters to two-to-three years each; levied fines of $75,000; and, worst of all, doomed the prisoners to five years' probation after their release.

This double-cross, as the mob regarded it, was the turning point in the Jersey drama. Willie Moretti went berserk. "What the hell you doing to my brother?" he screamed at Stamler. "Who the hell you think you are? You can't do that to my brother."

Stamler insisted that Willie Moretti was so enraged by this treatment of Solly that he was ready to testify about the payoffs he had made to politicians. But he never got the chance. On October 4, 1951, Willie was having a leisurely lunch in Joe's Elbow Room, not far from the now-closed Duke's, when two gunmen walked in, blasted away, and left Willie dead on the floor under a sign reading: CHICKEN IN THE ROUGH—$1.50.

The Moretti murder was pivotal. Stamler wasn't allowed to handle the investigation; Parsons ruled that the scandal-tainted Bergen County prosecutor's office should take charge. The murder investigation went nowhere.

In reaction to all of this, Stamler resolved to expose the corruption that riddled Bergen County. He wrote in *The Saturday Evening Post* that the law had been so corrupted that "the most flagrant offenses went unpunished." Stamler wanted to give the county a thorough housecleaning, and so did two grand juries that he guided.

A member of the first grand jury described the sudden chill that set in: "At first we were clicking one-two-three. Everything was going right. Then we started reaching out to go higher. But all of a sudden something went wrong. We ran into a blank wall. I don't know what happened or what the connection was, but it was tied up with the Moretti murder. After that, we couldn't get anywhere."

The second grand jury took up the cold trail of the $228,000 bribe; it indicted Harold John Adonis and the dead Willie Moretti for conspiring to obstruct justice. Then it went further and indicted Adonis for common-law bribery. With this indictment, the bribe story made the newspaper front pages.

On January 27, 1953, Parsons went before the second grand jury and told the jurors that he was firing Stamler. The jurors were angry—their efforts had already met with plenty of obstruction. A State Police witness had tried to block their inquiry into the bribe scandal; they had obtained what evidence they had only through their own perseverance. As one juror told Parsons, "We feel—it is my opinion, and I think the rest of the grand jury is of the same mind—that we are getting awful close to home and people are going to squirm." Parsons insisted that his firing of Stamler had to stand. From that minute on, no one had to squirm.

The administration attempted to avoid scandal—and the rumor mills went into action. One tactic was to impugn the mental capacity of the dead Willie Moretti; another, to discredit Stamler. Moretti, it was said, had a brain so badly eaten away by paresis that his uncontrolled babbling had made him a threat to the mob. The evidence cited was Willie's testimony before the Kefauver Committee. I read that testimony, and found his repartee so sharp and clever that it was no wonder he had the hearing room convulsed in laughter: he had made monkeys of the senators trying to question him.

The Stamler rumor was even more vicious and desperate. A State House correspondent described how representatives of the governor and the attorney general had visited newspaper offices to tell publishers and editors "all sorts of horrible things about Stamler: At least seven of the deputy attorney generals and a dozen of the top State Police officials have been doing *nothing else* for several weeks other than working up the case against Stamler. It even dwarfs what went on there during the Lindbergh baby kidnapping and trial."

This State House pressure seemed obvious to those of us who tried to report on the state investigation. The Associated Press coverage was so bland that our city desk distrusted it and sent my reporting partner, Bill Longgood, to Trenton to cover the hearings firsthand. Bill soon found himself being tailed around the State House by an AP staffer who seemed more interested in what Bill was doing than in covering the hearings himself.

Now was the time to use the letter John Winberry had given me. After Driscoll's re-election, Winberry had learned that the governor intended to reappoint Walter Winne as prosecutor in Bergen County. What he had written Driscoll was that "the book-making kings of the nation, Frank Erickson, Frank Costello and Joe Adonis" had set up shop in Bergen County with the blessing of law enforcement agencies. In a paragraph intended to touch Driscoll's prickly pride about his new state constitution and re-formed judicial system, Winberry had written: ". . . The con-temptuous flouting of the law in Bergen has greatly decreased the respect for our model court system. Efficiency in our court system becomes a mockery if the breakdown in law enforcement in Bergen is whitewashed by the Governor through the appoint-ment of a Prosecutor who has proved himself incapable of coping with the situation."

A little gremlin in Stamler's office sneaked me a copy of a letter that Winne had written in response. The letter had gone to Par-sons, and it seemed that Parsons had asked Winne for his opinion of Winne. We could guess, but not prove, that Driscoll had for-warded Winberry's letter to Parsons and that Parsons had sent it to Winne, the man accused. We had what seemed like two ends of a chain, the beginning and the end; but there was a gap in the middle.

Bill Longgood and I discussed what we should do. Bill had developed considerable respect for the investigating committee's chief counsel, whom he felt to be a man of integrity. The com-mittee, of course, had subpoena powers and could fill in the gap for us. We decided that Bill should take the copies of the two letters that we had and deliver them to the committee's counsel. Bill's estimate of the man proved correct; he demanded and got the Driscoll–Parsons correspondence. This established that the governor *had* turned over Winberry's complaint to Parsons; that Parsons had sent it to Winne without conducting any investigation of his own; that Winne had found himself as pure as the driven snow—and that Parsons had then advised the governor that there was no reason for him not to reappoint Winne.

Winne's exculpation of himself contained these incredible par-agraphs: "As far as Frank Erickson and Frank Costello being in this county, *I doubt very much if they know where Bergen County is.* It is true that Adonis lives in Bergen County and has a very

substantial business in Cliffside [hauling Ford cars to be delivered
to dealers], but I have never had any evidence of his activity in
New Jersey in any illegal matters. . . . I conferred many times
with Hogan's office and they absolutely refused to furnish me with
any information regarding the alleged gambling place in Lodi. *I
am of the opinion that no such place existed.* [Italics added]"

The committee frowned upon the Driscoll–Parsons–Winne
runaround, and wrote in its final report: ". . . Parsons is to be
censured for having referred this complaint about Winne to Winne
himself, instead of having a thorough and independent investigation made. Such an investigation would have disclosed that the
charges made by Winberry in his letter to the Governor were
based upon fact."

The committee was equally harsh with virtually everyone involved in handling the Moretti bribe. The committee declared
that "it is apparent that the investigation, from its inception, was
mishandled. . . . The inquiry into the charges growing out of the
Moretti–Dickerson meeting suggests a desire on the part of those
responsible to avoid a public disclosure of the underlying facts,
due to their embarrassing nature, rather than a desire to utilize
the full power of their respective offices for the purpose of establishing who the offenders were and bringing them to the bar of
justice."

The committee report was a triumph for us. It substantiated
every charge we had made; it even devoted a special section to
the Winberry letter sequence in its censure of Parsons. The trouble was that we didn't know it.

The report was issued very late one afternoon, too late for any
of our editions. I was occupied with my exposé of the New York
harness tracks, and the city desk decided to rely on the Associated
Press to pick up and relay the final report of the Jersey committee—a fateful mistake.

I couldn't believe what I saw the next morning when I entered
the newsroom. The first edition was rolling off the press, its lead
story the Jersey report. It was a ho-hum piece stating that the
state committee had submitted its report and, ho-hum, nobody
much cared. I blew my stack and so did Bill Longgood.

A little investigation showed that night rewrite had followed
the line set by the AP story out of Trenton. Examining the wire
copy, we found that one had to wade through seventeen para-

graphs of ho-hum to get to the first mention that the committee
had censured anybody for anything. I went to work and whipped
up a story for the next edition, featuring what the report had
really said. But even then I did not have the full details about
the committee's censure of Parsons until I read the Newark *Evening News* on the way home that night. I was so disgusted that I
wanted to kick some of those play-along-to-get-along cretins in
the AP's Trenton bureau. I had rejected that kind of news philosophy when I was a green reporter in Ocean County, but apparently it lived and flourished around the State House.

13

Rackets, Raceways, and the Crime Cabinet

<hr>

THERE HAD BEEN A MURDER. SO WHAT? THERE ARE MUR-
ders every day in New York. The victim this time—on
August 29, 1953—was Thomas F. Lewis, a man unknown
to the general public but actually a powerful boss of the labor
union controlling employment at Yonkers Raceway, one of the
largest harness-racing tracks in the state.

The hit man, a hood named Edward (Snakes) Ryan, had been
shot and killed by a traffic cop as he was fleeing from the apartment
hallway where he had just gunned down Lewis. Detectives felt
certain that underworld forces had ordered Lewis's execution.

All of this had taken place during a weekend when I was busy
working on a magazine article at home. I had read the headlines,
skimmed the story, but been so busy getting my own words on
paper that I had not thought about the details. It never occurred
to me that I was about to be plunged into my second page-one
exposé series of the year, another in the familiar pattern linking
base crime to high politics.

I was sitting at my rewrite desk at the *World-Telegram and
Sun* in midmorning on Monday when Lee B. Wood, our executive
editor, came charging out of his front office. A big man, over six
feet, with a burly build, Lee reminded me of one of Teddy Roosevelt's Rough Riders charging up San Juan Hill. He bore the not

entirely worshipful sobriquets of the Bull Moose or the Caribou, because he always moved under a full head of steam, arms pumping furiously, powerful legs churning as he headed directly for his target of the moment. Today, I was his target.

"What about this Lewis murder in Yonkers? Isn't there more to it than has come out so far?" he demanded of me.

He had caught me in a state of monumental unpreparedness and I had to do some fast thinking (a feat for which I am not always noted, but in this case the brain cells clicked in desperation and to some purpose). I could somehow smell the ex-convict taint that ran through the entire affair, and, grasping at the first glimmer of an idea, I said to Lee, "Well, I always thought that ex-convicts were supposed to be barred from working at the racetracks."

He thought for a moment, grunted and said, "Good. Maybe that's an angle. Let's look into it." Then he was gone, back to his front office.

I had to bring myself up-to-date in a hurry. The clips told me that not only had Snakes Ryan been gunned down, but police had also spotted and arrested another man, William Howell, who had been waiting for Ryan in a getaway car. Howell, also an ex-convict, was linked to a much more powerful and strangely prosperous ex-convict, Lawrence (Lar or Lala) Lynch.

Lar Lynch was not the kind of man you would invite to dinner. Federal agents had arrested and jailed him for hijacking. Once released, he had taken gun in hand and stuck up the Latin Quarter, earning five-to-ten years in state prison. Again released on probation, he had soon mysteriously found a better road to fortune than sticking up nightclubs: he had become a $2000-a-month "troubleshooter" for Yonkers Raceway.

I knew just where to go next. Before I was put full time on the rewrite desk, I had been let loose on occasion to write feature stories. One series had involved the Pinkerton National Detective Agency, and I had acquired a good source there. I telephoned him—and what he told me in that first call was enough to lift the lid on the whole simmering stew of crime, labor rackets and politics.

The Pinkertons fingerprinted and ran police-file checks on all of their employees, but they had no control over the hiring of clerks, cashiers and other personnel at Yonkers even though they were supposed to protect the racetracks from criminal elements.

As for Yonkers itself, it made no checks at all, but the Pinkertons had outlined a fingerprinting and record-checking system for all raceway employees and submitted the proposal to the State Harness Racing Commission, repeating their suggestions at two-year intervals. They had been ignored.

A second state body had been just as blind. A state legislative committee headed by Senator Arthur H. Wicks had conducted a two-year "investigation" of harness racing and had found nothing wrong. When we tackled Wicks, he was obviously shaken. He sputtered that he knew nothing about the hiring of ex-convicts at the Yonkers track and that he had never heard that "troubleshooters" were paid fancy salaries for doing next to nothing.

There was no valid excuse for such obdurate official blindness in the face of the warnings the Pinkertons had issued. My source told me that the failure to maintain proper standards at Yonkers was caused by heavy pressure from Local 32-E, Building Service Employees Union (AFL), which the murdered ex-convict Lewis had headed.

"The union put the heat on the management when they built the track," my informant said. "And when it became a tremendous success and the money came rolling in, the pressure was really put on. The only outfit that fought Lewis and the union and tried to resist the pressure was the Pinkertons."

This was the opening wedge in a two-month-long, page-one exposé series that had Governor Dewey squirming in Albany. Dewey's entire political career had been founded on his sensational prosecutions of the mob hierarchy in New York City in the 1930s, and he was extremely sensitive about disclosures that his own state administration was sheltering the mob. Yet that was what we were discovering, and the harder we looked, the worse it got.

Under our badgering, Yonkers Raceway was forced to admit that twenty-two convicted bookmakers worked as sellers and cashiers at the track. (Later investigation showed the track's payroll had a total of thirty-three ex-convicts.) The raceway also conceded that it had paid out $167,500 to five labor "troubleshooters" in just three and a half years. Lar Lynch had received $42,000 in eighteen months; the Bronx campaign manager for Vincent B. Impellitteri, then mayor of New York, had done even better, picking up $65,000 in a little over a year.

The expanding investigation shot off in all directions, and it began to take up the best reporters on our staff. I wrote the lead stories, but a lot of the digging was done by Fred Woltman, who also wrote some of the sidebar articles; Walter MacDonald, a bulldog of an interviewer who had been our Albany correspondent; and Bill Longgood, my former partner in the Jersey probe.

I also had the surreptitious help of one of our sportswriters. I was busy at my desk one day when he paused in the aisle, looked around to make certain no one was within earshot, and said to me in a barely audible voice, "Look, Fred, I can give you some good tips on this racetrack story you're working on if you promise me not to tell any of *them*." He nodded his head in the direction of his own department. The implication was clear: he would trust me, but not his own editors. I promised to protect him.

"Here's something that perhaps you don't know," the sportswriter said. "You're concentrating on Yonkers Raceway, but the situation at Roosevelt Raceway on Long Island is just as bad. I'll keep in touch whenever I have anything for you by phoning in at night. I'll use a phony name, or perhaps I'll just say, 'This comes from a guy Fred knows,' but you'll know where the information comes from and you can trust it."

During the next several weeks, some of our most valuable tips came from him. When I came into the office at 8:30 in the morning I would find notes, typed out for me by the night side at 1 or 2 A.M. Our city editor was almost beside himself with curiosity to find out how I came to have such a valuable tipster, but I didn't tell him or anyone else. It remained a secret until now.

That first tip about Roosevelt Raceway was especially valuable, for Roosevelt and Yonkers were essentially one operation. In August 1952 Old Country Trotting Association, owners of the Roosevelt Raceway plant, bought the Algam Corporation, which owned the Yonkers plant, for a reported price of $2,300,000.

When Fred Woltman studied corporate and State Harness Racing Commission records, he uncovered an unholy alliance between wealthy men of the underworld, labor racketeers and state politicians.

Infamous Frank Costello's name was connected to both Yonkers and Roosevelt. Nathan Herzfeld, a New York garment manufacturer, controlled Yonkers before the Roosevelt acquisition. The Kefauver probe disclosed that the same underworld wiretapping expert who had been hired to check Costello's telephones had been engaged to double-check Herzfeld's; he found that Herzfeld was being tapped at the same time as Costello.

Joseph Henschel, another garment manufacturer and one of the original powers in Algam, had been the treasurer of Tammany Hall for a short time during the mob-speckled regime of Mayor William O'Dwyer. Henschel admitted to the Kefauver Committee that he had a close acquaintance with two of the five crime overlords of New York—Frank Costello and Thomas (Three-Finger Brown) Luchese. At the end of World War II, when purchasers of new cars had to get on waiting lists, he had had an option on a new Cadillac, which he had given to Mrs. Costello, and the gift, he said, had "made her very happy."

Henschel had been bankrolled in his original Algam investment by Benjamin (Benny) Levine, also known as Benjamin Cohen, a millionaire garment manufacturer who had been convicted in connection with the extortion rackets run by Louis (Lepke) Buchalter and Gurrah Shapiro. Levine disclosed that he had lent Costello's friend Henschel $150,000 to help him get started in Algam. When Roosevelt Raceway subsequently bought 51 percent of Algam's shares (the State Harness Racing Commission had no idea who held the remaining 49 percent of the stock, though Henschel was reported to have retained a block of it), the $2,300,000 that the raceway paid for Algam (and so for Yonkers) was principally split between Herzfeld, Henschel and Max Getz of Cincinnati.

The same shadowy underworld–Costello taint besmirched Roosevelt Raceway. The ostensible boss of Roosevelt was George Morton Levy, a Freeport, Long Island, lawyer who had admitted to the Kefauver Committee that he was a golf-playing companion of Frank Costello. Levy acted as trustee, holding blocks of stock for the real, unnamed owners of Roosevelt.

Fred Woltman's examination of stockholders' lists showed that huge multithousand blocks of stock were held by some of the most powerful politicians in the state. One was J. Russel Sprague, the Republican national committeeman, the boss of Nassau County and a close political associate of Governor Dewey. A former attorney for Assemblyman Irwin Steingut (Steingut had been minority leader in the Assembly when it passed legislation beneficial to racing interests) held 17,100 shares in Old Country Trotting and 5200 shares in Nassau Trotting, a separate corporation that actually ran the races at Roosevelt. In addition, a Sprague political aide who held 5700 shares in Yonkers had transferred 500 of his shares to Steingut's daughter.

Another power in the stockholders' group was William C. DeKoning, Sr., czar of AFL construction unions on Long Island for twenty years and the holder of a charter to unionize pari-mutuel clerks at Roosevelt. DeKoning and his wife owned 8200 shares of Old Country Trotting, 350 shares of Yonkers Trotting and 1000 shares of Nassau Trotting. DeKoning had a personal interest in both management and labor at the tracks, and his charter to unionize the work force game him complete control of hiring and firing at Roosevelt—a power he used in the most unprincipled and ruthless ways.

Our disclosures pressured Governor Dewey, and he became restive. On September 22, 1953, he closed down Yonkers Race-way pending a resolution of the questions about employment of ex-convicts and highly paid "troubleshooters," and ordered the district attorneys of Westchester and Nassau counties to start investigations. At the same time, however, as if trying to belittle the scandal, he indicated clearly that he thought the trouble was confined to Yonkers and did not affect any other harness track, and he claimed that there was no secret about stock ownership since all stock was registered. We happened to know that George Morton Levy was not the only attorney who held stock in trust for undisclosed parties.

The day after the governor's action, I wrote a page-one article, based on Woltman's research, that disclosed the heavy interests of high politicos in both tracks, and then I focused on the highly suspect DeKoning control of labor at Roosevelt.

The DeKoning connection caused the most embarrassment to the politicians. With Walter MacDonald investigating, we learned that 1200 workers at Roosevelt Raceway were forced to kick back to DeKoning if they wanted to hold their jobs. Employees re-vealed that they had to spend $8 every Friday night in the Mule Club, headquartered in DeKoning's Labor Lyceum Bar in Union-dale, and that they had to kick in regularly at the Mule Club during the off-season as well. If they didn't, they lost their jobs. We estimated—and felt the estimate was conservative—that these kickbacks added up to some $345,000 a year.

We broke the kickback story on Monday, September 28, and on Wednesday night Roosevelt Raceway workers were ordered by telegram to report to DeKoning's Mule Club. There they were harangued, told that they must be indignant "about the lies that have appeared in the newspapers" and at "the reflection" on their integrity. Then they were ordered to sign a prepared statement denying that any kickback racket existed, and were reminded, "You want to work at the track next year?" As one informant told us, "What could we do? We signed." When two of our reporters arrived at the scene, the bartender immediately ordered the premises closed. "A short night tonight," he said.

A week later, on October 18, Governor Dewey superseded the county prosecutors and appointed a special three-man commission to probe the track scandals. On the same day, a Nassau County grand jury indicted DeKoning and twelve of his underlings on charges of extortion in the kickback racket.

Even so, the damage to politicians could not be contained, for in spite of the pressures of the scandal and the indictments, the mob's influence was not checked. Residing in a prison cell in Sing Sing was a union racketeer so powerful that politicians of two states paid obeisance to him: Joseph S. Fay, ruler of the AFL's building trades, who was serving a sentence of seven and a half to fifteen years after being convicted by District Attorney Hogan of extorting $368,000 from contractors on the city's Delaware Aqueduct project. Fay was DeKoning's superior in the AFL pecking order, and DeKoning visited him faithfully. So did DeKoning's son—and nephew. Another visitor was Arthur Wicks, the senator who had found nothing wrong on the harness tracks and had now risen to become acting lieutenant governor. Wicks acknowledged that he had paid four visits to Fay in Sing Sing: "I went to see Joe about the labor situation in my district." Others who had beaten a path to Fay's cell were Senator William F. Condon of Yonkers and former Supreme Court Justice William F. Bleakley, counsel for Algam. In addition, Paul L. Troast, the Republican candidate for governor in New Jersey, had written a letter to Governor Dewey urging him to commute Fay's sentence. I felt that our exposé of the corruption in New Jersey and our disclosure of Troast's support for Fay contributed to his defeat and the election of his little-known opponent, Robert B. Meyner. Embarrassed by the disclosure of Fay's power, Governor Dewey refused to commute his sentence and instead ordered him transferred to upstate Dannemora, the "Siberia" of New York state prisons.

Throughout the two months that we had been hammering at the racetrack scandal, Dewey had been pressuring our publisher,

Roy W. Howard. According to Lee Wood, Dewey had phoned Howard repeatedly, urging that the two of them get together for lunch or dinner. Howard, sensing what Dewey wanted, had kept stalling, offering one excuse or another.

Then one day (for reasons I have never understood, presumably an innocent mistake) a headline writer went way beyond Fred Woltman's perfectly straightforward sidebar on the racetrack imbroglio to put a title on it that reflected directly on Dewey. The first edition had hardly hit the streets before Dewey was on the telephone threatening to sue for libel. In midmorning, all hell broke loose as the Bull Moose came rampaging out of his front office and corralled all of us—Woltman, me, the managing editor, the city editor and his assistants, the news editor and his assistants. "We're running into trouble on this racetrack story," Lee told us. "We're going to have to be more careful about what we're writing. We've been all right so far, but we're going to have to be more careful in the future."

Everyone in that group got the message: the plug had been pulled on our exposé. I went back to my desk ready to chew up the copy paper, for this was the same day we flubbed the final report on the New Jersey crime investigation. To have two long-running exposés emasculated in one morning put me in such a black mood that I vowed to myself I'd never get involved in another.

The event seemed to demonstrate that the mob itself had been following the articles I had written; for, when murder at the top began to change the face of the underworld, the emerging new order decided to use me to telegraph its punches. It was a new technique and Assistant District Attorney Alfred J. Scotti, who was in charge of Hogan's rackets bureau, was as baffled by it as I was.

Frank Costello had served eleven months in prison for income tax evasion; when he was released in March 1957 he found a changed world. Vito Genovese had returned from Italy, where he had hobnobbed with Benito Mussolini, and had a New York murder charge against him aborted by having the principal witness knocked off while he was presumably in protective custody in prison. Genovese assumed the role of boss over the dethroned Costello.

The old Crime Cabinet that had ruled from Duke's was scattered. Willie Moretti had been murdered; Solly Moretti died in prison; and Joe Adonis had been deported. Only Albert Anastasia and Tony Bender Strollo were left; and Strollo had always been Vito Genovese's lieutenant. The odds were against Frank Costello, but still the former prime minister of the underworld balked at stepping down. So, on the night of May 2, 1957, at about eleven, as Costello was returning to his apartment in the Majestic, at 115 Central Park West, a hit man followed him into the lobby and announced, "This is for you, Frank." Costello hearing the man behind him, had started to turn just as the man fired a shot at his head. The .38-caliber slug, instead of braining him, merely ripped a slash along the right side of Costello's head, beginning just behind the ear.

About two hours later a tough-talking caller tried to reach me by phone at the office. The night side took the brief message: "They stepped on some good guys' toes. All I can say is that if Albert or Freddie steps in, they'll get it too." The reference to "Freddie" puzzled Al Scotti, but no one had any doubt about the identity of "Albert"—it could only be Albert Anastasia, the one-time field commander of Murder Inc.

The threat became a reality less than six months later, on October 25, 1957, when Anastasia was having "the works" in the Hotel Sheraton barbershop at Seventh Avenue and 55th Street at about 10:15 A.M. Two gunmen strolled in, walked up behind him and blasted away with such a fusillade of shots that Anastasia was catapulted right out of the barber chair. His executioners cruised out of the shop and mixed with the crowds on the street, as the victim lay dead on the floor.

The assassination of the Lord High Executioner occurred just before our second edition deadline, and I went into the last-minute deadline drill, pounding furiously at my typewriter with a copyboy standing by to grab the story a paragraph at a time. I had only a short breather before another telephone call came, about two hours later. The message was tough, fast and to the point: "You remember I called you last spring right after Costello was shot, and you printed a warning we issued to Anastasia not to butt in?"

"Yes," I replied.

"Well, we're delivering another warning now. This time we're telling Frankie—and I don't mean Costello—not to interfere. And we're not fooling."

"Who do you mean by Frankie?" I asked.

"Frankie C., but it's not Costello," the caller said.

Before I could ask another question, he slammed down the phone.

This second warning baffled authorities. Who was Frankie C.? And why had the mobsters chosen me to convey their warning? The first question was never answered; Frankie C., whoever he was, apparently heeded the threat—and lived. As for the second question, I remained as puzzled as anyone. I could only surmise that I had some fans in the underworld who knew that a message delivered through me would reach the right eyes.

14

Our Cloak-and-Dagger Heroes

MANY AMERICANS BELIEVE THAT THE MEDIA ARE SOME-
how captive to insidious liberal forces. My experience,
however, suggests that the very reverse is true.

On the *World-Telegram and Sun*, the political reporting was
entrusted to types who could be expected to reflect the solidly
conservative, Republican views of the front office. On rewrite,
the handling of the day's fast-breaking political development was
entrusted to a writer who had joined our staff in 1950 after Roy
Howard bought the *Sun*. But in the 1952 presidential race between Adlai Stevenson and Dwight D. Eisenhower, even he had
trouble fulfilling the dictates of the front office.

In an attempt to discredit Stevenson, the paper embarked on
a Red-smear campaign and tried to tie Harry Bridges, the West
Coast longshore leader who was then being denounced as a Communist agitator, to Stevenson's coattails. The story our political
writer was ordered to track down was that Stevenson and Bridges
had been in Chicago at the same time—*and even had stayed at
the same hotel!* The reporter struggled all morning attempting to
verify the story, but he could find absolutely no evidence to show
that Stevenson and Bridges had ever met or talked. He told the
city desk that the verifiable facts did not justify publishing the
rumor, but he was directed to write the story anyhow, and the
paper splashed it on page one.

Other instances of distortion during that campaign are there for the citing. And then came the 1954 New York gubernatorial campaign between U.S. Senator Irving Ives and W. Averell Harriman. Dewey decided that he'd had enough of Albany and had persuaded Ives to run as his hand-picked successor. Since Harriman was not a colorful campaigner, Ives might have won—if Dewey had been content to leave well enough alone instead of going for the jugular.

In the closing days of the campaign, the governor tried a canard dating back to post–World War I days involving the disposal of excess maritime shipping of which Harriman was in charge. First, our highly conservative, Republican-oriented political reporter checked the Dewey-fed "facts." He decided he was dealing with a very flimsy smear story and that there was no hard evidence Harriman had ever done anything illegal or unethical in disposing of the excess shipping. The city desk refused to run the smear.

This did not stop Dewey. He got the story planted in a Buffalo newspaper; then the Associated Press was pressured to pick up the tale, quoting the Buffalo paper. We were next. Lee Wood came charging out of the front office in midafternoon and told the city desk that the Associated Press wires were carrying the story all over the state, that Dewey was demanding to know why we weren't using it, and that we were just going to *have* to run it. Bert MacDonald, our city editor, emitted a disgusted groan, but he was helpless. Our own research had indicated that the story was an example of phony, last-minute blackguarding, but it wound up on our front page anyway.

When the votes were counted, Harriman eked out a narrow victory over Ives. Indeed, some postmortems concluded that Dewey's last-minute effort to besmirch Harriman's reputation might well have backfired.

By this time I was pretty well disenchanted with the distortions of the newspaper I had been putting so much effort into. So when I received a letter from Carey McWilliams, editor of *The Nation*, inviting me to write for that small liberal periodical, I was certainly—though guardedly—open to the possibility.

I had not read *The Nation* for some twenty years. I knew vaguely that the far right had tried to label it a pro-Communist rag. I didn't know whether I wanted to get involved, and I didn't reply to the inquiry for several days. But, at lunch with several colleagues one day, I happened to mention McWilliams's suggestion that I do some writing for him.

George Montgomery, a friend on rewrite, let out a large guffaw. "That's all you would need to get yourself in good with Roy Howard," he said. "Writing for *The Nation!*"

I guess I must be a perverse, stubborn individual, for that's all I needed to hear. I was spurred, not deterred. "To hell with Roy Howard," I muttered to myself silently. As soon as I got back to the office, I telephoned Carey and told him I'd be delighted to write for *The Nation,* thus beginning an association that has lasted for more than a quarter of a century.

I didn't find out until much later that it was Bernard (Bud) Nossiter, a young reporter with whom I had collaborated on a number of stories, who had recommended that his friend McWilliams approach me.

Carey McWilliams will always be special to me. He was a one-man staff at *The Nation* in those days, and the work he did was incredible. He clipped newspapers from all over the country, compiled voluminous files, and seemed to inhale with every breath a sense of developing national issues that others hadn't yet discovered.

Carey was a fighter for the underdog; he believed in causes; and he was not to be deterred. Early in his career, he had written a trail-blazing book called *Factories in the Field,* the nonfiction counterpart of John Steinbeck's *Grapes of Wrath,* published at the same time, and another titled *Prejudice,* written after World War II, a study of the discrimination against Japanese-Americans who were interned. Carey McWilliams was my kind of man.

Short and stocky, with a roundish face that broke into a pleasant smile as he said, "Hi, fellow," when you walked into his office, he was usually to be found at his desk in shirtsleeves, his heavy-rimmed glasses sliding down his nose as he peered closely at some manuscript he was reading.

He provided a kind of catharsis for me. When I became frustrated at having a perfectly good story killed at the paper, I found an outlet by telling it the way it should have been told in *The Nation.*

A good example was my experience with the case of Boris Morros, champion counterspy for the FBI. Morros sprang from obscurity into headline prominence in winter 1957, when a federal grand jury in New York indicted Myra and Jack Soble and Jacob

Albam as kingpins in a Soviet spy ring operating in this country. Two more important figures allegedly involved in the ring had already fled behind the Iron Curtain: Alfred Stern, an American millionaire, and his wife, Martha Dodd Stern, the daughter of former Ambassador to Berlin William E. Dodd and the author of *Through Embassy Eyes*, a best-selling account of the early days of Adolf Hitler's regime in Germany. Morros was the government's key witness in the case.

According to the legend, Morros, in his sixties at the time, a pudgy, bull-necked hulk of a man, had been a musical prodigy in his youth in Russia; had composed the well-known "Parade of the Wooden Soldiers"; had scored the music for almost four hundred movies; and had become famous as the producer of such major movies as *Tales of Manhattan* and *Carnegie Hall*. He had given it all up—had sacrificed his career at a cost of some $2 million—and, out of sheer patriotism, had become a counterspy for the FBI. He had spent ten years undercover, had outfoxed the wiliest Russian agents, and had penetrated to the heart of the Soviet espionage networks in Europe. What a story!

But there was another side to Boris Morros, one with decidedly less of Hollywood in it. Our paper received a tip that a detective agency in downtown Manhattan had compiled a dossier on the real Boris Morros, and I was sent to investigate.

I found that the detective agency had put together a very thorough file, indeed. I learned that Boris Morros had not composed the "Parade of the Wooden Soldiers" (that was credited to Leon Jessel), and when he went to live on the FBI payroll, he was not a famous and wealthy movie producer, but a bankrupt man harassed by a flock of lawsuits.

In 1923, shortly after he came to the United States, Morros filed for bankruptcy, listing $15,600 in debts and no assets. On January 28, 1930, he filed a second bankruptcy petition in New York County, listing $13,666.19 in liabilities and again, no assets.

In September 1945, some twenty months before he entered the service of his adopted country, Morros formed Federal Films, Inc., and produced *Carnegie Hall*, a gaudy project that cost a fortune and bombed at the box office. The Security First National Bank of Los Angeles foreclosed on the film company, which then went out of business. On November 14, 1946, some eight months before Morros went to the FBI, a night watchman named Joseph Steiner sued Federal Films for $4987.39 in unpaid back wages.

And Carnegie Hall, Inc. sued the film company and Morros for $8,123.02, obtained a judgment—and found one Morros bank account with just $50 in it, an amount it attached.

I came back to the office with this disillusioning portrait of the FBI's new super hero and described it all to our managing editor. He hemmed and hawed and finally said, "We don't want to do anything to prejudice the government's case with trial coming up. So just hold the material in your file. Perhaps we'll get a chance to use it later."

I dutifully put the file away in my desk drawer and waited. Then, on August 12, 1957, I came back from lunch and noticed that my typewriter was overflowing with copy—a pile of United Press and Associated Press wire stories, plus notes from our own reporters, spilled from the typewriter to the desk.

The Sobles and Albam had walked into Federal Court and pleaded guilty. Once the pleas had been entered, U.S. Attorney Paul L. Williams trotted out Boris Morros and praised him as a self-sacrificing patriot. Morros took over, adding details to the federal statement, and claiming that the sacrifice of his flourishing career as a movie producer had cost him $2 million and left him bankrupt.

I turned to the city desk. "We know all this isn't true," I said. "What am I going to do with the material on this guy that I've been holding?"

The assistant city editor never raised his head or looked at me. "Just write the story," he said. "We have to meet competition."

Meet competition! And to hell with the facts? "All right," I growled, "I'll write the story, but I'm damned if I'm going to say that this phony bastard sacrificed $2 million to serve his country."

I sat down at my desk and, swallowing my bile, wrote a story that I'm afraid didn't do very much to "meet competition." I eliminated all reference to $2-million patriotism and treated Boris Morros far more tepidly than most of our competition—our afternoon rivals and the morning New York *Times* as well swallowed the Boris Morros myth whole. But perhaps no one else knew as much as we did.

As time went on, some newsmen made efforts to set the record straight. Columnists Walter Winchell and Dorothy Kilgallen wrote some tart comments that indicated they were not entirely hoodwinked; and Bob Thomas, of the Associated Press, writing from

Hollywood, did a three-part series that wound up in our morgue instead of in the paper. Thomas really shredded the image, writing that Morros was not a composer and had never conducted anything, that his only big studio job had been as head of Paramount's Music Department, "a supervisory post" in which he had had the task of lining up the right composers and orchestrators for specific projects (in other words, a glorified talent scout).

It was during the Paramount period that Morros became involved with Soviet secret agents. He said he wanted to get his father out of Russia, and the Soviets demanded a reward: they insisted that Morris furnish their agents with identification so that they could go all over the world posing as representatives of Paramount. Morros obliged. After his Paramount job folded, his Soviet superior came to him and said in effect, "Well, you have a small music company. We will make it a big music company." Morros was agreeable. He went to New York, where he met Alfred and Martha Stern and accepted $130,000 to make the Boris Morros Music Company "a big music company." In return, he continued to furnish ID for Soviet agents. The music company, like Morros's other ventures, did not prosper, and the Sterns wanted their money back. At first Morros refused to reimburse them, but his Soviet spymaster talked him into returning $100,000. Morros and the Sterns had ceased to trust each other, and a bankrupt Morros went to the FBI.

On October 17, 1957, the Associated Press reported from Los Angeles that Morros's wife, Catherine, had brought suit for separate maintenance. The story did not attract much attention in the press, but Mrs. Morros alleged cruelty and charged "Morros had failed in recent years to provide for his own father . . ." The New York *Times* printed that Mrs. Morros was demanding the return of "an undisclosed sum of personal funds she says she contributed toward the support of her husband's father."

None of these piecemeal disclosures affected the high-riding career of Boris Morros. He strode across the American stage larger than life. He went on the lecture circuit and spoke to rapt audiences about the Communist menace. He testified as a qualified expert before the House Un-American Activities Committee. The Associated Press, quoting Chairman Francis E. Walter, reported: "Counterspy Boris Morros foresees the fall of Soviet Communist Party chief Nikita S. Khrushchev within the next eight months.

He predicts that the successor will be a military dictatorship headed by Marshal Georgi K. Zhukov." Rep. Walter added that Morros had told the committee that all Soviet spy networks were being consolidated under the direction of the Red Army, a shift of power that was most ominous for the West.

In less than two months, the very reverse of expert Morros's predictions came to pass: Khrushchev hatcheted Zhukov. But did this discredit the know-all counterspy? Not in the least. One national news agency reported this development as if it confirmed what Morros had told HUAC, noting that he had predicted two months previously that there would be a showdown between Khrushchev and Zhukov and said, "Zhukov could become a rival to Khrushchev." Omitting the vital detail that Morros had gotten the outcome all wrong, that he had picked Zhukov to win, the news dispatch made it appear that the new development in Russia confirmed everything Morros had said.

During these months, I watched developments and steamed. I resented the phoniness; I burned in silent outrage at the manner in which my notes on the real Boris Morros still lay discarded in my desk. Finally, fed up beyond endurance, I wrote a thorough debunking of the Morros myth for *The Nation* issue of January 25, 1958. Carey published it under the title "Boris Morros: Myth of a Hero."

The sequel demonstrated that, in the America of the time, the myth was the message. Viking Press was about to publish Morros's *My Ten Years as a Counterspy*, written in collaboration with Charles Samuels, a well-known writer. *The Nation* article may have given Viking a jolt, but it went right ahead with the book. In press releases sent out on the date of publication, it noted that Morros had been vouched for by the highest authorities and that only a certain (unnamed) "left-wing" publication had tried to smear the hero. That veiled "left-wing" smear incensed me again because, as far as I could see, *The Nation*'s only sin was that it had printed the truth that mainstream publications had smothered. But in those days one did not have to meet an opponent's facts; all anyone had to do to win the battle was to pin a pejorative label like "left-wing" or "pinko" or "pseudo-liberal" on an annoying critic. Labels did the work, critics were demolished, and the anointed remained protected.

15

Alger Hiss

CAREY MCWILLIAMS HAD READ MY ARTICLE ON THE WILliam Remington miscarriage of justice; and he was so impressed by it that he telephoned me in spring 1957 and asked if I would be willing to do a similar study of the Hiss case for *The Nation*.

"Carey, I wouldn't touch it with a ten-foot pole," I told him. "I think Hiss was guilty as hell, and I don't want any part of it."

A week or so later Carey approached me again. Wouldn't I take a look at the Hiss case for *The Nation?* Again, I said, "Carey, I don't want to touch it."

He argued with me this time: "I'm told that if one really looks at the evidence, he'll come away with a different feeling about the case."

"I don't see how," I replied. "How can anyone get around those documents that Whittaker Chambers produced?"

Carey said he didn't know, but perhaps on close examination the documents might not be all that they seemed.

I still said I wanted nothing to do with the Hiss case.

A short time later, Carey telephoned me again, but this time couched his request in the form of a challenge that no conscientious reporter could ignore. "Look, Fred," he said, "we'd still like to get a piece on the Hiss case. I understand how you feel,

but will you at least do this for us: Will you look at the record?
There's no obligation. If you still don't like what you find, that
ends it. But will you at least take a look?"

I was hooked. A newspaperman always has an obligation to look
at the facts. How could I refuse even to look? All right, I told
Carey, I would study the record, although I didn't expect it to
change my opinion. But once I looked, I was shocked at what I
found.

More than thirty years after the Hiss case became a *cause
célèbre,* its significance can be understood only if one appreciates
the political turmoil of the times. The Republicans and arch-
conservative big business forces that had been operating through
The Committee for the Constitution had become paranoid. In
election after election, they had been frustrated by the personal
charisma of Franklin Roosevelt and such innovations as Social
Security and the forty-hour week. "The Roosevelt revolution" had
them raving, and from the mid-1930s on they conducted an unremitting campaign against dangerous foreign "isms," a catch phrase
designed to foster the belief that the Roosevelt Administration
was tinged pink by Moscow.

Then Roosevelt died, and Harry S Truman became president.
Truman ran in 1948 at the head of a divided party, split by the
Dixiecrat revolt in the South and by Henry Wallace's campaign
in the North. Republicans, with Governor Dewey as their standard bearer, smelled victory, and they stepped up their propaganda
barrage. The Republicans controlled Congress, and the Republican national chairman urged their investigating committees to
keep spy hearings going throughout the summer to put the heat
on the Democrats. Spy scare followed spy scare in headlines
generated by these committees. Years later, when I wrote my
first book about this period, I studied newspaper files for that
hectic summer, and I was amazed at the number of headlined
disclosures that, having made their impact in type, faded and
were forgotten.

But the Hiss and Remington cases did not. These were flaunted
as irrefutable proof and justification for the demagogic outcry
"twenty years of treason." According to those prize informers,
Elizabeth Bentley and Whittaker Chambers, both had been Communists; both had been spies; both had given secret government
information to Russia. Both had been convicted of perjury in

defending themselves against these charges, the statute of limitations against espionage having expired, and these convictions were fodder for the propaganda campaign. Alger Hiss, by reason of his background, education, high government positions, and even his name, was an ideal target for the hate brigades that capitalized on the common man's prejudices.

Hiss, born in Baltimore in 1904, had a prep school education and attended Harvard Law School, where he was on the Law Review. He served as secretary to Supreme Court Justice Oliver Wendell Holmes before going into government service. He was counsel to the Nye Committee in pre-World War II days—another suspect connection since that committee had focused on war profiteering, with emphasis on the powerful du Ponts. Next, Hiss entered the State Department, which conservatives charged had been soft on Communism, and in State he had been the Golden Boy who rose rapidly: secretary to the Dumbarton Oaks Economic Conference in 1944; a member of the American delegation to Yalta (where political opponents alleged Roosevelt had sold out to Stalin), and finally secretary general of the San Francisco conference at which the United Nations had been born. In December 1946 Hiss had left government service and become president of the prestigious Carnegie Endowment for International Peace at a salary of $20,000 a year.

Whittaker Chambers couldn't have been more different from the Golden Boy he came to accuse in testimony before the House Un-American Activities Committee in August 1948. Chambers was a beefy, bloated senior editor of *Time*. While Hiss came from a middle- to upper-class society, Chambers had emerged from the netherworld, as he admitted during the Hiss trials. When he was seventeen he had lived in a New Orleans dive that was the home of a prostitute known as One-Eyed Annie. While he was a student at Columbia University, he had written a "Play for Puppets" that blasphemed Christ and held Christianity to be "a sadistic religion." He had stolen books from the Columbia University Library. He had frequently committed perjury.

This last admission began to give me trouble with my preconceptions about the Hiss case. The record showed that Chambers in repeated questioning by the FBI and in testimony before HUAC and a federal grand jury had made one consistent charge and only one: that Hiss had belonged to a Communist cell in Washington in the mid-1930s. Chambers had denied time and again under oath that there had ever been any hint of espionage. He had been interviewed some fourteen or fifteen times by FBI agents before he ever took the witness stand, and had each time insisted that Hiss had belonged to an "elite, policy-making, top-level group . . . not a spy ring, but far more important and cunning because its members helped to shape policy in their Departments."

Chambers admitted that he had been a spy courier. By 1948, however, the statute of limitations had expired and he could be prosecuted only if he committed perjury on the witness stand. Yet, if his final charge that Hiss had been a spy was correct, this was precisely what he had done when he testified before HUAC that Hiss and others in the alleged Communist cell "were *specifically* not wanted to act as sources of information. These people were an elite group" whom the Communist Party expected to rise to high positions and influence policy.

Even after Hiss had challenged Chambers to make his Communist charge in a public forum, outside the sanctum of a Congressional hearing, Chambers had stuck to the same line. Appearing on "Meet the Press" on August 27, he repeated his charge that Hiss had been a Communist. But when he was asked about espionage, he said, "That was a group, not, as I think is in the back of your minds, for the purpose of espionage, but for the purpose of infiltrating government policy."

Q. It was not, then, by definition, conspiracy?
A. No, it was not.

After this broadcast, Hiss sued Chambers for libel. Chambers later admitted in his book, *Witness,* that he knew he was in danger and might lose the libel suit, but he persisted in his denials that Hiss had ever been a spy. When Chambers testified before a federal grand jury in New York on October 14, 1948 (a little more than a month before he was to produce his documents in a pretrial libel hearing in Baltimore), this sequence occurred:

JUROR: Could you give me one name of anybody who, in your opinion, was positively guilty of espionage against the United States?
CHAMBERS: Let me think for a moment and I will try to

answer that. I don't think so, but would like to have the opportunity to answer you tomorrow more definitely. Let me think it over, overnight.

The next day Chambers acted on his night-long meditation.

CHAMBERS: I assume that espionage means in this case the turning over of secret confidential documents.
JUROR: Or information—oral information.
CHAMBERS: Or oral information. I do not believe I do know such a name.

I read this testimony in 1957 with a feeling of *déjà vu*—here was the Remington case all over again. Here again was the prosecution making a 180-degree turn from what it had never been to what, it was ultimately contended, it had always been. If Chambers's final accusation that Hiss had been a spy ever since the mid-1930s was true, then he had lied repeatedly to the FBI over a period of years; he had committed perjury time and time again— the last time before a federal grand jury only a month before he was to do his startling about-face, spring his trap, produce the documents and declare that Hiss had always been a spy.

I had covered courtroom trials and had studied trial transcripts. I had seen witnesses become entangled in untruths, but I had never seen the basic foundation of a case change from white to black overnight as had happened in the Remington and Hiss cases. Whittaker Chambers's sudden and inexplicable change from denial to accusation convinced me that Hiss, like Remington, had been framed for political purposes. Now I knew: I was going to have to write this story.

This did not mean I was entirely satisfied with the conduct of Alger Hiss. He had demanded to be heard as soon as Chambers testified on August 3. When he appeared before HUAC two days later, he emphatically denied ever knowing a man named Whittaker Chambers. He insisted that he had never been a Communist, had never followed the line of any Communist-front organizations, and had never, so far as he knew, had a friend who was a Communist. As for Chambers, he would like the opportunity to meet him face-to-face. The hearing ended with the implicit understanding that this confrontation would be the next procedure.

But Rep. Richard M. Nixon, an opportunist intent on forwarding his own political career, was not about to keep this implied promise. Instead of letting the two men confront each other, he had the committee call Chambers to a secret session in the Federal Court House on Foley Square in New York on Saturday, August 7. Word soon leaked out to the press that Chambers had testified "for hours" about all kinds of intimate details proving his close association with Alger Hiss.

Hiss knew only what he read in the papers. When he was recalled by the house committee on August 16, he had no knowledge of the content of this secret testimony, so had no way of refuting the charges. For example, in his secret testimony Chambers had said he had been known to Hiss only as "Carl" because Communists never used their last names with each other. When the committee asked Hiss if he had ever known a man named "Carl," he was clearly baffled, and when he was finally asked if he had ever known anyone between 1934 and 1937 just by the name of "Carl," he said, "Absolutely not."

Also in his secret testimony Chambers had contended that he had lived for long periods in Hiss's home, that he had made it his unofficial headquarters in Washington, and that he had spent hours reading in Hiss's library. The committee asked Hiss to explain how a man could have spent so much time in his home and he not know him. Hiss now had a recollection: in 1934–35, when he was working for the Nye committee, he had met a freelance writer named George Crosley; the Hisses were moving from their 28th Street apartment and still had a month left on their lease, and since Crosley needed a place to stay, Hiss had let him have the apartment. Later, he said, when Crosley needed a car, he had given Crosley his old Model A Ford, which was worth about $25 as scrap metal. Under hostile questioning, Hiss conceded that he had come to consider Crosley "a welsher" because he had not paid the apartment rent nor repaid small loans—but even then Hiss had let him have the old Ford.

The questioning switched to Hiss's hobbies. He said they were "tennis and ornithology." Rep. John McDowell, a Pennsylvania Republican, slipped in an apparently innocent question. Had Hiss, he asked, ever seen a rare bird known as the prothonotary warbler? "I have, right here on the Potomac," Hiss exclaimed. "Do you know the place? . . . They come back and nest in these swamps. Beautiful yellow head, a gorgeous bird—" Nixon cut him off.

Hiss's eager confirmation of this obscure ornithological detail elevated the prothonotary warbler to a unique niche in legal history. This rare bird, by itself, seems to have convinced McDowell, Nixon and the rest of the committee (if anyone needed any further convincing) that Chambers had been telling the truth and Hiss had been evasive.

The next development was the long-promised confrontation, at the Hotel Commodore in New York on August 17. Chambers's appearance had changed considerably between 1935 and 1948; he was much heavier, more jowled, balder than he had been in the 1930s.

Hiss walked up to Chambers and asked, "Would you mind opening your mouth wider?" He explained that his most vivid recollection of George Crosley was that the man had very bad teeth. After examining Chambers's incisors, Hiss said that it appeared a lot of dental work had been done, and he added, "I believe, I am not prepared without further checking to take an absolute oath, that he must be George Crosley."

Nixon wondered sarcastically whether Hiss wanted the name of Chambers's dentist so that he could check further, but Chambers finally settled the issue by identifying himself as the man who had stayed in Hiss's former apartment in 1935. But, he said, he had not been supposed to pay rent; Hiss, he said, as a dedicated Communist, had donated the apartment to Chambers as his superior in the hierarchy of the Communist Party. Hiss was so enraged that he advanced on Chambers as if about to strike him, but then he said that on the basis of Chambers's own admission he was prepared to acknowledge that Chambers was the man he had known as George Crosley in 1935.

The public hearings continued with further ruthless grillings of Hiss. The onesidedness of the performance was later described by the English journalist Alistair Cooke in his book *A Generation on Trial: U.S.A. Vs. Alger Hiss*. He commented on the angry tone of Nixon's accusatory grilling which "put the burden of proof on Hiss." He observed that the hearing took on "the pervasive psychological force . . . of a cross- examination in court," and, he added: "The spectator had to shake himself from time to time out of this trance to appreciate that he was not in a court of law, that Hiss was not a defendant, that there was no right of rebuttal, no cross-examination of the accuser; in a word, it was the heyday of the public prosecutor."

All the time, buried in the background, not to be released for months—and then to be ignored by a press absorbed in later sensations—there was a fundamental truth test: the August 7 secret testimony of Whittaker Chambers. To me, from the moment I read this transcript down to the present day, this was the most revealing testimony in the entire case, the vital key to understanding. By any process of logic that I can conceive, one would have to conclude that the "real" Whittaker Chambers must have told all that he knew in this testimony given in the almost fraternal atmosphere of a committee baying on the trail of Hiss. Chambers had already perfected his story in those numerous interviews with the FBI, in talks with others, in his first witness-stand testimony; and so it is inevitable, in any rational assessment of the case, to conclude that what facts he had—*all* the facts—must have been firmly fixed in his mind. Thus the August 7 testimony became the basic testimony by which all else must be judged. Yet when I read this crucial transcript, I was amazed both by its skimpiness and the manner in which this testimony of the "real" Whittaker Chambers collided in virtually every detail with the later accounts of the witness-stand Chambers.

As in all of Chambers's testimony, dates are of crucial importance. The copies of secret State Department documents that he had produced at the Baltimore libel hearing ran from January 1938 to April 1, 1938. These were all documents, Chambers contended, that Hiss had brought home and that Mrs. Hiss had copied on an old Woodstock typewriter. If there had been any truth to these charges, Chambers would have had intimate knowledge of the Hisses and their home, which, he claimed, he was constantly visiting until mid-April 1938. But when Chambers gave his secret testimony on August 7, 1948, he was in the phase of his story in which he was insisting there were no such documents; in the phase in which, as he testified repeatedly, he had left the Communist Party in 1937; the phase in which he claimed to have known Hiss only between 1934 and 1937. So clear was this time element that Nixon later asked Hiss for his recollection of his dealings with Chambers only between 1934 and 1937 because nothing else was at stake. Again a fundamental basis of the case was changed later to make it seem possible for Chambers to have received 1938 documents despite his many prior statements that he had left the party in 1937.

Such contradictions made checkpoints of Chambers's veracity, as revealed in this secret session, especially significant. He had testified accurately that Hiss called his wife, Priscilla, by the pet names "Hilly" and sometimes "Pross." He had been accurate about the prothonotary warbler. He had told of accompanying Mrs. Hiss on an automobile trip to Paoli, Pennsylvania, where her father lived. He denied Hiss had given him the Ford, but insisted that Hiss had donated the car to the party for the use of some loyal party worker. Motor vehicle records were murky; they showed that someone had transferred title through an automobile agency to a mysterious man named Rosen, who apparently had been a Communist.

Beyond this, Chambers's testimony was notable for its absence of specifics. Asked about Hiss's library, where he said he had spent days at a time reading, all he could offer was the vague statement: "Very nondescript as I recall." Asked if the Hisses had a piano, he felt "reasonably sure that they did not." (They did.) Asked about their furniture, all he could recall was "a small leather cigarette box . . . with gold tooling on it. It seems to me the box was made of red leather." I got the impression from the transcript that committee members were virtually panting for Chambers to tell them more, but these skimpy details, not all of them accurate, were all that he could offer.

Perhaps in his effort to please, he came up with an additional item, one that branded him an arrant liar. Priscilla, before her marriage to Hiss, had been the wife of New York publisher Thayer Hobson. They had had a son, Timothy, who lived with the Hisses and was sent to a private school, for which Thayer Hobson paid the tuition costs. Elaborating on these facts, Chambers told the committee that the Hisses had taken Timothy out of an expensive private school and had sent him to a cheaper one so that they could pilfer tuition money from Thayer Hobson and send it to the Communist Party.

Thayer Hobson later said, "I knew Chambers was lying the instant I read that quote." The very reverse of Chambers's tuition-swindling yarn was true, according to Hobson. The Hisses had transferred Timothy from a less expensive to a more expensive private school; Hobson had protested against this extravagance; and the Hisses had made up the difference out of their own pockets.

Chambers's only explanation for the complete about-face in his testimony was that he was a man of sensitive moral character, one so humanistic that he could not bring himself to destroy the life of another until Hiss drove him to the deed with his threat of a libel suit. I had good reason to remember this bit of self-justification. Victor Lasky occupied the rewrite desk directly in front of me at the *World-Telegram and Sun;* and, when he was researching his book, *Seeds of Treason,* written with Ralph de Toledano, he had visited Chambers at Chambers's farm in Maryland. When he returned, some of us asked him how Chambers explained the complete turn-around in his testimony, and Lasky snapped, "He was just trying to save the son of a bitch, that's all."

Incidentally, Lasky's book couldn't be published unless Hiss was convicted, another echo of the Remington case and a book grand jury foreman Brunini and Elizabeth Bentley had been writing. Thirty years after the trials, Hiss obtained through a Freedom of Information action the copy of a two-page letter Lasky had written to U.S. Attorney Thomas F. Murphy, who was prosecuting Hiss. In this, Lasky told of a long telephone conversation he had had the previous night with Richard Nixon. He noted that "Dick has a heck of a lot at stake in the outcome" (as did Lasky), and he passed along to Murphy detailed advice from Nixon concerning the manner in which Murphy should harass Hiss in cross-examination.

When my analytical critique of the Hiss case, which took up an entire issue of *The Nation* in fall 1957, had barely circulated I received a telephone call from an editor at William Morrow & Co., Thayer Hobson's firm. The editor wanted to know whether I would be willing to expand the article into a book.

Thayer Hobson had always been convinced of Hiss's innocence and had long wanted to do something about the case. And so I wrote *The Unfinished Story of Alger Hiss,* which was published by Morrow in spring 1958.

Another revealing aspect of Chambers's secret August 7 account was that, if his ultimate courtroom testimony about the passing and copying of documents in 1938 was true, he must have known a lot about the Hisses during the period when he was supposedly making regular visits to their home in his role as spy courier. But the transcript showed that Chambers's recollection failed him by

1937. In February of that year, Timothy Hobson was nearly killed in an automobile accident while riding his bicycle. He was bed-ridden for weeks and then cast-bound for months in the home to which the Hisses had moved in July 1936. Had Chambers known the Hisses in 1937, the year *before* the alleged document passing, he could hardly have been unaware of this traumatic accident; yet even with his friendly inquisitors literally begging him for just such specifics, he never mentioned it. Obviously, he had not known—and, if he had not, then his entire later tale of espionage and document-copying appeared to have been concocted.

The more deeply I probed and analyzed this case, the more I became convinced that Whittaker Chambers was a pathological liar who could not tell the same story the same way twice. The proof was there in his August 7 testimony, which revealed his contradictions of himself in his account of the collection of Com-munist Party dues. Chambers, in the public hearing of August 3, had testified that seven men were in the high-level cell to which Hiss belonged. They met at the apartment of Henry Collins, a boyhood friend of Hiss's.

> Q. When you met these men at Mr. Collins's apartment, did you collect Communist Party dues from them?
> A. *I did not,* but the Communist Party dues were handed over to me by Collins, who was the treasurer of that group.

Just four days later, under friendly questioning by Nixon, there occurred this sequence:

> NIXON: Did you obtain his [Hiss's] party dues from him?
> CHAMBERS: Yes, I did.
> NIXON: Over what period of time?
> CHAMBERS: Two or three years, as long as I knew him.
> . . . NIXON: How often?
> CHAMBERS: Once a month.
> NIXON: And once a month over a period of two years, ap-proximately, he gave you an envelope which contained the dues?
> CHAMBERS: That is right . . .

Even Nixon seemed to see that this complete conflict in his ace witness's testimony had to be patched up. The press and public, of course, had no idea of the conflict; only Nixon and the members of the committee did. On August 25, with Chambers back on the stand, Nixon engineered a bit of cover-up testimony that resulted in yet a *third* version. Nixon asked Chambers if he had ever collected party dues from Hiss. Chambers now said that he had.

> NIXON: On one occasion or more occasions than one?
> CHAMBERS: At least on one occasion, and I would think on at least three occasions. [Not once a month, now, for a period of approximately two years.]
> . . . NIXON: Who collected dues from Mr. Hiss generally?
> CHAMBERS: Henry Collins.

A tangled, contentious web of testimony characterized this infinitely complicated case. But in the end it all came down to the documents that Chambers had produced and to the ancient Woodstock typewriter on which he contended that they had been typed.

In the innocence of the age, Americans of varying political allegiances regarded documents as sacred evidence. To understand the effect the documents made on the public mind in this case, it is important to realize that Chambers dropped two bombshells—that there were two entirely separate sets of documents. In early questioning, Hiss's attorneys had grilled Chambers relentlessly, giving him such a bad time that his own lawyers, as he later wrote, warned him that if he had any hard evidence he had better produce it. And so at a pre-trial libel deposition hearing in Baltimore on November 17, 1948, Chambers suddenly produced sixty-five typed pages of State Department documents and four brief memoranda in Hiss's own handwriting. Hiss immediately turned this material over to federal authorities.

Since the hearing had not been public, it was not until December 1, 1948, that hints of some new development leaked into the press. A Washington gossip column reported that "new and sensational" information had been developed in the libel case. On the same day, the United Press queried Justice Department officials and quoted them as saying that the Hiss-Chambers case was as good as dead unless "something new turned up soon."

Nixon and Robert E. Stripling, HUAC's chief investigator, hurried out to Chambers's Westminster farm. Chambers said his lawyers had told him not to talk, but he admitted he had dropped "a bombshell" at the Baltimore hearing. And then, according to Stripling, he added the tantalizing information that "the first one was nothing compared to the second." Stripling quoted Nixon as saying, "I'm here for the second one."

Uncharacteristically, Nixon didn't wait for the production of "the second bombshell." He had been scheduled to take a vacation cruise, and he went. Stripling returned to Washington, got a subpoena, and went back to Chambers's farm at 10:30 the next night, December 2, 1948. Chambers led Stripling out into his pumpkin patch. He went over to a hollowed-out pumpkin, reached inside and plucked out five rolls of microfilm. Three rolls had never been developed, but the two that had showed reproductions of official documents.

"The Pumpkin Papers" as all of Chambers's documents were immediately labeled in the sensationalized headlines of the day blew the "dead" case into the courts. Stripling wired Nixon to get off his cruise ship, and Nixon rushed back by Coast Guard crash boat and seaplane. Hollywood never wrote a more dramatic script, and press reporters and photographers covered every moment of it. Nixon captured the headlines and demanded the indictment of Alger Hiss.

Something I hadn't realized—and that I think most of the general public hadn't—was that the late-night drama in Chambers's pumpkin patch produced no worthwhile evidence. The three strips of undeveloped microfilm were useless, and the two developed rolls yielded just fifty-eight pages of documents that could not be traced to any specific espionage source. But that did not matter. Official statements fed the public hysteria. Stripling told the New York *Times* that "he had a stack of papers, developed from the film, about three feet high." Even this hyperbole didn't satisfy Chambers, who wrote in *Witness* that "the enlargements made a pile almost four feet high." Never had fifty-eight pages been more puffed up into a veritable pyramid of evidence; but the publicity windfall, as Chambers later chuckled in *Witness*, forced the hand of the Justice Department and led to the indictment and ultimate conviction of Hiss on charges of perjury.

In my study of the case, I disregarded the widely publicized "Pumpkin Papers" and concentrated on the only real documentary evidence: the sixty-five typed State Department documents and four handwritten memoranda that Chambers had produced in Baltimore. And here again I confronted the enigma of Whittaker Chambers and ran into testimony that defied belief.

Chambers's version was that when he left the Communist Party he squirreled away the last of the documents he had obtained from Hiss as "a life preserver" against future retribution. They had been hidden for years, he said, in the dumbwaiter shaft of the Brooklyn home of Nathan Levine, his wife's nephew, and he had even forgotten what he had until, under the pressure of the libel suit, he had retrieved the dirt-caked envelope in which the papers had been stored. Once again I found Chambers in conflict with Chambers.

All of the documents Chambers had produced were dated between January and April 1, 1938; but in repeated accounts and in testimony under oath he had insisted that he had left the party in 1937. In *Witness*, he wrote a dramatic account of how he had sat at night with a gun in his lap, watching for his Communist ex-comrades if they came to kill him. So traumatic an experience, by any rational measurement, must have fixed the date when it occurred indelibly in the mind; yet Chambers, from his first disclosure to Assistant Secretary of State Adolph A. Berle, in 1939 soon after his defection, in his later fourteen to fifteen interviews with the FBI, and in his original HUAC testimony, had always fixed 1937 as the year when he had abandoned Communism. But if Chambers had left the party in 1937, it was impossible for him to have obtained 1938-typed documents from Hiss.

The four memoranda were unquestionably in Hiss's handwriting. But had Hiss given them to Chambers or had one of Chambers's other contacts—he claimed to have had several—scrounged them from a wastebasket? Hiss's explanation was that he often made notes to remind himself of details when he had to report to his superior, Francis B. Sayre. The notes had all been folded in half as they might have been if they had been stuck in a pocket for just such a purpose; they were cryptic, virtually meaningless to anyone except the person who had written them; and it seemed to me that they could have served just one purpose for Chambers—not to pass on vital espionage information, but to incriminate Alger Hiss. I had difficulty believing that a man of Hiss's undoubted intelligence would have given Chambers such hand-written memos that could serve just one purpose for Hiss—to hang himself.

The sixty-five typewritten pages presented other difficulties. Chambers's testimony was that, although the spy network had photographic facilities available to it (as the Pumpkin microfilm showed) and although it was much easier, faster and more reliable to film documents than to copy them, Chambers never tried to make such copies. According to Chambers, his superiors in the party felt there might be a gap in their document collection; so Hiss brought documents home at night and Mrs. Hiss typed them on an old typewriter that her father, Thomas Fansler, had given her.

At this point there was introduced into the case one of the most mysterious and famous typewriters ever built—Woodstock N 230,099. Once Chambers testified that Mrs. Hiss had typed the documents, a frantic nationwide search began to find the old Woodstock. Hiss gave authorities copies of letters his wife had typed on the Woodstock before it became so unworkable that they discarded it. If the machine could be found, it could be determined whether its typing matched that of the Baltimore documents. So a seemingly uneven contest began: scores of FBI agents sought the Woodstock in the effort to prove Hiss's guilt; Hiss's attorneys sought it in the expectation it would prove his innocence. Amazingly, the FBI with all its resources failed; Hiss's attorneys, working alone, followed a tortuous trail until the machine almost fell into their laps—a mover named Ira Lockey said he had found the Woodstock N 230,099 sitting in the rain in a junkyard.

Documents examiners did some test-typing and shocked the Hisses with their verdict: the typing done on Woodstock N 230,099 matched that of the Baltimore documents. Hiss then notified the FBI that he had found the machine; and at his two trials (the first ended in a hung jury), it was the defense, not the prosecution, that put Woodstock N 230,099 into evidence. Yet here is one of the great ironies of the trials: this typewriter, produced by the defense, sat in court like an accusing witness and was adopted by the prosecution as its very own.

In the first trial, U.S. Attorney Thomas F. Murphy made the mistake in summation of telling the jury that, if it didn't believe Whittaker Chambers, the government had no case. This was asking too much, and the jury split, four holding out for acquittal. In the second trial, Murphy did not repeat the blunder. Instead, he bore down hard on what he called "the immutable witnesses"— the documents and the typewriter on which he claimed they had been produced. The defense did not know at the time that there was nothing "immutable" about these silent witnesses. But the truth was that the government's case was based on a lie, and it seems impossible that the prosecution did not know it. The lie, endlessly repeated by Richard Nixon in his prideful rehashings of the Hiss case, lay in the official assertion that each typewriter leaves its individual imprint as identifiable and unchallengeable as a fingerprint. This simply is not so.*

But when Hiss went on trial for a second time in November 1949, the defense had literally hanged itself by the typewriter it had produced and by its uncritical acceptance of the government's false assertion that typewriters left their own fingerprints. The result was the conviction of Alger Hiss on two counts of perjury in January 1950 and his subsequent sentence to five years in federal prison.

Though I did not know that typewriter forgery was a proven technique when I wrote my *Nation* article, I found sufficient discrepancies in the documents themselves to make me doubt their authenticity. Chambers had insisted that he had obtained *all* of the documents from Hiss and that *all* had been copied on Hiss's Woodstock. Even one black sheep would cast doubt on Chambers's testimony—and there *was* a black sheep, an important one.

This was exhibit No. 10, a nine-page summary of the ticklish relations between Japan and the United States in 1937. The report had been sent to the Far Eastern Section of the State Department: receiving stamps and routing notations showed that the document had never been sent to Sayre's office, which meant that Hiss could never have had it. Even more destructive to Chambers's asser-

---

*During World War II, the secret services of several countries indulged in forgery by typewriter. The British secret service, with which the FBI worked closely, established a forgery factory in Canada. William Stephenson, head of the British secret service in North America, has since described the activities of this unit in the book, *The Man Called Intrepid.* H. Montgomery Hyde, in another book, *Room 3603*, had previously disclosed the activities of the Canadian forgery factory known as Station M. It was headed by Eric Maschwitz, the lyricist who later wrote that he had been associated with "an industrial chemist and two ruffians who could reproduce faultlessly the imprint of any typewriter on earth."

One of the exploits of Station M played a major role in switching Brazil from the Axis to the Allied camp. L.A.T.I., the Italian airline, was the Axis link to Brazil, and the British wanted to destroy this connection. They managed to purloin a letter written by General Aurelio Liotta, head of the airline. Then they acquired exactly the right kind of paper. "The embossing was copied with microscopic accuracy," Hyde wrote, "and a typewriter was rebuilt to conform to the exact mechanical imperfections of the machine upon which the General's secretary had typed the original letter." A forged letter was concocted indicating that L.A.T.I. was plotting against Brazilian President Getulio Vargas; and when secret agents managed to get this forgery into Brazilian hands, Vargas was so enraged he broke off all connections with the Axis powers.

tions was the undeniable fact that document No. 10 had *not* been typed on Hiss's Woodstock. Even the FBI's own expert testified that the typing must have been done on an Underwood or a Royal; personally, he favored the Royal.

Claude Cross, Hiss's attorney in the second trial, cross-examined Chambers rigorously on this. Chambers began by insisting he had received Exhibit No. 10, like all the others, from Hiss. Confronted with the typing discrepancy, he waffled and said he might have obtained it from someone else; badgered further, he switched back to his original version that the document had come from Hiss. Unable to explain how in that case it had been typed on either an Underwood or a Royal, he was finally reduced to saying, "I believe it was given to me by Mr. Hiss."

There were other conflicts between the story Chambers told and the story the documents told, but it was not until the late Chester T. Lane became Hiss's counsel on appeal that the Hisses had any idea of the kind of ball game the government had been playing. Chester Lane had been in government service in Washington during World War II and at one time had headed Lend-Lease. He knew too much about the activities of the secret services to accept the government's "immutable witnesses." He was not so naive as to believe N 230,099 must have been the machine that typed the Baltimore documents simply because the FBI's expert had testified that ten characters on the keyboard matched the typing. He discounted the accepted wisdom that forgery by typewriter was impossible and launched a two-pronged attack on the typewriter evidence: he backtracked on the history of N 230,099, and he engaged two highly regarded typewriter experts, Martin and Pearl Tytell, to try to manufacture a typewriter that would duplicate the typing of the Baltimore documents.

Lane's researches proved conclusively that the Woodstock typewriter the Hisses had found was *not* the real Hiss machine. It was, Lane concluded, a phony that had been planted on the defense in the most devious of plots designed to achieve exactly what it had: to put the Hiss defense at sea and to rob it of rational explanations to counter Chambers's charges.

The history of the legitimate Hiss Woodstock was this: Priscilla Hiss's father had been in the insurance business in Philadelphia with a partner named Harry L. Martin. In the late 1920s they had purchased a Woodstock typewriter. The earliest surviving example of typing produced by this machine was dated July 8,

1929. But a check of Woodstock records in Woodstock, Illinois, indicated that N 230,099 could not possibly have come off the assembly line before the first week in July—a date that meant it could not have been in use in the insurance office on July 8. Joseph Schmidt, the plant manager, stated in a letter to a document expert hired by Lane: "There is nothing more we can say other than that the machine in question was built approximately in July or August 1929."

There was more. When Lane's experts checked the typefaces on N 230,099, they found that this kind of type had been used by Woodstock in 1926, 1927, 1928 and possibly the very early part of 1929. Schmidt told Lane's investigator that this kind of type had been discarded by Woodstock at the end of 1928 and could not possibly have been used in a machine that would have had to be manufactured, according to its serial number, in the summer of 1929.

This was proof, it seemed to me, that Hiss had been the victim of an intricate plot; but getting the proof in the legal form necessary for submission to the court had been an insurmountable obstacle for Lane. Schmidt would not sign an affidavit; Lane's own investigators would not sign affidavits attesting to what they had learned; everyone connected with the case had either been warned by the FBI to say nothing or had become too frightened to have anything to do with so controversial an issue. Lane in his appeal brief put the facts in these pungent paragraphs:

> It is the handicaps surrounding the investigation that require the Court's attention. We search for records—the FBI has them. We ask questions—the FBI will not let people talk to us. We request access to ordinary documents in corporate files—corporate officials fear the wrath of their stockholders. We ask people to certify information in files they have shown us—they must consult counsel, and we hear no more from them. We pay experts to give us opinions—and they decline to back them up in court because "they cannot subscribe" to anything which might support the conclusions we believe the facts point to.
>
> And, even worse, honorable and patriotic citizens who have wanted to help have been deterred by the appearance— whether or not it is a reality—of official surveillance and

wiretapping, and others who have labored to gather information for us in the interests of justice are afraid to come
forward for fear of personal consequences which might result
to them from public association with the defense of Alger
Hiss.

When I read those paragraphs, when I re-examined in my mind
the suspicious conduct of the government, I began to wonder:
was the FBI becoming an American Gestapo?

Other facts developed by Lane only reinforced my apprehen-
sion. The Tytells did succeed in manufacturing a machine whose
typing, according to Lane's document experts, matched that of
the Baltimore documents so perfectly that the experts said they
would not have known they were dealing with a fabricated typewriter. Even more important was the affidavit submitted by Dr.
Daniel P. Norman, a Boston expert who had been frequently used
to test and analyze paper and other materials for the U.S. Armed
Forces and for federal, state and municipal agencies as well as
large industrial firms. After he made a thorough physical examination of mysterious Woodstock N 230,099, he reported that he
found large, irregular blobs of solder had been left on 29 out of
the 42 keys and that the keys on Woodstocks of similar vintage,
as well as the other 13 keys of N 230,099 were always smoothly
buffed. He subjected samples of the soldering from the apparently
tampered bars to spectographic analysis and determined that these
extra blobs of solder contained far more nickel and traces of other
metallic substances than did the untampered bars of N 230,099
or any of the other normally soldered Woodstocks produced during the 1928–29 period.

Citing Dr. Norman's analysis, Chester Lane declared in an
affidavit he submitted to the court: "I no longer question the
authenticity of Woodstock N 230,099. I now say to the court that
Woodstock N 230,099—the typewriter in evidence at the trials—
is a fake machine."

The array of evidence that Lane had collected under the most
adverse circumstances seemed to me incontrovertible proof that
Alger Hiss had been framed in a complicated plot—and that the
FBI, if it was not a partner in the deed, must at the very least
have been aware of it. My feeling about the culpability of the FBI
was reinforced by the way it and the prosecution attorneys ran

all around the Maypole to avoid meeting facts with facts. Instead of asking to examine the typewriter and make tests to controvert Dr. Norman's assertions about crude soldering, the FBI obtained affidavits from Woodstock workers based, not on any examination of the machine itself, but on *pictures* Lane himself had furnished. These obliging workers, after merely examining the pictures, signed affidavits that said, well, the soldering did not look all that suspicious to them; the soldering done at the plant was sometimes crude and uneven, etc., etc. The FBI supposedly had the most scientific detective tools in the nation. What accounted for this failure to use them?

As for the Tytell machine, the new U.S. Attorney, Myles Lane, ridiculed it as a Rube Goldberg experiment. He denied the possibility of forgery by typewriter and he argued that in any event even if the Tytell machine showed what *might* be done, it had no relevance because there was no proof such a thing *had* been done.

The judicial verdict was almost a foregone conclusion. Federal Judge Samuel H. Kaufman had presided at the first trial; when the jury failed to convict, Richard Nixon screamed for Judge Kaufman's impeachment. The second trial was conducted by Judge Henry W. Goddard, a stalwart Republican whose prejudice was evident throughout the trial. He had choice seats directly facing the jury reserved for Alice Roosevelt Longworth and her rigidly Republican handmaidens; and every morning, when he took the bench, he gave a little bow and welcomed them with a "Good morning, ladies." Throughout the trial, these Mesdames La Farges had stared at the jury as if challenging the jurors to do their duty.

Thus, when Judge Goddard got Chester Lane's appeal, he promptly threw it out of court. He accepted the government's most specious arguments and ruled that the defense could not raise the issue of forgery by typewriter at this late date. If it had intended to take that line, it had an obligation to do it at the time of trial; it could not retry the whole case on the basis of a contention that, if it had used due diligence, it should have raised during the trial. It was a ruling that, while judicially proper, ignored all the basic realities of the case, all the deceptions that had made it impossible for the defense to know and raise the issue at the time of trial.

My research into the Hiss case brought me to a crucial decision, and I was deeply disturbed. I had a wife and two children to support (my son was in college); I had no family money. Except for some additional but inadequate free-lance income, our livelihood depended on my salary from the *World-Telegram and Sun*, and I knew that the Hiss case was the most treasured trophy in Roy Howard's anti-Communist gun room. I knew, too, that FBI Director J. Edgar Hoover was to Howard a holy, irreproachable icon; and now I was convinced that the FBI had been deeply involved in the dirty tricks and repression of witnesses that had resulted in the framing of Alger Hiss. Did I dare even hint at such a thing?

Many nights I lay awake running through the whole chain of evidence. Couldn't there be some other explanation? But each time I reviewed the case, I found myself arriving at the same conclusion.

That much settled, I had yet another worry. Lane's appeal brief showed how FBI pressure had silenced and terrorized potential witnesses. I felt certain that if I wrote the article the way it was shaping up in my mind the FBI would subject me to the closest scrutiny. And so I felt forced to take a hard look at my own life. Fortunately, I had never been a joiner, I had never taken dirty money, I had never run around or been unfaithful to my wife. There was nothing in my past that even the most devilish of secret agents could use against me. When I reached this point in my self-examination, I began to get angry. Why should I, an American citizen in a free country, have to hesitate before doing what my conscience told me to do? I knew that I could never respect myself if I turned my back on the story, so I said to myself, "The devil with it"—and wrote the long, analytical article on the Alger Hiss case for *The Nation*.

16

Big Brother
Was Watching

HARASSMENTS BEGAN ALMOST IMMEDIATELY AFTER MY *Nation* article appeared and have continued intermittently ever since. Some were petty. Others involved brazen tampering with my mail, and others still—more serious, more devious—were attempts to discredit me and kill off sales of my books.

The first sign that some official omniscient eye had me in its sights came only days after the article was published. I had had a subscription to *The Nation* ever since I started writing for it in 1954; copies of the magazine had always been delivered to my home on time. But after I wrote the Hiss article, four of the next six issues failed to arrive.

Carey McWilliams and I both protested to the Post Office Department. All we got was a typically bureaucratic self-justification. The subscription, said the Post Office, had been improperly addressed. It had been mailed to my home in Interlaken, New Jersey, and it should have been sent to Interlaken in care of the Asbury Park Post Office. This official whitewash did not take into account the fact that I had lived at the same address since 1938; that my wife and I had subscribed to innumerable magazines, all addressed just to Interlaken as *The Nation*'s copies had been— and that, in all those years, I had never had any trouble with the mail until I wrote about Alger Hiss.

This minor scuffle with the Post Office was just the first sign of trouble. In the *World-Telegram and Sun* office, my managing editor asked me for a copy of the magazine, which I gave him. Some three weeks passed before, one morning as I came to work, I found the rolled-up copy of *The Nation* in my mailbox with the cryptic comment "Scandalum Magnificum" written across the top.

The managing editor never said anything more about it to me, but Fred Woltman, long afterward, told me that it had been touch-and-go whether I would be fired. It was finally decided, he said, that there would be too much trouble with the New York Newspaper Guild if I were dismissed for daring to write about Alger Hiss—so I was allowed to keep my job for the time being.

When I compounded my offense by writing *The Unfinished Story of Alger Hiss*, published by William Morrow & Co., I encountered some devious and sophisticated plotting designed to kill the book. I was at my rewrite desk on March 25, 1958, when John Willey, my editor at Morrow, phoned.

"Fred," he said, "we have been warned by a very old and very trusted friend of the firm that we have a bad one in your book, and we will look foolish if we publish it."

A few hours later, an extremely worried editor and an equally concerned writer sat down to lunch. I asked John Willey to spell out the details of the charges that had been leveled against my forthcoming book.

"I can't tell you who this comes from," he began. "You will just have to take my word for it that it comes from a very old and very trusted friend of the firm, a man whose integrity is beyond question and whom we trust completely. He knows a private investigator who says he was hired by a law firm, not the present Hiss law firm, to help investigate the case. In the course of his work, he obtained photostats of the typing produced by the Tytell machine, and the typing does not match that of the documents at all. Any expert could detect the fraud in a minute, and we will look extremely foolish if we publish your book."

"Look, John," I said. "Two things strike me about this right off the bat. In the first place, the Hiss defense quickly discovered that it could not trust private investigators. Everyone they tried appeared to be hooked directly into the FBI; and whenever they sought a particular piece of information, they found that the FBI, obviously tipped off, had gotten there just one step ahead of them. For instance, they employed Ray Schindler at one point in the investigation; his bills were so huge that he almost bankrupted the law firm—and he refused to sign an affidavit about what he had done for them."

Willey started at the mention of Schindler's name.

"The second point, John," I went on, "is that no expert worthy of the name will put his reputation on the line on the basis of photostats. Document experts insist on working with originals because there is too much loss of detail in a photostat. And the Hiss defense had given up on private detectives before the Tytell machine was made. Information about this was tightly held in their own office, and no private detective could possibly have had photostats of the typing."

One incident described in my book constituted outright thievery of some of Tytell's test-typing. He had picked up some copies of typing done on his machine from a secretary in Lane's office, had stuck the pages in the jacket of his coat and hung the coat up on a coat-tree outside his office door. Shortly afterward, he had heard steps coming up the stairs to his second-floor office, but when no one appeared, he had gone out and found that his jacket and the typed pages had been stolen. All of this had happened during the testing period before Tytell had finished work on his machine.

Before John Willey and I parted, I told him that I would check with Mrs. Helen Buttenwieser, Chester Lane's law partner, and write him a confirming letter.

On the way back to my office, I puzzled over John's reaction to my reference to Raymond Schindler. Then I remembered: Schindler and Erle Stanley Gardner, the creator of Perry Mason and for years one of Morrow's most successful authors, had collaborated on a project called "The Court of Last Resort," investigating cases in which justice might have gone awry and presenting their findings as a regular feature of *Argosy* magazine.

The following morning, after Mrs. Buttenwieser had confirmed everything I had told John and had extended an invitation to Morrow to examine all the records and correspondence if it wished, I wrote John Willey a letter (I still have a copy) that began: "If I am right, the report you discussed with me yesterday was written by Raymond Schindler and came to you through Schindler's 'Court of Last Resort' buddy, Erle Stanley Gardner."

John Willey telephoned me after reading the letter. "Fred,"

he said, "that was an interesting letter you wrote. A *very* interesting letter."

He chuckled (a confirmation that my deduction had been correct) and I chuckled. Morrow went ahead and published the book. It attracted a lot of favorable attention (three articles in one issue of *The Saturday Review*, for instance), but Morrow did virtually nothing to promote it. I never knew whether the devious Gardner-Schindler ploy had left a damaging residue of doubt or whether it was simply a publishing decision not to throw good money after bad; but Barthold Fles, my agent, and I could not understand why a firm that had wanted the book so badly because of its publisher's own convictions dropped it so quickly despite the wide notice it received. One thing seemed certain to me: the Gardner-Schindler plot to kill off the book before it could be put into hard covers could hardly have been the product of immaculate conception. Schindler was a double agent, hooked into the FBI network; and, given this tie, it seemed obvious that the attempted roadblock had been an official ploy. It followed that, if the government's case against Hiss had been valid, it would not have had to resort to such an extreme to avoid criticism; and the whole episode convinced me more than Hiss himself had done that he had been innocent—that he had been framed.

And so I kept dogging the Hiss case through the years. I compounded all my other offenses by writing a scathing analysis of J. Edgar Hoover and his FBI for *The Nation*, something I probably would never have done had I not been disgusted by the FBI's nonperformance where big-time crime was concerned and by what I had learned about its partisan role in the Remington and Hiss cases. Such an article, topping all others, made me a marked man.

Counterattack, one of the right-wing smear sheets of the time, devoted an entire issue to excoriating me and *The Nation*. It tried to tie a pro-Communist tag to Carey McWilliams and the magazine; as for me, it conceded that I was known as "a nonpolitical writer" but pictured me as a cheap crime reporter who had suddenly become an expert on national issues. Right-wing yahoos salivated over such attacks, which were widely circulated and were designed to intimidate anyone who dared to speak out.

Harassments by official sources continued on several fronts. First-class mail from my agent, Bart Fles, began arriving unsealed. Sometimes it was just crudely ripped open and patched with tape as if the gremlin who was reading my mail wanted me to know that I was being watched.

The FBI began to check up on me. A business executive with whom I regularly commuted to New York told me how he had been called by a former FBI agent who was the security chief for the textile firm for which he had formerly worked. After some trivial preliminaries, the ex-FBI sleuth wanted to know what my friend could tell him about Fred Cook, specifically who had put me up to writing the article criticizing the FBI in *The Nation*.

Years afterward, my daughter-in-law encountered a former neighbor of mine who told her what trouble I had caused him. At the time he was a young lawyer serving as an Assistant U.S. Attorney in Newark. The FBI called him in and demanded that he tell everything he knew about me. Since he had nothing detrimental to say, the agents thought he was lying. "Why are you protecting him?" they demanded. "We *know* he's a Communist. What are you standing up for him for?" According to the former Assistant U.S. Attorney, another government lawyer living in my neighborhood had been put through the same FBI wringer. Fortunately, neither of my neighbors would make up any tale to satisfy the FBI interrogators.

By all signs, nothing convinced the FBI. Through the years, my mail continued to arrive in tampered condition. In 1972, when I wrote *The Nightmare Decade*, a hard look at the era of Joe McCarthy, a batch of proofs arrived from my publisher with the heavy manila envelope ripped and the proofs almost falling out. I could only conclude that some official snoop wanted to see what I was writing. And even later, in 1979, when the Hiss defense sent me a notice about an upcoming hearing, the envelope containing this routine information had been torn open, then clumsily sealed with tape. Such incidents occurring over a span of years convinced me that "1984" was a misnomer; the spirit was alive and active in this great democracy well in advance of Orwell's date.

During these years, Alger Hiss kept battling for vindication. Once released from prison, he began a campaign to clear his name that continues to this day. His marriage to Priscilla broke up as a result—the worst thing, he has said, that happened to him during the whole ordeal. Hiss describes Priscilla as "a very private person," psychologically unnerved by being put in such a harsh spotlight. After he came out of prison, he says, she wanted them to change their names, go off to some small remote college and devote their lives to teaching. Hiss refused.

There can be no question that Hiss was utterly devoted to Priscilla and prized their marriage; but, to me when I studied the case, Priscilla Hiss seemed a strange and enigmatic figure. And it seemed to me from the transcripts of the Congressional hearings and trials that much of Hiss's entanglement in trying to belittle his early association with Chambers, the loan of the apartment, the gift of the car, stemmed in some obscure way from a desire to protect Priscilla. From what I could not tell, but I picked up a strange thread that ran through all the testimony of Chambers and his wife.

In his original testimony Chambers was more accurate in dealing with Mrs. Hiss than with her husband. He knew the details of her former marriage, the name of her father, her family home, the nature of her ex-husband's job. But when he turned to the Hiss side of the family, he thought Hiss's sister was living in Baltimore with her mother (actually she had been teaching at a university in Texas for twenty years), and he couldn't recall the name of Donald Hiss's wife. During the trials, the Chamberses' testimony, for whatever it is worth, focused more on Mrs. Hiss than on Hiss. According to them, Mrs. Hiss made a long visit to them at a summer cabin they occupied; she stayed in Baltimore to take care of their baby while Mrs. Chambers went to New York; she visited the Chamberses on several occasions, while the best they could allege was that Hiss came only once.

In his 1977 book* about his father, Tony Hiss, the son of Alger and Priscilla, wrote that Judge Kaufman, who presided over the first trial, "thought that Chambers told more than the truth and Al less than the truth. But he said he thought Al was an honest man. . . . I have found it very interesting to discover, in talking to people associated with the case, how many people on all sides of the case thought that the real truth was that Al was innocent but was covering up for something that Prossy had done. In addition to Judge Kaufman, several of Al's own lawyers believed in their heart of hearts that this was what had really happened and one of the top FBI men investigating the case thought exactly the same thing."

---

* *Laughing Last: Alger Hiss* by Tony Hiss. Boston: Houghton Mifflin, 1977.

I may be partly responsible for the feeling among some of Hiss's attorneys. I had never met Hiss and had had only one brief contact with Chester Lane's office to pick up a transcript before I wrote *The Nation* article. I was so wary at the time that I wanted to avoid all contact and base my conclusions solely on what the record showed. After the article and the book, however, I met from time to time with Hiss, Chester Lane, Helen Buttenwieser and a secretary at the law firm. One day, sometime in 1958, Helen Buttenwieser telephoned me and asked if I could have lunch with them. I got to the old Barclay Restaurant on Barclay Street sometime before they did. I had a Manhattan, and when they arrived, I had another. Blame what took place later on two Manhattans.

The attorneys, it seemed, were having trouble with Hiss. He had written his book even before I became interested in the case; and, though it read like a dry lawyer's treatise that I thought did him little good, it had sparked some media interest. "Meet the Press" wanted him, Mike Wallace wanted to interview him, so did Martin Agronsky. But Hiss had rejected all such overtures. The lawyers thought Hiss should not shun such attention.

"Look, Goddamn it," I said—the voice of two Manhattans— "I stuck my neck out for you, and I think you owe me something. I risked my job to write what I did, and I didn't do it because I love you, but because I'm convinced you got a dirty deal. And so I say you owe it to me and to yourself to show yourself. If you go off and hide in a corner and won't show yourself on television with anybody, everybody's going to think you're guilty as hell."

"But these people will want to bring their cameras into my home," Hiss protested. "They'll invade my private life."

"So what?" I said. "What have you got to lose? If you don't want to go on 'Meet the Press,' all right; I wouldn't blame you. That might be a gang-up job. But there's no reason you shouldn't talk to Mike Wallace or Agronsky in a straight interview."

"But they'll insist on bringing their camera crews into my home," Hiss persisted. "They'll want to take pictures of my home and family."

"So what?" I said again. "Let them. What harm can that do?"

Hiss continued to protest, and the discussion continued along the same lines, getting nowhere. As we parted on the sidewalk outside the restaurant, Hiss promised to consider what I had said, but Chester Lane whispered to me in an aside, "He'll never do it."

The following day, Helen Buttenwieser telephoned me, and we had lunch together. "I've always insisted," she said, "that there was nothing in this case, absolutely nothing, that it was all made up out of whole cloth. But after that discussion yesterday"—she shook her head—"I have to agree with you. What came out of it was that there must be some private, personal thing. Every time you pressed him, it came back to that."

I apologized for my rudeness of the previous day, putting the blame on the Manhattans; but Mrs. Buttenwieser said she was glad that I had spoken as roughly as I had. Alger, she said, was always surrounded by a coterie of close friends; and one reason they had wanted the luncheon with me was to see how he would react in a different atmosphere.

In more recent years, since his irrevocable break with Priscilla, Alger Hiss has indeed shown himself as I had recommended. He speaks regularly on college campuses, making fifteen or more speeches a year, with the proceeds going to finance his continuing appeals.

One piece of legislation passed by Congress has aided him greatly. In the early 1970s, two investigations of the nation's intelligence agencies, the FBI and CIA, shocked the nation with exposures of the manner in which both had broken the laws of the land for years. The CIA, in futile plotting to overthrow the regime of Fidel Castro in Cuba, had actually gone into partnership with the Mafia; the FBI had pulled off innumerable "black bag jobs," burglarizing homes and offices in search of possible evidence; and the CIA and FBI between them had established a watch on international mail, especially at Kennedy Airport, and had not hesitated to open, read and even purloin any communications they wanted.* The Freedom of Information Act granted aggrieved persons and institutions the right to force the release of information about them in the secret files. Taking advantage of this, Hiss and his latest appeals attorney, Victor Rabinowitz, engaged in a years-long battle to force the FBI and

---

* I had a personal experience that, it seems in retrospect, must have been the result of this activity. In 1966 I wrote a book, *The Secret Rulers,* an exposé of the Mafia, and my Brazilian publishers, who had issued two of my earlier books, wanted reprint rights. They sent a contract to my agent, Barthold Fles. I signed the contract and mailed it. A month or so later, Fles received a complaint from the Brazilian publishers that they hadn't received the contract. So I signed and mailed another. More weeks passed, and Fles received another complaint: the second contract, like the first, had failed to arrive. The military dictatorship was then coming into power in Brazil, and we assumed that this

CIA to turn over documents to which Congress has said they are entitled.

The disclosures show that virtually every principle of a free society dedicated to justice was violated by agencies of the government in Hiss's case. Even a brief capsule of the major findings is sufficient to show the seriousness of the issue. Hiss's home telephone in Washington, D.C., had been tapped for nearly two years; the intercepts covered some 2500 pages, including conversations with friends about everything from intimate family details to the Hisses' dinner table menus. Hiss had been subjected at times to round-the-clock surveillance; a mail cover had been put on his correspondence, and in some cases messages addressed to him had been intercepted and never reached their destination. In 1950, one letter addressed to Claude Cross, Hiss's second trial counsel—a letter dealing with the highly important issue of just when Chambers had left the Communist Party—was forwarded to U.S. Attorney Murphy by someone in the Post Office with instructions that neither Murphy nor the FBI was to inform the Justice Department. Even telegrams sent to Hiss were intercepted, and the residence of an unidentified person (much is blacked out in FOIA releases) had been burglarized and documents photographed. In the end, what was produced by this monumental effort that invaded every right of privacy guaranteed by the Constitution? Virtually nothing. The final trial and conviction of Hiss had to depend on the uncertain word of Whittaker Chambers and "the immutable witness."

The disclosures forced out of the FBI files prove two points destructive to the prosecution's case against Alger Hiss: (1) The Woodstock machine that Hiss found and produced in good faith was a fraudulent product, one known to be so by the FBI before the trials, yet one that the FBI accepted as legitimate; (2) Whittaker Chambers, in private sessions with FBI agents before the trials, waffled on such vital points as whether Alger Hiss had been a Communist and whether Chambers had really gotten his documents from Hiss.

---

authoritarian regime might have intercepted the contract. However, on a hunch, I mailed a third contract in a plain envelope without my name and return address on it. And this third contract sailed through without any trouble, and my book finally was published in Brazil. The sequence convinced me that I had done the military dictatorship in Brazil an injustice by suspecting *them*.

On the Woodstock: One revealing FBI report dated December 23, 1948, pointed out that no accurate record of serial numbers was kept by Woodstock, but that a "trade-in manual for the use of dealers" listed the approximate serial numbers for each year. According to this manual, Woodstocks coming off the line at the beginning of 1929 started with the serial numbers 204,000; in 1930, the starting number was 240,000. In other words, N 230,099 would have been manufactured in the latter part of 1929, as Schmidt had written Lane's investigator—and so could not possibly have been the machine in operation in the Fansler-Martin insurance office in July 1929. The FBI had also found the salesman who had sold the Woodstock to the insurance firm—Thomas Grady, a Woodstock salesman who had resigned on December 2, 1927. The FBI had concluded: "it would appear, therefore, that the serial number on the typewriter sold to Fansler-Martin would be less than 177,000."

After Hiss produced N 230,099, FBI agents across the nation re-examined their original research and arrived at the same conclusion. On May 20, 1949, the Chicago office sent to Director Hoover a list of serial numbers furnished by Schmidt, "indicating the serial numbers being used at times technical changes were made in Woodstock typewriters." Schmidt, the Chicago FBI said, vouched for the accuracy of the numbers. They showed that a highly significant changeover had been made in March 1929 when machines labeled "New Style Action" were first produced, beginning with serial number 220,000. This, it would seem, was the reason that Schmidt could have written so positively to Lane's investigator that N 230,099 could not have been manufactured before August or September 1929.

Even more devastating to the government's case was the FBI re-interview of Grady, the Milwaukee salesman who had sold the Woodstock to the Fansler office. He insisted "that he could not have sold this typewriter [N 230,099] as he sold no typewriters subsequent to leaving the employ of Woodstock in December 1927."

With "the immutable witnesses" impugned, there remained only Chambers, whom President Ronald Reagan has since praised as representing "the conscience of America." Chambers's pretrial questioning by the FBI resulted in such waffling and wavering that it should have scratched at someone's conscience. Telexes between the FBI in New York and FBI headquarters in Washington tell the story.

In New York Chambers was questioned again about the membership of the Communist cell in Washington to which, he had alleged, Hiss had belonged in the 1930s. In this new pre-trial questioning, Chambers mentioned Hiss's brother, Donald, whom he had previously denounced without presenting any proof, but had omitted the name of Alger. The results of Chambers's January 13 questioning were telexed to Washington where it had apparently shaken up headquarters, for the New York telex in reply to a question about its accuracy read: "He [Laughlin] stated that the Director had questioned whether the name of Donald Hiss should have been included in the group. . . . I advised him, after checking with S[pecial] A[gent] Thomas Spencer, who was at the moment interviewing Chambers, that the teletype as sent was correct, that Donald Hiss was, according to Chambers, in the group. I also advised that he [Chambers] had not put Alger Hiss in the group because *he was not sure Alger Hiss was in the group. Consequently, no statement was made regarding Alger Hiss.* [Italics added]"

Chambers had charged for years, even before he first testified in public before HUAC, that Alger Hiss had been a Communist who belonged to this Washington cell headed by Harold Ware. He had testified about the collection of Communist Party dues from Hiss before the grand jury that had indicted him. Yet suddenly, almost on the eve of the first trial, he was certain that Donald Hiss belonged to the group, but *he was not sure about Alger Hiss.*

Worse was to follow. The New York FBI bureau on February 2, 1949, drafted a long, pre-trial scenario, outlining the evidence needed to convict Hiss and discussing the manner in which it should be handled. A section labeled "Documentary Evidence" dealt with the core of the case—the famous documents that Chambers had testified he had obtained from Hiss. Discussing this, the New York bureau included a parenthetical note that should have jarred J. Edgar Hoover had he been a man of probity. "It is not clear at this time if Chambers can testify that he received these particular 69 documents from Hiss, but upon establishing the facts of this situation, decision can thereafter be reached as to who is in a position to introduce these documents."

Once again, Chambers was attempting to retreat from testimony he had given under oath. He was the only one to testify that the documents he had produced had all come from Hiss, yet virtually on the eve of trial, he was unwilling to reiterate such testimony. In time, of course, under FBI and prosecution pressure, Chambers flopped back to his original accusatory stance and testified that Hiss had been a Communist and that he had given him the documents. But the point that nags at the mind and the conscience is simply this: How could any honest and conscientious prosecution have gone to trial relying on a chief witness who gave such clear indications that he was lying?

The answer is that this was not a conscientious prosecution but one that was out to hang its designated victim at whatever cost. The prosecution headed by Thomas Murphy, who was to be elevated to the federal bench on the wings of his great achievement in convicting Hiss, stopped at nothing. The purloined letter forwarded to Murphy by some snoop in the Post Office is just one example. Throughout the case, the prosecution did not hesitate to invade the defense in defiance of its rights by using double agents.

Information dragged out of FBI files under FOIA shows that, as Hiss's attorneys had come to suspect, private detectives employed by them had betrayed them and acted as informants for the FBI. The first double agent, early in the case, was Horace W. Schmahl, an investigator for the famous private eye John G. (Steve) Broady, who had assigned him to the Hiss case. The second was a detective famous in his own right, Raymond Schindler, Erle Stanley Gardner's partner and my hidden Nemesis. An FBI report to Washington headquarters on April 5, 1951, described how Schindler had come to the New York bureau to inform the FBI about the work he was doing for Chester Lane. The report said in part: "Schindler advised that he had come to this office voluntarily because he wanted us to know the facts of this matter and his connection therewith and that he also wanted to furnish any additional information that might come to him."

Horace Schmahl's double-agent activities were of longer duration. Engaged by Hiss's original attorneys even before Hiss was indicted, he immediately volunteered to spy for the FBI; and he continued, as FBI telexes to Washington show, to furnish "information of a confidential basis." On November 18, 1950, New York

advised Washington that Schmahl had kept the FBI advised about
Hiss's appeal strategy and it added: "As previously stated, Schmahl
will keep our New York office advised of any particular developments."

Besides the use of double agents, the prosecution practiced
what can only be called outright deceit on the defense and the
court. There is a well-established principle of law that the prosecution, if it has in its files any information that might be exculpatory, has an obligation to furnish it to the defense. In the second
trial, Claude Cross had asked the prosecution for any statements
made to the FBI or government lawyers by Chambers. Murphy
furnished just two relatively brief statements that Chambers had
signed. He assured the court that was all there was.

It simply was not true. FBI files now reveal that in January,
February and March 1949, in preparation for the first trial, Chambers himself wrote out a 184-page document giving an account of
his life. In this, he admitted he had been a homosexual, something
the defense had suspected but had been unable to prove. Public
attitude toward homosexuality in 1949–50 was eons removed from
the more tolerant view of the 1980s; disclosure of Chambers's
homosexuality might well have affected the outcome of the trial.
How did the prosecutors avoid producing this document? They
told Chambers not to sign it; and so the 184-page statement written by Chambers himself became a non-statement.

All of this information has become public knowledge because
Alger Hiss has continued to fight. In 1978, he and his attorney
filed a *coram nobis* action in Federal Court in New York, seeking
the reversal of his 1950 conviction. *Coram nobis*, a rarely resorted
to legal action and one that by its very nature is difficult to sustain,
is an appeal to the courts for the rectification of gross judicial
error so that justice may be served. In essence, it requires the
judiciary to castigate itself for its past performance. In 1980, Rabinowitz filed a supplementary brief, based on additionally discovered evidence.

Personally, I was convinced that the federal judiciary lacked
the conscience and the principle to right any wrong done to Alger
Hiss. To do so, judges would have to reflect, by implication at
least, on the conduct of one of their own brethren on the bench,
Thomas Murphy. When the Asbury Park *Press* asked me in November 1980 for my opinion about the outcome of the *coram
nobis* action, I said, "Maybe I'm a cynic, but when the courts

have to admit these kinds of shenanigans, particularly involving one of their own, I don't think they will reopen the case. I doubt the courts will want to admit to previous error."

That, unfortunately, was one of my better predictions. On July 19, 1982, Federal Judge Richard Owen rejected Hiss's appeal in an 82-page decision in which he declared "the trial was a fair one by any standard." Judge Owen dismissed all of Hiss's arguments. The double agents, he said, "could not have had the slightest impact on the outcome" of the trial; the withheld statements by Chambers were insignificant or irrelevant. The typewriter, he admitted, posed some "puzzling" questions, but it did not matter because Hiss had conceded the documents were typed on it and "consequently, any evidence as to its origins is irrelevant."

Early in summer 1983, the U.S. courts confirmed my belief that nothing that could be adduced in the Hiss case would be considered "relevant." The three-judge U.S. Court of Appeals upheld Judge Owen's ruling in a brusque, 25-word statement; and on October 11, 1983, the U.S. Supreme Court refused to review the case. Thus, by ignoring the evidence, it upheld the ruling of the lower courts and in all probability brought to an end Alger Hiss's thirty-year battle for vindication.

In a statement on October 20, Hiss reacted to this final setback: "I am bitterly disappointed and angry. Neither the disappointment nor the anger is for purely personal reasons—not by any means. . . . When serious charges of a miscarriage of justice are treated lightly or with prejudice, the result is to encourage public cynicism and to discourage reliance on our courts."

His eight-and-a-half-year legal battle that had forced an obdurate FBI to release documents under the Freedom of Information Act had uncovered "sufficient documentary evidence of gross misconduct," he said. He spelled these out:

"The transgressions we documented—including withholding of important exculpatory evidence, misleading judge and jury as to the identity and authenticity of the typewriter that was a crucial exhibit, flat misrepresentation of fact—were magnified by the identities of the perpetrators—J. Edgar Hoover and the prosecutor, Thomas Murphy, now a judge. Each had full responsibility for his acts; each was sworn to further the administration of justice."

Hiss recognized that his case had become the litmus test of

politics, having been "used by the right wing . . . to discredit our liberal political tradition" and "to denigrate the values of the New Deal and of the United Nations, in both of which I took a part." He was indisputably correct. Richard Nixon's ascendancy to the presidency resulted from the Hiss case; the whole Republican and arch-conservative battle cry of "twenty years of treason" depended upon it. In the context of the times, then and now, Alger Hiss simply *had* to be found guilty—and still *has* to remain so. The highest reputations, the fate of a party and a conservative political movement were at stake; and, in such circumstances, as the record has repeatedly shown, the courts, instead of serving justice, become the cats-paws of the passions of their times.

17

Sacco and Vanzetti

I N THE CHARLESTOWN PRISON IN BOSTON MINUTES AFTER midnight on the morning of August 23, 1927, Nicola Sacco and Bartolomeo Vanzetti—the "good shoemaker" and the "poor fish peddler"—were sent to their deaths in the electric chair for a holdup-murder that the accumulated evidence of more than half a century says they did not commit.

The state can engage in no more horrible crime in my opinion than the execution of innocent citizens, and in the Sacco-Vanzetti case the horror is compounded by the knowledge that many of the officials involved were convinced that both men were innocent.

No other case—not the Remington case, not the Hiss case in more modern times—so clearly illustrates the American dichotomy. Sacco-Vanzetti was not just the *cause célèbre* of the 1920s; it has retained for nearly sixty years the power sharply to divide in bitter controversy those moved by the tragedy of colossal injustice and those unable to conceive that constituted authority could ever have been so wrong, so blind, so utterly perverted.*

---

* In this age of wide public clamor for reinstatement of the death penalty, few Americans, I think, have any conception of the fallibility of our judicial system. The record is replete with cases in which faulty eyewitness identification or the distortion of evidence by unscrupulous prosecutors resulted in the conviction of innocent persons. The New York

In the early 1960s, more than thirty years after the executions of Sacco and Vanzetti, the doubts that would not die led to a number of reassessments of their guilt from predominantly conservative viewpoints. Robert H. Montgomery, a Boston corporation lawyer, wrote *Sacco-Vanzetti: The Murder and the Myth* in which he concluded that, of all great lies, "the Sacco-Vanzetti Myth is the greatest lie of all." William F. Buckley, Jr., the publisher of the *National Review*, taking the Montgomery book for his Bible, promptly proclaimed in an article in the *American Legion Magazine* that the trial had been fair and Sacco and Vanzetti had indeed been guilty. In a slight modification of this theme, James Grossman reasoned in a January 1962 article in *Commentary* that Sacco had been guilty, Vanzetti innocent. This was followed in the summer of 1962 by a massive reappraisal of the crime and trial by the historian Francis Russell in his book *Tragedy in Dedham: the Story of the Sacco-Vanzetti Case*. And this was where I become involved.

I was only sixteen when Sacco and Vanzetti were executed, and, like most others of that age, I was more concerned with the problems of adolescence than with the intellectual and emotional ferment of the times. My honest, hardworking, conservative parents distrusted agitators; placid by nature, they instinctively shunned anything that smacked of violence or rabble-rousing. Thus, as far as I can recall, the Sacco-Vanzetti case was never discussed in our home, or if it was, it was in such an insignificant way that it made no impression on me.

During my years as a newspaperman, I had read brief and inconclusive accounts of the famous case, but none had made any impact on me. Then Carey McWilliams asked me to review Francis Russell's book. It was, I thought, a routine assignment, just a book review; but Russell's ambivalent account—he, too, concluded that Sacco had been guilty but Vanzetti innocent despite

---

Times, in a single issue on August 5, 1983, cited four such cases. Isidore Zimmerman, whose death sentence had been commuted at the last instant to life imprisonment, had had his 1937 murder conviction overturned in 1962 on the grounds of prosecutorial misconduct. He was later permitted to sue the state, and the New York Court of Claims in June had awarded $1 million in damages. On August 4, Governor Cuomo vetoed bills passed by the legislature that would have permitted three other wrongfully convicted persons to bring similar suits. One case involved a man who had served eleven years in prison for manslaughter before his conviction was overturned in 1958 when a judge ruled that the prosecutor had knowingly used false evidence and withheld other evidence.

the mass of evidence he cited about the unfairness of the trial—
pricked my curiosity and led eventually to a discovery of my own.
The simple "book review" became an 8000-word article that *The
Nation* headlined on its cover: NEW LIGHT ON SACCO-VANZETTI.
THE MISSING FINGERPRINTS.

The Sacco-Vanzetti case can be understood only in relation to
its times. The mood of the early 1920s was much like that of the
1950s, lacking only a supreme demagogue like Joe McCarthy.
During World War I, the Bolsheviks had overthrown the cen-
turies-long rule of the czars, and conservatives everywhere were
hag-ridden by visions of a world-threatening Red menace. Spo-
radic outbreaks of violence, bomb plantings, and the mailing of
bombs to prominent officials lent substance to these fears and
helped to create a nationwide wave of hysteria. Though the bomb
incidents were apparently the work of only a few fanatic individuals (the perpetrators were never identified), Attorney General
A. Mitchell Palmer launched a nationwide dragnet, the so-called
Palmer Red raids directed by J. Edgar Hoover. Some 10,000
foreigners were swept up in cities across the nation and herded
by the hundreds into bullpens so crowded that each individual
was allowed only about half a foot of space. Caught in the roundup
were high-school girls and some immigrants who were attending
English classes. In the indiscriminate mood of the time, all were
considered dangerous foreign anarchists. An uncritical press fed
the frenzy: Bolsheviki were everywhere; one day they were about
to seize control of Chester, Pennsylvania; the next day the item
disappeared from the press never to be mentioned again.

Such was the atmosphere when, shortly after 3 P.M., April 15,
1920, the payroll holdup-murder that was to doom Sacco and
Vanzetti took place in South Braintree, on the outskirts of Boston.
Frederick Parmenter, the paymaster for the Slater & Morrill shoe
factory, and his detective guard, Alessandro Berardelli, were walking
to the factory carrying two steel cashboxes containing a $15,776.51
payroll. They passed a fence where two squat, dark-complexioned
men were loitering. As they went past, the pair sprang out behind
them, pulled revolvers and began firing. Berardelli fell first; Parmenter staggered out into the street and collapsed. A touring car,
its rear curtain down, came up the street, and a third man jumped
out and administered the coup de grâce to the still-struggling
Berardelli. The two original gunmen grabbed the fallen cashboxes,

and all clambered into the touring car, which sped away with one gunman in the front seat beside the driver spraying bullets as they went.

There were many eyewitnesses and almost as many versions of the bandits' appearance and their car. Authorities lacked hard clues, but soon an accident of fate led one frustrated policeman to form the hunch that was to become the foundation of the Sacco-Vanzetti case.

The originator of the tragedy in Dedham was the police chief of Bridgewater, Michael E. Stewart. Chief Stewart had no use for foreigners and he had arrested six the previous year when he aided immigration authorities in the Red witch-hunt. When the South Braintree murders occurred, Chief Stewart had been struggling for months—and getting nowhere—in an attempt to solve a similar, but abortive, payroll-holdup incident in his own town.

On December 24, 1919, four gunmen had tried to ambush a payroll delivery truck in Bridgewater. Three highwaymen had jumped from a black touring car and started spraying bullets at the delivery truck. The quick-thinking driver had thwarted the thugs by jerking his truck across streetcar tracks just as a trolley was approaching. The trolley had intervened between truck and bandits, and the gunmen had to scramble back into their car and make good their escape. They had left behind them two tenuous clues: their shotgun-firing leader was a man with a black mustache, and the license plates on the touring car, noted by one witness, had been stolen from Hassam's Garage in Needham.

Pinkerton detectives working on the Bridgewater case had come up with a man named V. A. Barr (though the Pinkertons didn't know it, his real name was Carmine A. Barasso), who claimed that he had invented a marvelous crime machine. One look into this unlikely gadget, according to Barr, was enough to let one identify the persons who had committed a crime. Barr said he had tested his crime machine with a neighborhood woman (actually, she told fortunes from tea leaves) and, though his device hadn't worked with total clarity, the woman had "seen" the Italian anarchists who had been involved in the Bridgewater case living in a shack near the Fore River Shipyard in Quincy.

On such a slender thread can rest human fate. Among the six men whom Chief Stewart had arrested in the Red witch-hunt was an Italian named Ferruccio Coacci, who had lived in Quincy at the time; he had also been employed in the Slater & Morrill plant in South Braintree but had quit his job after he was released on bail to await deportation. Coacci had been scheduled to report to immigration officers in East Boston on April 15, 1920—the date of the South Braintree murders—but he had telephoned that his wife was seriously ill and he had to stay home to take care of her.

Immigration investigated. An inspector contacted Chief Stewart, and the chief sent one of his own men with the inspector to West Bridgewater, where the Coacci family was then staying in a home rented by another Italian, Mike Boda. The investigators discovered that Coacci's wife did not appear to have been seriously ill; and when the immigration official offered to have the deportation postponed for a week, Coacci wouldn't hear of it. He was packed and ready to go; he wanted, he said, to get back to Italy in time to see his sick father; and he left with the immigration inspector, his wife and children crying on the doorstep behind him. The instant Chief Stewart learned about all this, a sudden light went off in his brain. "Something hit me," he said in a 1952 interview, "about the dates involved: the fifteenth deadline for Coacci's bond, the holdup and the phony illness."

Chief Stewart became convinced in that instant that the Bridgewater and South Braintree crimes were both the work of a single gang of Italian anarchists. He soon found support for his suspicion when the getaway Buick used in South Braintree was found abandoned in a woods only about two miles from the house in which Boda and Coacci lived. The car had been stolen in Needham in November and Chief Stewart was sure that it was the car used in both the Bridgewater and South Braintree jobs.

Stewart felt certain that Coacci had been involved in both cases, but Coacci was out of reach on the high seas. Boda remained, and Stewart began to make repeated visits to Boda's West Bridgewater home. Not welcoming these attentions, Boda fled, but he left behind him a link: an old Overland car badly in need of repair. Chief Stewart arranged with the mechanic to tip him off when Boda returned for the car. The plan worked. On the night of May 5, 1920, Boda came to get his Overland. He was riding in the side seat of a motorcycle driven by one Ricardo Orciani; and hovering in the background were two mysterious, foreign-looking strangers.

Boda became alarmed when the mechanic tried to stall him,

and he and Orciani drove off into the night. The two mysterious
strangers simply walked away, crossed a railroad bridge and boarded
a trolley. Chief Stewart, alerted by a phone call, had them picked
up. They were Sacco and Vanzetti. Both were armed. Sacco had
a .32-caliber Colt in his pocket with eight cartridges in the clip
and one in the chamber; Vanzetti had a .38 Harrington & Richardson, also loaded, and in his pocket police found four shotgun
shells.

With these arrests, Chief Stewart was satisfied that he had
solved both the Bridgewater and South Braintree crimes. He felt
certain that the same five men had been involved in both; and
now he had five suspects—Coacci, Boda, Orciani, Sacco and Vanzetti. Convincing as Stewart's theory might appear in the abstract,
it began to encounter difficulties the instant it was spot-checked
against fact.

The first collision of theory with fact occurred in the case of
Orciani. The motorcycle driver was picked up May 6, 1920, the
day after the arrest of Sacco and Vanzetti. Eyewitnesses positively
identified him as one of the holdup men at both Bridgewater and
South Braintree. Chief Stewart insisted (as the prosecution, in-
deed, implied at one point during the Sacco-Vanzetti trial) that
Orciani was one of the gunmen who had shot the payroll guard,
Alessandro Berardelli; that he then snatched Berardelli's gun, a
Harrington & Richardson; and that this was the very gun found
in Vanzetti's pocket when he was arrested.

In this reconstruction of the crime, Orciani loomed as the central figure, so it is instructive to see just what happened to him.
Arrested on May 6, he was released on May 12. Why? Because
the time card in the small foundry where he worked gave him a
perfect alibi: it showed that he had been laboring at this regular
job on both December 24, 1919, and April 15, 1920, the dates of
the crimes in question.

Here, then, at the very outset was a flaw in Stewart's theory.
If as vital a linchpin to the theory as Orciani could be eliminated
by a time card, the theory as a whole should logically have become
suspect. But logic no longer operated once Stewart's reputation
was staked on his theory. Chief Stewart theorized that someone
"must have" punched the time clock for Orciani to give him an
alibi—and "must have" punched it not on one day but on two.
Francis Russell in *Tragedy in Dedham* seemed to accept this

theory *in toto*, and it was at this point that I began to part company with Russell.

After talking to Carey McWilliams, I wrote Tom O'Connor, who had been a young reporter in Boston at the time of the Sacco-Vanzetti case. At this point one of the most dedicated men I have ever met came into my life. Horrified at what he perceived as a colossal injustice, O'Connor had devoted his entire life to the case and had unearthed the Pinkerton reports, of which not even the defense attorneys had been aware. In mid-July 1962 he was the secretary of the Committee for the Vindication of Sacco and Vanzetti. "There seems to me," I wrote to O'Connor, "to be a curious ambivalence about Russell. It is almost as if, having served on a jury in the same courtroom, he has become a dedicated disciple of the theory of the infallibility of the jury system. He admits that, whatever you believe, the one overriding impression left by the case is doubt—yet, if he had been on the jury, he would have voted as the jurors did to take a man's life, a deed that can be justified, if it ever can, by the absolute absence of all doubt."

The next thing I knew, on a bright Sunday morning a week later, a taxi deposited Tom O'Connor at my doorstep. He was a short, roly-poly, feisty man, then in his seventies; the kind of man whose life-long dedication to principle, at whatever personal sacrifice, earned him my total respect. I gathered that his crusade had sapped his financial resources; whenever he traveled from Auburndale, Massachusetts, to my home in New Jersey, he made the long trip by bus, sometimes breaking it with an overnight stay at the Sloane House YMCA in New York. On occasions when he rode buses straight through, he would arrive rumpled, a half-eaten pizza in his hand, apparently his principal sustenance on the journey. The return trip would be equally grueling. As he wrote in one letter: "As you see, I made it back o.k. Got the 1:15 A.M. Greyhound bus to Providence. Got to Providence around six, had breakfast there and drove direct to the office." It must have been an exhausting weekend grind for a man in his seventies, but Tom O'Connor made it cheerfully, his zest for his cause unabated.

On his first visit, he sat down in my sunny dining room and had a cup of coffee and a bite to eat while we talked. We first discussed Orciani. Knowing from experience how hard police will work to substantiate a theory to which they are committed, I felt

certain that they would have spared no effort in combing the
Norwood foundry where Orciani worked in the attempt to find
the accomplice who "must have" punched the time clock for him.
This was, indeed, Tom O'Connor said, exactly what had happened.

"The foundry in which Orciani worked was a relatively small
one," Tom said. "It probably employed something like twenty to
twenty-five men, and State Police checked with the owners and
Orciani's boss trying to prove that someone had given Orciani a
time-card alibi. But they couldn't do it. It would have been almost
impossible in a small place like that anyhow; a man would be
missed. But the police tried so hard to prove their theory that
the workers finally got up in arms. On one occasion the workers
threatened to leave their jobs en masse and picket in support of
Orciani. Can you imagine an entire factory doing this for an Italian
immigrant if he was guilty?"

Another angle had occurred to me that I wanted to discuss with
O'Connor. Though the South Braintree murders were committed
in 1920, four years before the FBI established its massive fingerprint collection, I knew from my police work that major departments around the nation already considered fingerprints the
most reliable means of identification. The bandits' getaway car in
South Braintree had been taken directly to police headquarters
after it was found, and so, I reasoned, there should have been
fingerprints on it. But I could find no mention of fingerprints in
the entire case and I asked Tom about it.

"Why do you ask that?" he wondered, somewhat surprised.

"Well," I said, "I know that fingerprints were in use at that
time, and I should think from the way the car was handled that
there should have been prints."

"Fred Cook," Tom sputtered, "you must be a damned smart
man. There *were* fingerprints."

"There were?"

"Yes. The local newspaper in the early days of the investigation
carried several articles about fingerprints found in the car. I always
intended to do something about it, but I got off on other things
and never did. I'd forgotten it until you mentioned it just now."

I started to get excited. "Tom, don't you understand what this
means? If there were prints and the prosecution didn't use the
evidence at the trial, it means that those prints must have belonged to *someone else,* not Sacco and Vanzetti—and not Coacci,

Boda or Orciani either. You can bet your bottom dollar that if the prosecution had had the *right prints,* prints of any of the five fitting Stewart's theory, it would have introduced them into evidence. It would have clinched the case, ended all doubt."

Tom O'Connor went back to Boston to check up on the fingerprints, and I continued my study of the Sacco-Vanzetti case. Sacco and Vanzetti, originally regarded as bystanders, were the only ones available for the state to prosecute. Coacci had been deported to Italy; Boda had hidden out and then escaped to Italy; Orciani had been cleared by the time cards.

Admittedly, Sacco and Vanzetti had lied to police when they were first picked up. Vanzetti said they had gone to Bridgewater to visit a friend called "Poppy" whose right name and address he admitted he did not know. Both denied acquaintance with either Boda or Coacci, and Sacco tried to explain the Colt and cartridges found in his pocket by saying he had just been going to have some target shooting with friends. The prosecution later was to build a cornerstone of its case on the contention that these transparent lies showed "a consciousness of guilt," when all they may really have shown was fear.

The Red raids against foreigners and anarchists were still going on; prejudice and hysteria were at their height. Only two days before Sacco and Vanzetti were arrested, an anarchist acquaintance of theirs, Andrea Salsedo, had plunged to his death from a fourteenth-floor window of the Justice Department's office in New York. There was much evidence that Salsedo, who had printed an anarchist pamphlet and was being held in the hope that he could identify the bomb plotters, had been savagely beaten in an effort to get him to "cooperate." Attorney General Palmer and J. Edgar Hoover later assured Congress that Salsedo had been treated with country club courtesy while he was being held incommunicado and that he had jumped to his death of his own free will, much to their distress. Understandably, Sacco and Vanzetti were scared. They insisted at their trial that they had gone with Orciani to pick up Boda's car only because, in view of Salsedo's fate, they wanted to use the car to collect and destroy all radical literature their friends might possess.

In any event, Sacco and Vanzetti remained in Chief Stewart's trap, and the state decided to try Vanzetti first in Plymouth for the abortive Bridgewater holdup. The state contended that Vanzetti had been the shotgun-firing bandit leader. Eyewitnesses

identified him positively. It was not until years afterward, virtually
on the eve of the executions, that the indefatigable Tom O'Connor
discovered the original Pinkerton reports and showed how this
case against Vanzetti had been rigged.

One witness who had told the Pinkertons he "did not get much
of a look" and could not describe the shotgun bandit's face gave
a letter-perfect description of Vanzetti when he testified in court.
Several other witnesses had originally described the distinguish-
ing feature of the bandit's face as a "close-cropped" mustache.
Vanzetti, however, had one of the most flourishing hirsute growths
ever to adorn an upper lip; his mustache drooped down to the
corners of his mouth. So, one after another, the state's witnesses
solved this difficulty by testifying that the bandit leader's mustache looked as if it had been "trimmed."

Vanzetti did not take the stand in this first trial in Plymouth,
relying solely on alibi witnesses. In most cases, these are as suspect and unreliable as eyewitnesses except in the rare instances
where there is some positive, checkable point of reference—as
there was in this case. On December 24, from long custom, Italian
immigrants dined on eels, so this was a big day for fish-peddler
Vanzetti. On the hour and day of the Bridgewater holdup, Vanzetti had had such a demand for eels that he had engaged his
landlady's thirteen-year-old son, Beltrano Brini, to help him make
deliveries on the streets of Plymouth. Brini testified for Vanzetti;
and more than forty years later, when he was a respected school
principal, Brini insisted in an interview with Francis Russell that
Vanzetti was peddling eels in Plymouth just when the state contended he was leading the Bridgewater holdup gang. Brini comes
through as a thoroughly honest witness. He told Russell: "Young
as I was, I knew what a disadvantage it would be for me to get
mixed up in it. I wanted to be a musician, and whatever I might
want, once I testified, I knew I'd find the way blocked. And it's
shadowed me ever since."

Documentary evidence corroborated Brini. Shortly before the
executions, Governor Alvan T. Fuller, a pompous Cadillac dealer,
conducted his own investigation. With all the prejudice of class,
Fuller sneered that the defense hadn't produced one shred of
documentary evidence to support Vanzetti's alibi. Taking up the
challenge, defense investigators belatedly scoured the Boston docks,
and finally, among the fish wholesalers with whom Vanzetti dealt,
they found one whose records disclosed that a shipment of eels

had been sent to Vanzetti at a time that coincided perfectly with Vanzetti's need to satisfy the traditional wants of his Italian clientele on December 24.

The evidence seems clear. Vanzetti was framed in the Bridgewater case that served as a trial run for the South Braintree case in Dedham. He was convicted and sentenced to twelve to fifteen years at hard labor by Judge Webster Thayer, who was to become his personal Nemesis.

Given the public prejudices and the official mental rigidities of the times, Sacco and Vanzetti never had a chance in the second trial in Dedham. The American system of justice has never been more disgraced than it was then in Massachusetts by the judge, the prosecuting officer, and the state's evidence they presented and ruled on.

The bias of Judge Webster Thayer was unmistakable, even in court. Newspapermen and fellow members of the bar were shocked time after time by his intemperate, off-bench remarks while the trial was in progress. At one point he made a remark so prejudicial and outrageous that he himself ordered it expunged from the record and demanded that newspapers that had printed it retract their stories. Capping all was the infamous remark he made after denying defense motions for a new trial: "Did you see what I did to those anarchistic bastards the other day?"

District Attorney Frederick Gunn Katzmann was a prosecutor hell-bent on conviction, regardless of how he had to torture the evidence. With men on trial for their lives, Katzmann put on the stand a Pinkerton detective who testified from specially made "notes," never disclosing the existence of the basic, original reports that disagreed with the testimony. Four bullet shells had been recovered at the South Braintree scene. Three could not be traced to any specific gun, but one, labeled No. 3 at the trial, was the bullet, the state contended, that had killed Berardelli. Captain William Proctor, the State Police ballistics expert and the officer who had been in direct charge of the investigation at the beginning, disclosed in a post-trial affidavit that he had "repeatedly" told Katzmann he would say, if asked the direct question, that he did *not* believe this fatal slug had come from Sacco's gun. So Katzmann, adept at framing a question deliberately intended to deceive judge and jury, concocted a weasel question: He asked Proctor if it was "consistent" with his findings that the shot had come from Sacco's gun; and, since Sacco's gun and the murder weapon were both .32-caliber Colts, Proctor could and did answer, "Yes." The false impression was thus created that Sacco had fired the fatal shot. When Proctor later filed his affidavit exposing the fraud, what did Katzmann do? He did not deny. He merely insisted that Proctor had not "repeatedly" told him. When Felix Frankfurter, then a Harvard Law School professor and later a U.S. Supreme Court Justice, read Proctor's charge and Katzmann's non-denial, he became convinced that the entire Sacco-Vanzetti case represented a colossal miscarriage of justice. In the March 1927 issue of the staid *Atlantic Monthly,* he wrote an article burning with outrage that caused a reaction like a lighted fuse to a powder keg.

As for the evidence, according to the prosecution, Sacco was, first, one of the loiterers who had shot the payroll master and his guard in their backs. This Sacco was wearing a cap, and this Sacco was the man who had pumped three bullets into Berardelli's body. But Berardelli had not been killed, he was writhing on the pavement. Enter the second Sacco. This was the gunman, the state soberly insisted, who had leaped from the car and fired the final, fatal shot—that No. 3 slug identified in court. This Sacco had jumped back on the running board and seated himself beside the driver of the getaway car. He had also started spraying the area with bullets, and he had bellowed at one spectator, "Get out of the way, you son-of-a-bitch!" Later he had yelled at a railroad crossing guard, "What the hell are you holding us up for?" Both guard and spectator agreed that this Sacco had yelled at them in clear, unaccented, earthy English; but Sacco, the real Sacco on trial for his life, spoke such broken English that, when he testified in court, he had to have an interpreter.

In linking Sacco to the scene of the crime, Katzmann relied heavily on a cap found there, just such a cap as Sacco was known to wear. This cap, so the state contended, had been on the head of the first Sacco when he leaped at Berardelli from behind. Katzmann labored mightily to show that Sacco had worn this cap. A similar cap had been found in Sacco's home, and the two caps had a striking similarity. Each had a hole in the back of the lining, apparently worn there when Sacco hung the cap on a hook when he went to work as a shoemaker. This effort to show that Sacco was "the man in the cap" got its first exposure in court when Sacco was asked to don the cap found at the murder scene. It perched on top of his head in ridiculous fashion, obviously too small for him ever to have worn it. The second exposure of the cap evidence came in July 1927, shortly before the executions. Tom O'Connor learned from ex-Police Chief Jeremiah F. Gallivan, of Braintree, that the cap had been given to him two days after the murders and that it had been found only the night before. As for the tear in the back of the lining, Gallivan said that he had made that himself when he was trying to find any identifying marks inside the lining. Gallivan testified before the Lowell Advisory Committee that Governor Fuller had appointed: "Can any of you gentlemen make me believe that the hat lay there for thirty hours, with the State Police, the local police and two or three thousand people there?" Obviously, Gallivan said, the cap must have fallen from the head of a sightseer.

Katzmann also made a desperate effort to picture Vanzetti as the driver of the getaway car. He tried to establish this by eyewitness testimony, the only kind he had. The trouble was that so many of his eyewitnesses described the driver as a pale, thin-faced, sickly man, a description completely at odds with Vanzetti's appearance. Another problem with this Katzmann thesis was that Vanzetti did not know how to drive. And that was the case on which Vanzetti was sent to the electric chair.

In studying the record, I was intrigued by Captain Proctor's attitude. He kept telling anyone who would listen in the corridors of the courthouse during the trial that Katzmann was trying the wrong men. And he told his friend, Massachusetts Attorney General Harry C. Atwill, "They've got the wrong men." There was no chance of discovering what made Proctor so sure, for he died shortly after signing the affidavit that wrecked the ballistics evidence. But I felt certain that he must have had some very positive, private information that made him act as he did. I could not recall in my experience a single case in which the principal police officer in charge of an investigation had switched sides and denounced his own case. Invariably, in such circumstances, the officer became the most dedicated witness for the prosecution. Why had Proctor broken the mold?

I had reached this point in my musings when Tom O'Connor delivered the photostats of the Brockton *Times* that carried the stories of the slayings and subsequent arrests. Reading these, I believed that I had uncovered the clue to Captain Proctor's otherwise inexplicable conduct.

The issue of April 20, 1920, reported: "The car [the Buick getaway car] was brought to the Brockton police garage in City Hall Square, from where it was later taken to Boston by the state officers. Photos of fingerprints were first made."

On the following day the Brockton *Times* returned to the theme. Its story said: "The experts of the identification bureau of the state police were busy today making records of the fingerprint tracings and photographs taken from the bandit auto at the Brockton police station Monday noon in an effort to learn by this system if any one of the bandits had left a trace to indicate the identity as a man known to the criminal identification bureaus of the country as a professional 'gun' in holdup or other work."

On April 25, the paper reported that Captain Proctor and his detectives were hoping the fingerprint evidence would turn up some suspects. "This work represents one of the keener elements of the job of fixing the identity of the bandits," the article said. "If fingerprints from the bandit car show favorably with those of any gunmen known to the criminal experts, a most valuable clue will have been obtained."

Clearly, fingerprints had been obtained in sufficient number and clarity to represent the major hope of breaking the case. Then, out of the blue, as the result of Stewart's theory, Sacco and Vanzetti were arrested. What happened next remains one of the most significant—and completely ignored—aspects of the entire case.

On May 6, the day after the arrests, the Brockton *Times* reported that Inspector George C. Chase was "at the State House" making a comparison of the fingerprints of Sacco and Vanzetti "with the fingerprint records taken off the South Braintree bandit car April 29 at the Brockton police station." This reference was no journalistic slip, for the following day the *Times*, a conservatively edited paper, ran a long, carefully detailed article on a major conference held by officials of the district attorney's office and high police officials: "Inspector George C. Chase has completed the comparisons of fingerprints taken since the arrests of the suspects and the marks obtained off the bandit car as directed by Eddie Sherlock, the State Police expert on criminal identification. Nothing is stated about the results. It is kept a close secret."

And it remained a close secret. In the six-volume, two-and-one-half-million-word record of the trial and subsequent motions, there is no mention of fingerprints. When Inspector Chase testified at the trial, his direct examination took up only half a page of the record. He was asked only to tell how Sacco and Vanzetti were photographed after their arrest. Neither he nor any of the other police witnesses was ever questioned about the development of fingerprints from the bandit car—the prints that, as the file of the Brockton *Times* shows, were considered the most important single clue in the case up to the very moment of the arrest of Sacco and Vanzetti. In all the literature of the case, fingerprints were never mentioned again until Tom O'Connor dug up the evidence for me.

With the conviction of Sacco and Vanzetti, the highest officials in Massachusetts achieved a vested interest in error. Throughout the world, Massachusetts justice was being denounced. Communist agitators touched off demonstrations in front of American embassies abroad. Anarchist bombings at home menaced officials who had any connection with the case. Many of America's leading writers and intellectuals sprang to the defense of Sacco and Vanzetti. This agitation, this violence, this worldwide frenzy, forced the officialdom of Massachusetts to retreat into its hardened shell much like a turtle.

Governor Fuller, impervious to reason, turned the task of whitewashing the deed over to a special committee headed by the distinguished A. Lawrence Lowell, president of Harvard University. The Lowells were one of Massachusetts' oldest and most aristocratic families. They claimed descent from an 11th-century Duke of Brittany, and Lowell himself was later described by his biographer as "a democratic aristocrat." He was a man who could be counted on to uphold the status of his privileged class—and he did.

Years later, Supreme Court Justice Michael A. Musmanno, of Pennsylvania, told a hostile Massachusetts investigating committee: "The attitude of Fuller and his Advisory Committee throughout their hearings and eventual findings lends credence to the fear often expressed that the purpose of the extra-judicial proceedings was to lend respectability to a discredited trial, and that the possible innocence of the subjects was of little consequence compared to upholding the institutions of Massachusetts."

This bias showed itself in many ways. The committee found that Judge Thayer's intemperate remarks were a mere "breach of decorum" that did not affect the outcome of the trial. The committee, with Lowell its dominating figure, either ignored or rationalized out of existence all defense testimony and accepted as valid the most incredible vaporings of unstable witnesses for the prosecution. It listened with approval to a woman so irresponsible that even Katzmann had not used her at the trial. She testified that she had seen Sacco at the murder scene twice on the day of the slayings, once at eleven o'clock in the morning and again at three in the afternoon. When asked how she happened to know Sacco, the witness replied, "Why I don't know, gentlemen. I talked with Governor Fuller, and I don't remember, my head is too full of music and things like that to remember." I am still stunned to think that a president of Harvard and his supposedly intelligent committee could conclude that, though this witness was obviously "eccentric," they believed "her testimony is well worth consideration."

The report of the Lowell committee gave Governor Fuller the excuse he needed to deny clemency on August 3, 1927, but touched off a wave of denunciation. An Episcopal minister wrote Lowell: "If Sacco and Vanzetti are executed, you will have to put a new and sinister meaning into the crimson of Harvard." The columnist Heywood Broun called Harvard "Hangman's House" and asked: "What more can these immigrants from Italy expect? It is not every prisoner who has the president of Harvard University throw the switch for him."

And so in Charlestown prison, "the good shoemaker" and "the poor fish peddler" awaited their inevitable fate. Admittedly, they were two quite different men: Sacco the peasant type, a man who had to work with his hands, a man limited in intellect and a radical anarchist (his wife was harboring the sister of a bomb-plotter killed in the bombing of Attorney General Palmer's home in Washington); Vanzetti, the intellectual, the philosopher, the poor fish-peddler touched with genius and possessing, even in the unfamiliar English language, a poet's feeling for the sheer cadence and beauty and meaning of words. Facing execution for a crime he had not committed, he could still express himself to Phil Strong, a visiting reporter, in words that have been compared for eloquence to Lincoln's Gettysburg Address:

> If it had not been for this thing, I might have live out my life talking at street corners to scorning men. I might have die, unmarked, unknown, a failure. Now we are not a failure.

This is our career and our triumph. Never in our full life can we hope to do such work for tolerance, for joostice, for man's onderstanding of man, as we now do by an accident.

Our words—our lives—our pains—nothing. The taking of our lives—lives of a good shoemaker and poor fish peddler—all!

That last moment belong to us—that agony is our triumph.

There can be no question now: not only did Sacco and Vanzetti not commit the crime for which they were executed, but the identity of the gangsters who did is known. South Braintree was just one in a series of holdups and freight-car robberies pulled off by the Morelli brothers, of Providence, Rhode Island. Even before the executions, the trail of evidence pointed to the Morellis, but officials, with their reputations at stake, refused to investigate.

Herbert H. Ehrmann, a junior defense counsel, tried to call attention to the Morelli gang before the executions, but he had found not only that officials would not listen but that they actively opposed any investigation of the Morelli angle. The record showed that members of the gang had been indicted for freight-car robberies in the area in 1919 and again in March 1920. Then a member of the gang, Celestino P. Madeiros, arrested in the slaying of a bank cashier in Wrentham, tried to communicate with Sacco in prison. Sacco distrusted prison inmates because authorities had planted an informer in a cell next to his and so refused to listen to Madeiros. However, William C. Thompson, the chief defense counsel on appeal, and Ehrmann were finally contacted, interviewed Madeiros in prison, and got a full confession from him.

Madeiros said he knew Sacco and Vanzetti were innocent because he had been the fifth man in the car at the South Braintree holdup. The Morelli gang, he said, had brought him along to provide extra firepower in case they ran into trouble. He gave a detailed account of how the South Braintree crime had been plotted and carried out, and though at first he tried to avoid naming any of the Morelli brothers, he told about the freight-car robberies for which they had been arrested. This was identification enough; and Ehrmann, in checking out Madeiros's confession, corroborated many details independently.

In 1969 Ehrmann described his researches in a perceptively titled book, *The Case That Will Not Die*. His meticulous account seemed to prove the case: Joseph Morelli, oldest of the Morelli brothers, who was later to serve time in the federal penitentiary for the freight-car robberies, had planned the South Braintree job with his younger brothers, Frank (Butsey) and Michael Morelli.

Corroboration of Ehrmann's account came in 1973 when Vincent Teresa, who had been the third-highest member in the pecking order of his Mafia family, told his life story to Thomas C. Renner. In *My Life in the Mafia,* Teresa described how he had mingled with many higher-up Mafiosi, including Butsey Morelli, the old "tough stone killer" who had bossed the Morelli gang after his older brother, Joe, had died.

Butsey Morelli had become incensed in 1951 because the Boston *Globe* had printed an article linking him to the South Braintree murders. Butsey, denying all, had threatened to sue the paper for libel because he wanted his past hidden from his "straight" adopted son, whom he adored. However, among mobsters, he made no secret of his role in South Braintree. Teresa told Renner of a conversation he had had with Butsey:

> I looked at Butsey. I didn't know much about the case except what I'd heard. But he was upset because of what was happening to his boy, not what happened to Sacco and Vanzetti. "We whacked them out, we killed those guys in the robbery," Butsey said. "These two greaseballs [Sacco and Vanzetti] took it on the chin. They [the payroll guards] got in our way so we just ran over them." I said: "Did you really do this?" He looked at me, right in my eyes, and said: "Absolutely, Vinnie. These two suckers took it on the chin for us. That just shows you how much justice there really is."

No one paid any attention to this belated confession, buried deep in the text of Renner's book, until I spotted it and wrote a short editorial for *The Nation.*

"The Case That Will Not Die" continued to produce more damning disclosures. In the summer of 1977, Lincoln A. Robbins, a historical researcher, found a black notebook that had been kept by Katzmann's assistant prosecutor, Harold P. Williams, who had donated it to the Harvard Law School Library. Other researchers had had access to the notebook, but all had missed its significance. Then Robbins, a forty-eight-year-old former history teacher from Buzzards Bay, came along, read more closely and was startled by what he found. "My eyes bugged out," he later told the Boston *Globe.* "I must have sworn out loud in the library. I simply could not believe what I was reading."

Williams's handwritten notes and a typewritten summary of the prosecution's case prepared in advance of trial made these two startling disclosures: Only *three* shell casings, not four as the jury had been told, had been found at the South Braintree scene; and the entire story of who found them and what was done with them had been changed for the purposes of the trial, presumably because the real finder of the evidence would not commit perjury on the witness stand.

Three shells had been found by John Shay, a Braintree policeman. Williams wrote: "Shay picked up 3 shells where Ber[ardelli] fell & gave them to Sherlock [the State Police detective]." At the trial, however, in response to Williams's questions, an entirely different witness, James Bostock, told the jury: "I picked up some shells . . . about two or three feet from the shooting." He said that he had given them not to Sherlock but to Thomas Fraher, a superintendent in the Slater & Morrill factory. Fraher confirmed receiving four shells from Bostock. However, when questioned at a pre-trial inquest, Fraher had never mentioned seeing any shells.

Since the prosecution had built its case against Sacco largely on the deceptive ballistics testimony about one shot fired from his Colt, Williams's notes indicating that an extra shell had been introduced into the chain of evidence adds an even more diabolical touch to the trickery Katzmann himself had tacitly admitted when he failed to deny Captain Proctor's charge. Robbins thought that Williams, who later became a justice of the Massachusetts Supreme Court, was as disturbed as Proctor but that he felt he had no choice except to go along with his boss, Katzmann. He cited Williams's strange reaction when a Brockton *Enterprise* reporter attempted to congratulate him after the guilty verdict had been returned. The *Enterprise* reported: "With tears streaming down his face, Williams replied, 'For God's sake, don't rub it in. This is the saddest thing that ever happened to me in my life.' "

Robbins's discovery was only one of the surprises of 1977. Governor Michael S. Dukakis, himself the son of Greek immigrant parents, realizing that the fiftieth anniversary of the controversial executions would be noted on August 23, ordered his chief legal counsel, Daniel Taylor, to restudy the case. Taylor began his work in fall 1976, and he concluded that, in addition to a prejudiced judge, legal authorities in the case had ignored or poorly handled vital testimony and evidence.

Taylor criticized Judge Thayer for limiting his charge to three pieces of evidence: the bullet allegedly fired from Sacco's gun, the revolver found in Var etti's possession, and the cap. "In the light of the evidence discovered after the trial, the tendency of each of the three to prove the guilt of the defendants is doubtful," Taylor wrote.

After receiving this report, Governor Dukakis proclaimed August 23 Nicola Sacco and Bartolomeo Vanzetti Memorial Day and declared: "The atmosphere of their trial and appeals was permeated by prejudice against foreigners and hostility toward unorthodox political views. . . . The conduct of the officials involved in the case sheds serious doubt on their willingness and ability to conduct the prosecution and trial of Sacco and Vanzetti impartially." The governor's proclamation concluded with a plea to the people of Massachusetts to "draw from their historic lessons the resolve to prevent the forces of intolerance, fear and hatred from ever again uniting to overcome the rationality, wisdom and fairness to which our legal system aspires."

The reaction was startling. Even after fifty years, even after the exposures of misconduct, it was still impossible to appeal to reason. Conservative and prejudiced minds remained in the frozen mold of 1927, and a storm of denunciation buffeted the governor. "We didn't think it would be quietly received," a Dukakis aide said, "but we certainly were surprised at the intensity of the reaction." The Massachusetts Senate, yielding to the hysterical public outcry, actually passed a resolution publicly censuring Governor Dukakis. In 1978, when Dukakis ran for re-election, he was defeated.

Fortunately, this is not quite the end of the story. In November 1982 Dukakis ran for governor again—and was elected. Since various political strands unite in any election victory, it is not possible to say that Dukakis's re-election was a complete vindication. What sticks in the mind as an evil symptom of the human condition is the irrational and hysterical denunciation of a governor who tried after fifty years to cleanse the record of his state, and it is still shocking that so many continued to refuse to recognize that the record needed cleansing.

18

"By Direction of the President"

DURING THE YEARS AFTER WORLD WAR II, I DETECTED A creeping authoritarianism in American life. It was as if, having won the greatest war ever fought against tyrannical regimes, we had ended up victims, adopting many of the attitudes and techniques of the dictatorships we had fought. Authority became holy. National good took precedence over independence. The FBI and CIA were virtually enshrined as secret agencies that were laws unto themselves. FBI Director J. Edgar Hoover was an untouchable icon, the irreplaceable public official, as unassailable as motherhood; and CIA Director Allen Dulles was publicly revered as he plotted the overthrow of legitimate governments and supplanted them with ruthless dictators. Joe McCarthy's wild attacks on anyone to the left of Torquemada were long accepted because he spoke with the aegis of a U.S. senator and the chairman of a powerful investigating committee. Dissent of any kind was regarded with suspicion.

Perhaps because I was known for my iconoclastic attitudes, I found myself frequently besieged by underdogs seeking a champion. Since I did all my own research and I was usually busy seven days a week with free-lance writing to earn enough to support my family, I probably passed up some cases I should have handled. But there were two I didn't pass up that gave me some of the greatest satisfactions of my writing career.

One spring day in 1962 I walked into the office of *The Nation,*
and Carey McWilliams told me that a former Air Force officer
had heard about some of the things I had written and had come
in with an extraordinary story. "It's something we can't handle,"
Carey told me, "but I told him that you sometimes write for *Saga*
magazine and suggested that *Saga* might be interested in it." *Saga*
was, and so I came to meet one of the most dogged, determined
fighters I ever encountered.

Former Air Force Major Marion Gray Denton impressed me
immediately. He was a prosperous businessman; the holder of a
number of patents; the proprietor of the Marden Manufacturing
Company in Auburndale, Florida, where he manufactured brush-
clearing and heavy earth-moving machines, some of which were
soon to be used in Vietnam. Denton was such a shining example
of a successful small businessman that the U.S. State Department
frequently called on him to entertain important visitors from
emerging Third World countries whom the department hoped to
impress with the virtues of the American way. Yet Marion Denton
was a man who had been on trial for nearly twenty years when I
met him in a futile effort to obtain justice from the most authoritarian of all authoritarian institutions, the U.S. Military.

Denton joined the Army Air Corps in World War I, but by the
time he finished his flight training, the war in Europe had ended.
He remained in the service and was one of the small band of
Army pilots who, flying by the seats of their pants in inadequately
equipped planes, ferried the first airmail service. After he left
active service, he remained in the Air Corps Reserve, and by
1937 had been promoted to major.

Pictures of the young aviator reminded me of a young Van
Johnson. When I met him, I could see that the passing years had
taken their toll. A stockily built man with thinning, graying hair,
he spoke with a soft Southern accent, and he told his story clearly and calmly. The only sign I could detect of the strains to
which he had been subjected was a nervous tic in one cheek.
He efficiently supplied full documentation—copies of his
orders, correspondence and the full transcript of court-martial
proceedings and of a later, futile Congressional hearing into his
case.

Denton was forty-four when he was recalled to active duty on
August 1, 1941. Nearly two years later, while he was attending

the Technical Inspectors School at Chanute Field, Illinois, he received what must be one of the weirdest orders ever issued by a high command. Special Order No. 156, dated June 8, 1943, from Maxwell Field, Alabama, was stamped across the top with a big red SECRET. The pertinent paragraph that was to be the basis of all of Denton's trouble read: "Maj. Marion G. Denton 0150435 is reld fr asgmt [relieved from assignment] to BAAF Fort Myers Fla and *by direction of the President* is asgd as Post Commander of the Greenland Base Command. He WP [will proceed] fr BAAF Fort Myers Fla to Presque Isle Maine reporting to CO North Atlantic Wing Air Transport Command not later than June 15, 1943 for T by air to destination. *Upon arrival at destination he will assume command.* [Italics added]"

Marion Denton had received many orders during his career, but he had never seen one that contained such an awesome phrase as "by direction of the President." The urgency of the order seemed to indicate that Denton had been tapped by the president himself; but when Denton arrived at Presque Isle, he found that no one in the Air Transport Command knew what to do with him. There were several bases in Greenland, and it was not clear where Air Transport was supposed to deposit him. Presque Isle officials said they would check with Washington. Then an officer told Denton, "We now know where we are going to take you. The War Department wants you to go to BW-1."

BW-1 was Bluie West-1, located on the west side of the island at Narsassuak. It was the command base for all U.S. flying fields and weather stations in Greenland. Major Denton landed there about 2 A.M. on June 18 and was given a bed in the transient officers' quarters.

In the morning, when Denton presented his orders, there was instant confusion. The War Department had failed to notify the base that it was to get a new commander. The existing commander was a regular Army colonel, a superior creature of whom all good little majors had better beware, especially one who came from the reserves. After what seemed an interminable delay, Denton was finally ushered into the presence of Colonel Robert W. C. Wimsatt. The colonel, a rugged man with a rosy complexion and a chubby face, was surrounded by his chosen brass: Captain Thomas L. Anderson, the post adjutant; a Major Lloyd; and Lieutenant Colonel Kelsey Reaves, the base executive officer.

Denton was given a seat, and Colonel Wimsatt said, "This is a crazy order. It looks like an Air Corps order."

"Well, Colonel," Major Denton replied mildly, "I did not write the order. I only came here to comply with it."

The colonel strode across the room to stand before a large wall map with the American bases in Greenland indicated. "There is no such thing as the post commander of the Greenland Base Command," he said, since the Greenland Base Command included a number of posts, fields and weather stations. "This is the Greenland Base Command," he said, sweeping his arm around the room.

Marion Denton was completely taken aback. It was quite obvious that this regular Army colonel wasn't about to relinquish his command to any upstart Air Corps Reserve major.

"Well, what am I supposed to do?" Denton asked.

"Just stay where you are," Wimsatt told him.

This settled nothing, and a very disturbed reserve major returned to his room in the transient officers' quarters. Major Denton would have been even more upset had he known that Colonel Wimsatt was noted as a harsh, blood-and-guts type who had once tried to court-martial a young lieutenant for driving a jeep five miles an hour too fast on the post (he had finally given up the court-martial but suspended the lieutenant's privileges for thirty days). Friday and Saturday passed without any word from Colonel Wimsatt. Denton grew deeply worried. He was supposed to take command *immediately* of whatever it was he was supposed to command, and one thing was certain: he was not doing anything *immediately*. Denton borrowed a typewriter and wrote to the "Air Inspector, Army Air Forces, Washington, D.C., Attention: Technical Division," describing the impossible situation and suggesting he be given the chance to discuss the situation "with appropriate authority in Washington." He closed by saying: "It is well understood that letters of this kind should move through channels, but at this exact writing there is no knowledge of any existing chain of command through which this letter can move." Then he sent the letter off on the next Air Transport plane.

Sunday passed with Denton still at loose ends. On Monday morning, he visited base headquarters, but Captain Anderson told him Colonel Wimsatt would not be available until afternoon. In midafternoon, Denton had his second session with the colonel.

"I . . . told the colonel," he subsequently testified, "that I had been ordered to this place, this destination, to do something which, at the time, I had not done; and that I wished to communicate that fact to the War Department that had issued the order."

Wimsatt's reply was: "That is not necessary. This is where you belong."

Since the colonel controlled all radio facilities at the base, there was no way for Denton to communicate speedily with Washington. He talked awhile longer with Wimsatt, who appeared friendly, and they parted with the understanding they would talk soon again.

Another day passed. Then, shortly before noon on June 23, 1943, when Major Denton was dining in the transient officers' mess hall, Lieutenant Frank Zitnick, Colonel Wimsatt's billeting officer, hurried breathlessly into the hall and informed Denton that "they" had been looking for him, and "they" had an airplane waiting for him, and "they" wanted him to get on it right away and take off.

"Wait a minute," Denton interrupted. "You're talking too fast. Who are 'they'?"

The messenger said "they" were Colonel Wimsatt and Captain Anderson, and wouldn't the major please hurry? As Denton was leaving the mess hall, he encountered a second breathless messenger, Lieutenant Robert H. Manley, Captain Anderson's assistant on the headquarters staff.

"Major Denton," Manley said, "I have an order to tell you that you are to go to APO #670 [also known as Bluie East-2, this was 500 miles away on the northeast coast of Greenland]. There is a plane waiting. You will have to hurry to catch it. If you will pack what things you need for the next few days, we will send the rest of your effects on the next plane."

"Wait a minute," Denton told him. "I was supposed to have a talk with the colonel before I left."

"Is that so, sir? I thought it had been all arranged."

"I'm not going anywhere until I have a talk with the colonel," Denton told him.

"Very well, sir," said Lieutenant Manley.

On his way to the transient officers' quarters, Denton encountered Captain Anderson, who had also been looking for him. He told Anderson what he had just told Manley, then went on into the quarters and sat down calmly in the day room. He did not

have long to wait. In a few minutes, Colonel Wimsatt stormed
in, Captain Anderson at his heels.

> WIMSATT: Major, I want you to get on that airplane. I have
> a sick commander. I want you to go to No. 2 and take over.
> DENTON: I understood, Colonel, that we were to have a
> conversation before I was sent anywhere.
> WIMSATT: That's the post you were picked out for, you were
> requisitioned for, anyhow.
> DENTON: In that case I request that you report me as unfit
> for duty.
> WIMSATT: I am not going to argue with you—you are going
> on that plane or I am going to charge you.
> DENTON: Then, sir, I suggest that you try me.
> WIMSATT: Prepare the charges, then, Captain.

The day after Colonel Wimsatt preferred charges against Major
Denton, the colonel himself was relieved as the commander of
the Greenland Base Command. What had happened in the mysterious labyrinth of the War Department? Had Major Denton's
letter alerted the high brass to their snafu? One that had to be
corrected to protect themselves? Was it possible that the old-boy
network had tipped off Wimsatt and inspired his sudden move
against Denton while he still had command?

Colonel Albert D. Smith was Wimsatt's replacement, but he
did not take over until July 10. In the interim, Major Denton was
at the mercy of Colonel Wimsatt. Denton was restricted to his
quarters and the transient officers' mess. He was charged with
violating the 64th Article of War—"wilfully" refusing to obey a
lawful order issued by his superior officer, an offense punishable
by death. Denton realized the seriousness of the charge, but he
still found it impossible to credit its reality.

Wimsatt moved swiftly while he still had control. War Department regulations provided that before a man could be brought
to trial there must be a pre-trial hearing in which the prosecution
must outline its whole case and the accused was to have the right
to confront and cross-examine his accuser. Major General Myron
C. Cramer, judge advocate general of the Army, had publicized
this pre-trial procedure as guaranteeing a military prisoner safe-
guards actually superior to those in civilian courts. Major Denton's
case was to prove such guarantees were worthless. Rank would
be served and upheld first.

The pre-trial hearing was held just three days after the alleged offense. Wimsatt had named one of his own subordinate officers, Major Edward A. Bosarge, to conduct the hearing. The transcript reveals that Bosarge's real task was to protect Wimsatt.

When the colonel testified, Denton cross-examined him. What authority did Wimsatt have to override Denton's "by direction of the President" order? "We have War Department orders on your being transferred here," Wimsatt testified. Denton wanted to see the orders, but Major Bosarge quickly intervened. "The investigating officer will examine any and all orders that are on file in Greenland Base Command headquarters, for the purpose of considering whether or not the accused was assigned to this command, and will rule on this feature of the case in his report," he said.

Denton protested that "my rights have been abridged." He felt, he said, that "the dodging of this question . . . is an attempt to avoid the main issue involved, and apparently is done on the part of the investigating officer, in order that he might protect the commanding officer from embarrassment." Bosarge ignored him and asked Wimsatt if he wished to say anything more. Wimsatt declared flatly: "At this time, copies of orders assigning Major Denton to this command, copies of orders both mail and radio, are on file in the headquarters of the Greenland Base Command."

As events were to show, there wasn't a word of truth in that statement, given under oath. Not a single order applying to Denton was on file at Greenland headquarters; and even in this one-sided hearing, the fact became obvious.

Wimsatt's adjutant, Thomas L. Anderson, who had been promoted to major after Denton's arrival at the base, testified that Wimsatt himself had issued an order attaching Denton to his command. But Denton hadn't been served with the order until *after* his arrest on June 23. Denton tried to find out what other orders might be hidden in the files, but Major Bosarge blocked him again. However, one vital question-and-answer sequence did slip through Bosarge's protective screen.

Q. Major Anderson, will you please state whether or not there was any other order, other than the one mentioned, on the 23rd of June 1943?
A. No.

It was a flat refutation of Wimsatt's testimony. Subsequently, the Congressional investigating committee would ask the War Department for any "mail or radio orders" relating to Denton, receiving the response that "no orders concerning Major Denton could be found."

Wimsatt's only justification for bringing Denton up on charges was his own order of June 23. Denton cross-examined Anderson closely on this point. Anderson admitted that special orders had been published on June 19, 20, 21 and 22—but not the one in question. He claimed that the order had been "thought of" and issued "verbally" by Wimsatt on June 19, but it hadn't been published due to a lapse by his assistant adjutant. Denton demanded whether Anderson wanted to take full responsibility for that statement. Major Bosarge intervened, reminding Anderson that "no witness shall be required to incriminate himself"; and Major Anderson swiftly declared: "I do not wish to answer this question in view of the fact that same may tend to incriminate myself."

The hearing ended with this Army major pleading the Fifth Amendment—clearly Wimsatt's case was in shambles. But Denton's obvious innocence was immaterial in a case in which rank and the system must be upheld.

The first indication that the brass would go to any extreme to protect itself came after Colonel Smith arrived in Greenland. Smith, a considerate officer, told Denton that if he had jurisdiction, he would dispose of the case, but he didn't have the authority. Then he showed Denton an "amended" order that indicated dirty work was afoot in the highest echelons of the War Department. The order had been issued from Maxwell Field July 8, 1943, more than two weeks after the offense for which Denton was being court-martialed. It was an afterthought that changed everything by eliminating the phrase "by direction of the President" and by stating "Upon arrival at destination he will report to the base commander for duty."

It was evident that the system was out to "get" Denton to uphold the sanctity of rank, but Denton couldn't really believe what was happening to him even after the Army ordered him to go on trial for his life before a court-martial board at Mitchel Field, Long Island, on September 27, 1943.

Years later, he told me, "I was confident that nothing could happen. Everybody in the service with whom I discussed my

case—and I talked with a number about it—had the same reaction. 'Why, that's the craziest thing I ever heard of!' they all
said. I never thought that the charges would come to trial, and
when they did, I never imagined they could be sustained. I was
unduly confident—I was overconfident."

He also underrated the unconscionable extremes to which the
system would go. First, the Army decided to ignore the pre-trial
hearing in Greenland and to start all over again with a second
one, violating every article in that code of military justice of which
General Cramer was so proud. Wimsatt was shipped off to Arkansas, so his accusing statement was read into the record, but
he was not "available" to testify. The authorities were taking no
chance with a direct confrontation and cross-examination.

General Cramer's rules provided that the accused man must
be furnished with counsel of his choice if at all possible. Denton
had asked that Captain John Conway Cook, a veteran trial lawyer
with wide court-martial experience, be appointed to defend him.
Denton had served with Cook on military boards and had
the highest regard for him. The Military Establishment was on
the spot. Denton's request had to be honored and forwarded
through the proper channels. And Captain Cook was available and
willing.

The high brass were determined to deny Denton skilled trial
counsel. The case Captain Cook had been busy with at Maxwell
Field had ended and he was ready to serve for a full week before
Denton's trial began. His superiors had notified the Army of his
availability, but the high brass ignored this notice.

Denton did not know about this flagrant double-cross until after
his trial. He was told simply that Captain Cook was tied up with
another case and, just like Wimsatt at the pre-trial hearing, he
was simply "unavailable." To bad, old man, Denton was told, but
the Army of course would see that he got the best available counsel. The Army's idea of the best was Lieutenant Colonel Gregory
C. Keenan—a flier famed for the curt message, "Sighted sub,
sank same"—who was not even an attorney.

Acutely aware of his limitations, Keenan appealed to Colonel
Henry J. Harmeling, the judge advocate of the First Air Force
at Mitchel Field, to be relieved of his assignment. As he later
testified, "I . . . requested that I be taken off the special court as
defense counsel because I did not feel myself qualified. I'm not

an attorney, and in a case of that nature I felt it was asking too much to be retained as defense counsel." But, Keenan continued, "Colonel Harmeling told me that he considered me as well qualified as any other officer they had, and that there was not anyone else available to take my place and that I would have to continue with the case."

Having done their best to destroy the defense, the brass now set about packing the court. The Mitchel Field officer who ordinarily would have served as law member (judge) was passed over in favor of Lieutenant Colonel Chester L. Fisher, Jr., who had built a career as a prosecutor. Then General Cramer's Judge Advocate General's Department in Washington, which ultimately would have to review the verdict, dispatched one of its own, Major Joseph Smith, to serve as trial judge advocate, or prosecutor. This action underlined the determination of high authority to convict: the judge advocate general's office, where impartiality should have been the prime consideration, became a partner in the prosecution.

Major Denton went on trial with Gregory Keenan as his counsel, assisted by Captain Adolph J. Eckhardt, a young lawyer. Keenan and Eckhardt denounced the procedure that required two pre-trial hearings, calling on the court-martial board to study the evidence of the first hearing. In opposing the motion, the prosecution made an amazing admission. "If the court does review the investigation, the whole case, I am afraid, would be thrown out because of the fact it could not help but prejudge it before hearing the evidence," Major Smith said. Keenan pounced. He argued that the prosecutor had now conceded that the case was so bad the trial never should have been authorized.

But Colonel Fisher, offering no justification, ruled abruptly: "Subject to objection by any member of the court, the motion of the defense is denied." There was no objection from *this* court (one member later admitted that his mind had been made up before the trial even started); and the legal farce proceeded.

The authoritarianism and injustice of the proceeding stands out glaringly on almost every page of the trial record. When Colonel Wimsatt testified, citing his mythical orders concerning Denton, the defense demanded to see the documents, but Colonel Fisher overruled it, saying, "The witness is answering of his own knowledge." On cross-examination, Wimsatt insisted that he had been advised by radio that a flying officer (he had assumed Denton was meant) was being sent to serve under him. Did the prosecution have a copy of that radiogram? "No," said Major Smith. It did not matter. This trial was forging a new rule of law: documentary proof was immaterial; whatever was in Colonel Wimsatt's mind was the only relevant evidence.

Denton testified that he acted in good faith in disobeying Wimsatt's order because his own order was "by direction of the President." The idea that an Air Corps Reserve major could have been named to supplant a regular Army colonel was so astonishing to the military mind that the prosecutor snorted indignantly: "That in itself is ridiculous. *Not even the President can do that.* [Italics added]"

This outburst was not an intemperate slip of the tongue; it represented the attitude of the entire court-martial board. It was accepted that no civilian authority, "not even the President," could interfere with the prerogatives of rank. Member after member harassed Denton on the seniority question. What was his conception of seniority? What had made him think that Colonel Wimsatt did not have authority over him, a mere major?

The board recalled Denton for one more go-around:

> Q. Major, did you know this: that no matter what the relative rank of two officers, the officer of the higher rank is superior to the junior?
> A. I know, sir, that he is of higher rank.
> Q. You know he is the superior officer within the meaning contemplated by the 64th Article of War?
> A. Not in every case. My answer would be, that is not an invariable assumption on my part. I believe, if I may explain that, by being superior in rank, there are some orders, we might say some courtesies, that might be due by a junior to a senior by reason of seniority, only I do not understand that such senior can issue orders conflicting with those of higher authority, no matter what the higher authority may be.

The trial ended on September 28. Denton, Keenan and Eckhardt were almost foolishly optimistic. "Well, we've certainly given them something to think about," Keenan said. "It ought to take them at least a good two to three hours."

Instead, it took only ten minutes. When the buzzer sounded indicating a verdict had been reached, Keenan slapped his knee in exultation. "Acquittal, by God!" he exclaimed.

Denton and his lawyers filed back into the trial room, where they confronted a grim-faced board of senior officers. "This doesn't look like acquittal to me," Denton said to himself. The verdict, quickly and sternly pronounced: guilty. The sentence: dismissal from the service, forfeiture of all pay and allowances, confinement at hard labor for twelve years.

Guards closed at once about the convicted Marion Denton. They led him back to his quarters, searched through all his possessions, and took him to the psychiatric ward of Santini Hospital at Mitchel Field. He was thrown into a stark, narrow, padded cell. Guards took away his money and possessions. "Watch out for suicide" was stamped on his chart.

Eckhardt, who had accompanied Denton, was so outraged that he wanted to make a violent protest, but Denton said mildly, "Well, you know, I don't want to get into any more trouble. So I guess I better do what they say." Eckhardt, who became Denton's life-long friend, recalled this scene for me long years later. "Can you imagine that?" he asked, marveling at Denton's composure. "With all the trouble he was in, he was still worried about getting into trouble."

Denton's first concern was for his wife, Caledia, who was at their home in Florida. "I hadn't told her anything about the court-martial," Marion said. "I was so certain that nothing could come of it that I hadn't wanted to worry her. But now I knew that she would have to be told."

Keenan and Eckhardt flew to Florida and broke the hard news to Mrs. Denton. An attractive and gracious woman, she bore the shock well and returned with them to Long Island. She was conducted to Denton's padded cell. Nearly twenty years later, the memory of that reunion overwhelmed Marion Denton. His voice broke, the tic in his cheek danced, his eyes watered, and he brushed his hand across his face in a self-conscious gesture. "That was quite an emotional scene," he said. "I remember one of the first things she said to me was, 'I know that, whatever happened, you didn't do anything wrong.' "

When Mrs. Denton carried word of her husband's plight back to Florida, trouble began to brew for the Army. Marion Denton was a well-respected businessman; he had some devoted and influential friends. One of them, James E. Williams, went to Washington and saw Senator Claude Pepper, a noted champion of the underdog. Pepper telephoned Eckhardt at Mitchel Field and asked for a transcript of the court-martial proceedings. Eckhardt didn't have one, so he telephoned Colonel Harmeling, the judge advocate.

Eckhardt later testified: "I immediately called Colonel Harmeling on the phone, and the colonel said something to the effect that 'he [Senator Pepper] is a civilian and we can't take orders from him.' But he talked on about it, and he talked about questioning the senator's authority for requesting the record. Finally, he said he would call me back and let me know."

A half-hour later, Colonel Harmeling changed his tune and informed Eckhardt that a copy of the record would be made available. Senator Pepper studied the record and filed a memorandum with the judge advocate's office denouncing the whole court-martial procedure. But even a U.S. senator couldn't make a dent in the rigid military minds, and General Cramer and his aides upheld the verdict they had helped to obtain. They did make some concessions, reducing Denton's twelve-year sentence to five, ordering his release from the psychiatric ward, and transferring him to Camp Upton.

The Army's troubles were only beginning. Denton's friends enlisted the aid of Representative Robert L. F. Sikes, of Florida, a member of the powerful House Military Affairs Committee, who, early in 1944, got the committee to authorize a full-scale investigation of Denton's case. Colonel Harmeling received a letter instructing him to send Major Denton to Washington to testify. "The colonel got on the telephone and started to raise hell with me," Eckhardt told me in 1963. "He told me about this letter he had from Congress that Denton was to come to Washington. 'They can go to hell down there,' he raged. 'Well, colonel,' I told him, 'I don't know very much about this—after all, I'm only a captain— but I don't think I would tell them that.' Harmeling roared, 'Well, I'm going to tell them that!'—and bang went the telephone."

This defiance of the House Military Affairs Committee was too brazen for even the authoritarian minds that had convicted Denton. The U.S. Military Establishment yielded, and Denton went to Washington, where he testified for two days.

The committee's investigation resulted in a scathing indictment of the military's conduct. It criticized Major Bosarge for ruling at the first pre-trial hearing that only he could see the documentary evidence. The Military Committee exposed the War Department's effort to cover up for Wimsatt by issuing that "amended" order that changed everything. It discovered that the phrase "by direction of the President" had been put in Denton's original order deliberately because someone had discovered belatedly that "an officer on the post [Wimsatt] ranked him." Denton had actually been sent to Greenland to replace Wimsatt; but, as the House committee pointed out, the order was ambiguous and nobody had thought to inform Wimsatt that he was being relieved.

In its severest blow, the committee found that in wartime the president had authority to issue an order without regard to the usual niceties of rank (after all, an officer named Eisenhower had been jumped over a lot of higher-ranking generals to exalted command); and the committee denounced the prosecution's statement, so wholeheartedly endorsed by the court-martial board, that "not even the President can do that."

The House committee found that the charges against Denton should never have been preferred; that the court-martial never should have been held; that the case represented "a serious miscarriage of justice."

But the Military Establishment felt that the members of the House committee were just a bunch of interfering civilians. What business did they have passing judgment? The brass would be damned if it was going to change the record, but it did decide to wash its hands of the troublesome Marion Denton. It transferred Denton to Atlantic City and then released him. But the court-martial verdict and the dishonorable discharge stood—and they still stood as if set in concrete when I talked to Denton in 1963.

The Army had tried to make a deal in October 1945, when the brass offered Marion a new commission as major, with the understanding that if he accepted he would be mustered out of service with an honorable discharge within a week. Recalling the offer, Denton shook his head in amazement and said with wry humor, "I guess I would have been the only major in history who would have been both dishonorably and honorably discharged."

Denton's family and some of his friends urged him to accept the offer, but to Denton "the big thing was that the court-martial verdict still stood. They weren't going to wipe that out." In other words, despite a presidential directive and the verdict of Congress, the principle would be engraved that rank must be upheld at all costs. There could not be, I thought, a clearer demonstration of uncontrolled authoritarianism.

Marion Denton rejected the Army's deal and spent thousands of dollars hiring lawyers and fighting a years-long battle in the attempt to wipe out the stain on his reputation. He fought his case in the U.S. Court of Claims, but the court refused to buck the military. He appealed to the U.S. Supreme Court, but the court refused to hear his case. Perhaps the court had weightier issues pending. But, I wondered, can the military consider itself beyond reproach? This was the issue that most troubled Adolph Eckhardt, who told me, "This whole case, as I see it, boils down to a simple question of presidential authority. Denton had a presidential order—no question about that. What is involved here is a challenge of the presidential authority by the military."

The challenge was still standing, the military still riding high in 1963, when *Saga* published my 10,000-word article. Al Silverman, then editor of *Saga*, made a sagacious move. He had copies of my article placed on the desks of every congressman and senator in Washington; he flooded the press of Florida with tear sheets. The explosion that followed rocked the Pentagon.

Most of Florida's press and public hadn't had any conception of Marion Denton's case and its dimensions until *Saga* hit the stands. The Auburndale *Star* said: "The story of Marion Denton's twenty-year battle with the high brass of the Pentagon hit Auburndale like an atomic blast." Irate citizens drafted a petition appealing to President John F. Kennedy to right the old wrong.

I don't know whether Kennedy made his displeasure known, but the fire was too hot for some high military britches. The military abruptly wiped out the record, credited Denton with his years of service, gave him his honorable discharge and allowed him to retire with his full rank, pay and privileges.

It was a complete vindication of Marion Denton, and I was elated. This one case may not prove that the pen is mightier than the sword, but the article I had written for *Saga* had accomplished something that not even Congress or the legal machinery of the nation could. And justice had been done at long last to a very deserving being.

19

The Ordeal of
Captain Kauffman

WHERE MARION DENTON'S CASE HAD EXPOSED THE STU-
pidity and viciousness of the military hierarchy, that of
Air Force Captain Joseph Patrick Kauffman was a spurious case much like the Remington and Hiss cases. Once more
I found the callous trampling of a defendant's rights: unremitting
third-degree questioning; official burglarizing of his home; the
taping of conversations with his counsel; reliance on the word of
an informer of dubious integrity.

Items about the case had appeared in the press, but I had paid
no attention until Carey McWilliams mentioned it to me in the
summer of 1963. Carey said that this might be another injustice
case and that Captain Kauffman's brother, who had changed his
name to Charles Keith, had the full transcript of the court-martial
trial and other records.

Keith conducted a real estate business from his basement
apartment-office on East 17th Street. Keith had been a Communist, but he had broken with the party years earlier, disillusioned, as many were, by the ruthless cruelties of the Stalin
regime. He had drifted into real estate, worked hard, prospered,
and no longer retained any of his former Communist connections.

I went to his apartment and he told me that his brother had
telephoned him on November 19, 1961.

"Pat told me that he had been arrested by the military and charged with having been a spy in Germany, that he had been taken into custody and that he was being subjected to incessant, third-degree-type questioning," Keith recalled. "He asked me to get him outside counsel."

Charlie Keith then loaded me with a mass of material, all the court-martial records, copies of legal motions, family memorabilia. I left with a bulging satchel.

As I waded through the material that Keith had given me, I began to develop a picture of the man I had never met, the man who was then in federal prison in Leavenworth, Kansas. There was a third brother, Michael Bernard Kauffman, of Salt Lake City, a department-store executive who was about to be promoted to major general in the Army Reserves.

Pat was born in Rutland, Vermont, August 10, 1918. His mother died while he was still an infant and his father abandoned the family and turned the boys over to a foundling home.

Young Pat Kauffman was passed from family to family, living in about fifteen different households. He started to work when he was ten and, as he later testified, had been working ever since. He attended a number of grade schools in New York City and State, and he had gone to Theodore Roosevelt High School in the Bronx. He never graduated from high school, but he managed to get himself accepted by the University of Wyoming, where he sometimes held six jobs at one time, existing on only three or four hours' sleep so that he could earn enough money for his college education.

He graduated from the University of Wyoming in June 1941 with a bachelor of science degree. U.S. Senator Joseph C. O'Mahoney, whom he had met while he was in college, got him a job with the Department of Agriculture in Washington, D.C. When the United States became involved in World War II, Pat Kauffman tried to enlist in the Navy but was rejected for deficient eyesight. In October 1942 the Army took him. He saw service in the Middle East and rose from private to commissioned officer. In 1945 he entered Officers Candidate School in medical administration in Carlisle, Pennsylvania, and in September 1946 returned to his job with the Department of Agriculture. When the Korean War broke out, he was recalled to service with his reserve unit. He had remained in the service ever since; had been promoted to captain in April 1953; had been awarded the Bronze Star, American Theatre; the World War II Victory Medal; the UN Service Medal and the Korean Service Medal.

I studied pictures of Captain Kauffman. He was forty-three in November 1961, when the Air Force charged him with espionage, but he looked much younger. He had close-cropped, jet black hair, parted on the left. His forehead was high, his eyes widely spaced. His face was long, yet with a hint of chubbiness about the cheeks; his mouth wide, with a downward droop at the corners that gave him at times a lugubrious look. His skin was clear and unmarred by lines.

What impressed me most were the Horatio Alger overtones in his life story. His career represented the kind of "Up from the Orphanage" success story that is a legend of the American dream. He had never been dismissed from a job; in fourteen years in military service he had never drawn a reprimand. The picture that emerged was of a man who was a workaholic; if anything, maybe too zealous.

These traits had caused minor trouble at the Elgin Air Force Base in Florida in 1956. Captain Kauffman had been sent there to work on a special project which was unfamiliar to him; and his own insecurity and obsession with detail had him in everyone's hair. He was haunted by a feeling of inefficiency; he was exercised by what he called the filthy conditions of the rest rooms; and he set out to change everything. His superior, not taking kindly to these endeavors, sent him to the base hospital for psychiatric examination.

The psychiatrist's report reflected the same man I had come to know from the records. The psychiatrist found that the captain had experienced "a great deal of trauma in his earlier life," and "while he feels he developed quite normally, he never had time to relate to other people in any close way." He had absorbed himself in his work and in one other overriding interest: he had always given of his time and money "to help support orphanages and homes of that nature" in the hope that other unfortunates might not have as hard a struggle as he had had.

Such was the man who was lounging in his cramped, three-room bungalow at 129½ Cedar Avenue, Atwater, California, on a night in November 1961. Three agents of the OSI (the Office

of Special Investigations, the investigative arm of the Air Force)
came gumshoeing out of the dark, snatched him from his home
and placed him under arrest. Why? Because an East German
secret service agent had defected to the West—and had come
bearing gifts.

We were to know this defector by name only—Guenter Karl
Maennel. Even when he testified at Captain Kauffman's court-
martial, he sported a disguise—false mustache, phony hairdo,
stage makeup, dark glasses; and his military mentors, enchanted
with their great spy case, threw a protective screen around him.
Only the most routine details slipped through this screen: Maennel was twenty-nine years old; he had been married for six years;
he did "not wish to talk about" his family; he did not know "at
the moment" where they were. He would be "sentenced to die"
if he ever had to return to East Berlin.

How had this good family man who did not even know where
his family was come to abandon them and defect to the West?
The best that I could learn from the record was that Maennel first
talked to an American officer about changing sides on May 30,
1961.

Q. Did you tell that official you would testify against Amer-
   icans if they pay you and protect you?
A. I did not say, "if you pay and protect me," but I said that
   I would have the opportunity to testify, and that I wanted
   to testify.
Q. And did you ask to be paid?
A. I did not ask to be paid.
Q. When were you first told that you would be paid?
A. On the 30th day of May.

So, a month later, on June 29, Maennel crossed over the border,
and on July 1, he went on Uncle Sam's payroll. He was paid about
$4.50 a day and furnished with clothing and allowances. Almost
at once, Guenter Maennel began to talk about spies. His most
sensational charge was that Captain Kauffman visited East Berlin
in late September–early October 1960 and had supplied Soviet-
bloc agents with military information and entered into a solemn
pact to conduct espionage for them.

Maennel's path and Captain Kauffman's had crossed by the
merest mischance. In September 1960 Kauffman had been wind-

ing up a one-year tour of duty at the Sondre Strom Air Base in
Greenland. The installation itself, probably one of the least secret
of America's overseas bases, was used as an emergency landing
field for the Military Air Transport Service and as a commercial
stop for the Scandinavian Airlines System. There were no security
regulations in force at the base, and Danish personnel, both those
stationed permanently at Sondre Strom and airlines personnel
flying in and out, were free to use all the buildings and facilities.

Captain Kauffman's next assignment was to the Castle Air Force
Base in Merced, California, but he had a leave to enjoy before
reporting and he decided to see something of Europe. He struck
up an acquaintance with Peter Borck, a guard at the Tomb of the
Unknown Soldier in Washington, and they did Paris together.
The queen city of France was crawling with tourists, however,
and Borck suggested they go to Hamburg, where he had relatives.
They toured Hamburg for four days, and then Captain Kauffman
decided that since he was so close to Berlin, he would go on and
see the former capital of Germany. On September 28 he purchased a train ticket to West Berlin. What he didn't know (and
no one told him) was that American military personnel were not
supposed to travel through the Russian-held East German cor-
ridor by train. At the first checkpoint, three East German policemen spotted Captain Kauffman and hustled him off the train.

He was held prisoner for nearly two days. A Soviet intelligence
officer tried to browbeat him for information; they got into a
shouting match (even Maennel confirmed this), and the Soviet
officer and his interpreter finally stormed out. They were followed
by two polite and considerate individuals. It was the old police
game: first the tough guy browbeats the victim, then his counterpart comes on the scene, exuding sympathy and offering to do
anything he can to help the prisoner. One of these sympathetic
interrogators was Maennel.

The kindly Maennel and his kindly partner seemed to have just
one object: to help Captain Kauffman, to release him—but first
he would have to sign a paper saying he had not been badly
treated. He would not be released unless he signed, they said—
so he signed. His former captors offered to show Captain Kauffman the sights of the capital if he'd accompany them to East
Berlin. As a condition of his release, the captain agreed, and
during the next two days, Maennel and his partner took him to
restaurants and nightclubs, showed him the site of the Hitler

bunker and other places of interest. On the final day of his stay Captain Kauffman learned that his guides were agents of the East German secret service trying to induce him to become a spy.

He beat it out of Berlin fast, with no further contact with the secret agents. He supplied no information (even Maennel was later to confirm this); but he realized that his superiors might view his version of this entanglement with suspicion. When he completed his travel form, he omitted Berlin. Months passed, nothing happened, and Captain Kauffman ceased to worry. He did not know that in Germany Guenter Maennel had switched sides.

The Air Force now began to hatch its own authoritarian plot against Captain Kauffman. The responsibility for their crusade could never be established, but it is obvious from the record that someone in the Pentagon had determined, on nothing more than Maennel's dubious word, to get Captain Kauffman.

In early November 1961 the captain received orders detaching him from Castle Field and sending him off on a two-week special assignment to Travis Air Force Base in Southern California. It was a ruse to enable military secret service agents, scrapping the Bill of Rights, to burglarize his home.

At 1 A.M. on November 8, 1961, three figures left a parked car and approached the locked, three-room bungalow. The leader— later identified in court-martial testimony as Lieutenant Colonel Raymond E. White, of the OSI—jimmied a window and crawled through, illuminating his way with the tiny beam of a pinpoint flashlight. Two other OSI agents squirmed after him. They searched the cramped quarters for hours; then they departed before dawn caught up with them.

They returned the next night, and the night after that. On each of these forays, they were led by the window-jimmying Colonel White; each time they spent two to three hours searching and then decamped. Some eight or nine hours were spent in these three illegal searches, a persistent and determined effort that proved fruitless. All evidentiary discoveries were made in a later— and "legal"—search.

Unaware of those who had been so active behind his back, Captain Kauffman returned from his phony assignment and settled down in his home. He had hardly made himself comfortable when the OSI agents came knocking at his door, spirited him away and questioned him all night. Captain Kauffman tried to explain to them exactly what had happened. The OSI agents just looked at him owlishly, obviously unsatisfied.

"But that was all there was to it," Captain Kauffman protested again and again. "There was really nothing to it, see?"

The OSI agents, knowing they had that invaluable defector in Germany, didn't see. They took the Captain to Castle Field, and the inquisition began in earnest. The questioning went on for days: the agents worked on Captain Kauffman in relays, alternating syrupy sympathy with brutal browbeating. Finally, Captain Kauffman, badgered, worn-out and infuriated, was driven to shout, "Let me out of here. I want to get a lawyer."

They would not let him go, of course, but they did have to honor his request for a lawyer. So Captain Kauffman made the telephone call to Charlie Keith.

Keith telephoned Benjamin Dreyfus, of the law firm of Gary, Dreyfus and McTernan, in San Francisco and Dreyfus agreed to represent Pat Kauffman.

The lawyer went to see his client, then being held in a room of the hospital at the Castle Air Force base. No formal charges had been preferred, but the OSI agents were harassing Captain Kauffman with daily rounds of questioning. Dreyfus instructed the captain not to answer questions, but no sooner had he left the base than the OSI agents resumed their interrogation in their effort to "break" him.

The following day, November 20, Dreyfus formally recorded himself with the Judge Advocate's Office as Pat's counsel, and he made a formal request that all questioning cease unless Pat's counsel was present. This, unquestionably, is another fundamental American right, but the OSI continued the remorseless inquisition.

On November 22 the OSI (Joe McCarthy would have been proud) really put the heat on Pat to get him to discharge his counsel. An OSI agent denounced Dreyfus, identifying him as president of the National Lawyers Guild, which the government had labeled a "Red" front and "the main bulwark of the Communist Party." If Pat continued to retain Dreyfus, he was told, the fact would be used against him at his trial; connection with such a man was virtual "proof" of Pat's guilt. In addition, Dreyfus's retention would be used by the government to make life difficult for Pat's brothers, Mike Kauffman and Charlie Keith.

This threat of retribution against innocent men reminded me of the tactics of Hitler, Stalin and other dictators. I wondered whether despite all the Fourth of July oratory those in power really cared about the Constitution and its guarantees of individual liberty. Pat Kauffman was similarly worried. He knew that his brother Mike could be made a scapegoat with his promotion at stake. Kauffman telephoned Charlie Keith again and urged him to fly to California. Keith took a plane the same night and landed in San Francisco on November 24.

Keith and Dreyfus talked. Dreyfus was, indeed, the president of the National Lawyers Guild and had represented many alleged Communists and sympathizers in civil rights cases on the West Coast. But there was not a shred of evidence to justify the OSI aspersions about him. His actions were consistently those of a lawyer trying to do the best for his clients.

After their conference, Dreyfus and Keith telephoned Colonel Leonard S. Dysinger, the commander at Castle, to make arrangements to see Pat, and this set off a new chain of events. Officials decided to file formal charges. They accused Captain Kauffman of conspiring with Maennel and others to commit espionage by passing along military information that would be injurious to the United States.

Dreyfus and Keith met with Pat, then called at headquarters. They were told that an investigating officer would be appointed by March Air Force Base and that a pre-trial hearing would probably begin on Tuesday, November 28. Dreyfus repeated his request that OSI agents stop their interrogation of Captain Kauffman. The OSI agents ignored this request and resumed their badgering the very next day.

This remorseless grilling was bad enough; worse was the fact that everything said in Captain Kauffman's hospital room was being preserved on tape. Conversations with his brothers and his attorney were taped—even his sneezes were recorded. OSI witnesses insisted at the court-martial that they hadn't violated his rights because they hadn't *tapped* his telephone; they had merely *tapped* his side of his conversations with his lawyer. Repeatedly, Captain Kauffman asked his interrogators whether their conversations were being recorded and they assured him, on their solemn word of honor as officers and gentlemen, that they were not.

"It's funny to listen to some of the tapes," Charlie Keith said to me later. "There they are pledging Pat on their honor that they aren't recording what is being said—and even the pledge as they gave it was being recorded."

November 28, Dreyfus and Keith had been told, was the day an investigating officer would be appointed. The day arrived and nothing happened. Dreyfus spent two days trying to contact Lieutenant Colonel John C. Chew, the judge advocate at Castle Field, and was finally told that March Field was going to name a senior officer to handle the preliminary hearing. Dreyfus was assured that he would be kept up to date.

Days passed, and no notification came. Then, on December 6, additional charges were filed against Captain Kauffman. Besides the original conspiracy charge, he was accused of traveling to Berlin without proper orders and failing to report his visit to his superior officers; of agreeing to commit espionage and to return to East Germany in 1963; and of actually transmitting to Guenter Maennel information "relating to the defense of the United States."

The following day, on an affidavit furnished by Paul W. Reed, the OSI agent who had taken the statements from Maennel, a "legal" search warrant was obtained permitting the OSI to search Captain Kauffman's much-searched home; and on December 8, a U.S. marshal, the window-jimmying Colonel White, Reed and other OSI agents ransacked the house by daylight. And they found—surprise, surprise!—a number of items they had had no idea existed, this on their word of honor as officers and gentlemen.

On this same eventful day, Captain Kauffman received another shocker: he was not going to be permitted to stand trial in the United States; he was going to be shanghaied to Germany to stand trial before a military court.

This meant that he would be separated from his brother and his attorney. And what's worse, if he had been held in this country on espionage charges, he would have stood trial in civilian court, but once he was in the hands of the military abroad he would be tried in a court-martial. In other words, the Military Establishment was insuring that they could obtain a conviction on the case they had brought up.

After he was informed of the hoodwinking, Dreyfus dispatched a sizzling protest to both Dysinger and Chew, but he was ignored again. The case had been taken out of the hands of Colonel Dysinger, he was told; "somebody up there" in the Air Force was calling the shots. So, on December 12, Captain Kauffman was flown under guard to face his next ordeal in Germany.

His brothers determined that he should have the best possible defense counsel, even though it strained all their resources. They sought out George W. Latimer, a former Utah Supreme Court Justice who had a distinguished reputation in Utah as a jurist and a former judge of the Court of Military Appeals. He agreed to represent Pat Kauffman. Dreyfus bowed out with characteristic grace, accepting the logic that impelled the move.

Almost as soon as Latimer took the case, the Air Force resorted to more cheap tactics. The Air Force planted a teaser in a Washington column on December 15, 1961, with an ambiguous reference to an Air Force captain who had been transferred to Germany in connection with a security investigation. This gossip item naturally spurred inquiries by the press, and the Air Force responded as the poor, helpless source yielding to reporters' importunities. On December 21, it spelled out the case against Captain Kauffman, and headlines hit across the nation. The public had a new spy sensation to savor.

Keith was still enraged about this development when I talked to him years later. He showed me a copy of a letter he had written to his brother Michael at the time: "The release of this material by the Air Force to the press is particularly dirty pool. When I was in California, the Base Judge Advocate made a very special point of asking Dreyfus that there be no publicity, for 'Pat's protection,' from our side . . . assuring us that from the Air Force side not only did they not want publicity but that they were prohibited from making the matter public, since all such stuff is 'restricted' until the conclusion of the case."

This "restriction" was apparently less than ironclad.

The pre-trial hearing and court-martial in Germany were hocus-pocus in gold braid. The Air Force began by insisting that agent Reed, Maennel's control officer, be present in the courtroom when Maennel testified. Latimer managed to have Reed barred. But Maennel appeared under heavy guard, as if the fate of the nation were at stake, wearing false face, phony mustache, weird hairdo and dark glasses. He had made two statements to OSI agent Reed, and he testified at both the pre-trial hearing and the court-martial. In his pre-trial testimony, he described how a So-

viet agent had tried to question Captain Kauffman, aided by a
woman interpreter. Maennel had heard "loud voices above me
coming from the room where the interrogation was taking place."
After an hour, the Soviet agent stormed out; and when Maennel
asked the interpreter why the voices had been so loud, she said,
"Those two are enemies." In his later court-martial testimony,
Maennel made no mention of this revealing quote and softened
his testimony by saying only that he had heard loud voices.

When Maennel himself took over the questioning of Captain
Kauffman, he testified that he had persuaded the captain to sign
an affidavit giving some information. Did he have a copy of the
document? Unfortunately, no. How valuable had the alleged information been? Maennel admitted that his Soviet liaison officer
had told him that the information he had received "was not of
much importance."

Major Baumgarner, Staff Judge Advocate, tried to rescue the
great spy case by asking Maennel if he could recall the answers
Kauffman had given to his questions. Maennel: "That is very
difficult now to repeat the answers entirely, after such a long
time." (The time lapse was from October 1960 to January 1962,
with many refresher recitals to agent Reed during the period.)

In his cross-examination Latimer tried to pin Maennel down.
Q. "Did Captain Kauffman furnish you with any information of a
political nature that was of any value to you?" A. "No." Well,
then, Latimer wanted to know, just what did Captain Kauffman
divulge? Maennel said the captain had talked about his colonel
in Greenland. Q. "What did he tell you?" A. "The question is
very difficult for me to answer." Q. "All right. Don't answer it.
Why is it difficult?" A. "First of all because it is that long ago
already. [October 1960 to January 1962 again] And to the other,
I did not try to retain all these things in my memory."

Latimer pressed on. Had the information Captain Kauffman
given been important enough to remember? "Yes," said Maennel,
but unfortunately he had not remembered it. Had Kauffman told
him anything about installations in Japan? "Today I can't give any
details any more," said Maennel. Q. "Do you remember any
military information given by Captain Kauffman?" A. "Very
dimly . . ."

As one can readily see, the national security of the United States
was at stake here.

By the time he had to testify at the court-martial, Maennel

replaced his vague statements with explicit ones. He contradicted his previous testimony, and his memory seemed to have miraculously revived. He recalled that Kauffman had told him the jet fighters stationed in Greenland were not the latest models, were small and of medium range; Kauffman had told him how many there were, "but it would be hard for me to recall precisely now"; and there were about a thousand American troops in Greenland.

OSI agent Reed testified he had discussed the case with Maennel some "fifteen or twenty times" for as long as half a day at a time. He had talked with Maennel for eight or nine days before the informer made his first statement; after getting it, Reed testified, there were another "eight or nine days" of discussions when Maennel gave Reed additional information for his second statement. As in the case of Whittaker Chambers and the FBI, this seems to have been a well-rehearsed scenario and Maennel's first story should have been complete and accurate. On the fourth go-round, when Maennel was testifying at the court-martial, he testified that he had talked to Reed only three times—and for brief interviews that had lasted for only "two to four hours." It became obvious that this star witness could not get his story straight.

For example, Maennel had first testified that he and his co-agent led Kauffman to believe that they were just ordinary policemen until their final meeting when they disclosed their secret agent status. He had described Kauffman as being startled and exclaiming, "My God! I might have thought so." But at the court-martial Maennel insisted that the two agents had disclosed their true status to the captain the second time they met and that Kauffman had knowingly gone along with their plans.

The prosecution's problems multiplied when Maennel said that he had wanted Kauffman to sign a spy contract but the captain had refused. However, Maennel said, they had shaken hands and agreed that Kauffman was to return to East Berlin in three years and disclose all he had learned in the meantime. Maennel said he had also taken the captain's notebook and had written down the name of Klara Weiss, a woman who lived in West Berlin. This, he said, was a "cover address" through which Kauffman could keep in touch. The trouble was, as Maennel had to admit, Klara Weiss, age eighty-four, had never been informed about the role she was supposed to play. OSI agents, who tracked her down, also had to admit that she knew nothing, had never received any mail from America, had never communicated with any secret agent in West Germany. What an espionage conduit!

When the cross-examination had Maennel wobbling, Latimer noticed that a man in the courtroom was making signals to the witness. During a recess, he protested to Colonel James S. Cheney, the Law Officer, or presiding judge. Prosecutors admitted the signaling but argued that it didn't mean a thing. They said they had been afraid that the questioning might get into vital national security areas, and so OSI agent Douglas Smith had been stationed with instructions to signal by removing his pocket handkerchief as a warning—but this had had nothing to do with the witness's testimony. Latimer was outraged. "I don't care if trial counsel can't run his case without signals from spectators," he said, "because then I don't know how an accused can get a fair trial. In this case, I think he has been denied one, fundamentally and substantially."

The Law Officer overruled the defense, and the trial continued—but with "Mr. Smith" banished from the courtroom.

Maennel contended that he had had a document signed by Captain Kauffman and some other documentary evidence in his East Berlin office. He had known for a month in advance that he was going to defect to the West; he had known he was going to inform about Kauffman—indeed, he had begun talking about Kauffman on the very day he arrived. Yet—

> Q. You have no written evidence of any kind to corroborate what you say on the witness stand?
> A. No.
> Q. You didn't bring any of those documents with you?
> A. No.

In other words, this whole case rested solely on Maennel's changing and uncertain words.

Another courtroom battle erupted over the final OSI entry into Captain Kauffman's house. Agent Reed testified that, in those "fourteen to fifteen" half-day sessions with Maennel that Maennel denied, he had obtained all the information necessary for the search warrant. He had had no help—heavens, no—from Colonel White, though as soon as they entered the house for their "legal" search, White discovered the evidence lying almost in front of them in the top drawer of Kauffman's dresser. This evidence consisted of a loose-leaf notebook with Klara Weiss's name written on it, a Berlin hotel bill receipt and the railroad ticket stub for Kauffman's trip from Hamburg to Berlin.

When Captain Kauffman took the stand in his own defense, the change in his appearance was startling. It looked as if he had aged more than a decade in a few months. The once glossy black hair was turning white, the youthful face was drawn and haggard, with deep-slashing lines running downward from the corners of nose and mouth.

On the witness stand he told the same story he had always told: the chance mistake that had put him on the train to Berlin; his angry shouting match with the Soviet officer; the denial that he had given anyone any national security information; his naive belief that Maennel and his companion were just two local police officers trying to make amends for his treatment—and his panicked haste to get away the instant he learned they were really secret agents.

In cross-examination, the Air Force prosecutor went for the jugular, trying in the most obvious way to smear Captain Kauffman because his brother, Charles Keith, had once been a Communist. He asked "how many years" Captain Kauffman had lived with Keith; the answer, "I didn't live with him for years—probably a matter of six or seven months." The hound dogs of the prosecution were sniffing on a hot trail. Who was the beneficiary of Kauffman's estate in the event of his death?

A. I'll answer the question this way, Colonel Morgan—
Q. Just a moment, Captain Kauffman, I want you to answer—
A. Would you not give me a chance to—
Q. I want you to answer the question, not some other question. . . . Do you want the question repeated?
A. No, my brother Charles is indicated as the beneficiary for my insurance. Now, may I continue?
Law Officer: You may explain that answer.
A. My brother also has a copy of my will, in which all of my possessions, including insurance, is left to the University of Wyoming to establish a trust fund for deserving individuals, so that they can continue their education and not go through what I had to go through working through college. Now, this can be confirmed, too.

The prosecution's McCarthyite tactic had backfired, and Colo-

nel Morgan dropped the subject like someone who had suddenly
noticed he was juggling a hand grenade.

In his summation Latimer tore Maennel's vague account to
shreds. He held up a map that the New York *Times* had printed
showing the precise location of American bases in Greenland and
giving the number of troops stationed there as 6000, not the 1000
Maennel had mentioned. Latimer acknowledged that Captain
Kauffman had been stupid to let himself be hoodwinked by Maennel and his partner, but he contrasted Kauffman's long spotless
career with the record of Maennel:

"We have a traitor, a deserter, a man that has sold out and
comes here in disguise and the trappings of a Hollywood actor.
And he comes in and gives us an oath, and we have the prosecution
insisting he is an honorable man because he tells the truth. Well,
I think maybe we had better give a little bit advantage to the
American officer. At least I have one that's not an admitted spy;
not an admitted Communist."

Latimer asked the court-martial board to weigh the characters
of the two men and decide. The board did. It abandoned the
American officer but honored the informer who delivered the
tales of treachery and subversion someone was panting to hear.
The court convicted Captain Kauffman on all four counts and
sentenced him to twenty years in prison.

Appeals from this verdict were getting nowhere when I wrote
my article for *The Nation*. I wrote:

> The ordeal of Captain Kauffman goes on. Probably no other
> case of our times has exposed such a range of callous disregard
> of the rights of the individual: illegal search; third-degree
> questioning in the absence of counsel and in defiance of
> counsel's request; the taping of at least one end of privileged
> conversations between the accused and his counsel; the spir-
> iting of the prisoner abroad to deprive him of a fair trial; the
> court-martial in an atmosphere loaded with the phony, ultra-
> security trappings of the totalitarian state; the exchange of
> signals in the courtroom while the accusing witness was on
> the stand, making a travesty of the most elementary processes
> of justice. Look well at that catalogue. The deeds in this
> unrelieved sequence are completely incompatible with the
> ideals of American democracy, with its primary emphasis
> upon the protection and liberty of the individual.

Carey McWilliams had an editor's nightmare trying to find space for the exceptionally long article I had written, but he finally published it in the issue of September 14, 1963, under the title "The Ordeal of Captain Kauffman." It was the lead article in the magazine, and I was proud of it. And it was the last I ever expected to hear of it.

Then, just two days before Christmas, I received an astounding phone call from Charles Keith. "Fred," he said, "I have someone here who would like to talk to you."

"Fred," another man said, "this is Captain Kauffman."

"Captain Kauffman!" I exclaimed in complete surprise. "But—but where are you? I thought you were in prison."

"I'm here in New York visiting Charlie," he said. "I've been released."

"You mean you're free?"

"Yes," he said. "Fred, you will never know what that *Nation* article did for me. I had been having a pretty rough time, but as soon as that magazine article hit the prison, the whole attitude toward me changed. It was amazing."

The ripple effect had gone all the way up to the highest echelons of the Pentagon, he said. He had been taken from Leavenworth and flown to Washington, where he had been conducted to the office of an assistant secretary of the Air Force. He told me: "The Secretary kept pounding his desk and demanding that I confess. 'We know you were a spy,' he said. 'We *know* that! Why don't you be a man and admit it?' "

Kauffman laughed. "I kept telling him what I had told them all along—that I had never been a spy, that I was innocent and I thought they knew it. But the Secretary just kept pounding his desk and demanding what he called 'the truth' from me. It was quite a scene."

Captain Kauffman had continued to insist on his innocence. "And so, finally," he said, "they let me go."

"You mean you're a completely free man now?"

"Yes," he said. "Of course, my Air Force career is ended, but I'm out of prison and free for good, thanks to you."

That Christmas I received the greatest gift a writer can be given: the satisfaction of freeing an innocent man from prison.

20

CIA, FBI, and
the Military-Industrial
Complex

T HE INJUSTICES BROUGHT ABOUT BY AUTHORITARIANISM
in American society in the 1950s and 1960s were not limited
to individual cases. There were some far-ranging effects,
as well. The FBI, the CIA and the Pentagon grew in importance
in both formulating policy and arousing public support for the
government. The little catlike steps the United States took on its
way into the Vietnam War illustrated the inevitable hazards of
this process.

In the 1960s I wrote exposés of all three of these mighty national
institutions. Looking back now, I think I am justified in taking
some pride in those unpopular endeavors; for, though I only lifted
the lid on certain situations, subsequent events have proved how
right those early perceptions were.

My first target was J. Edgar Hoover and the FBI. My discoveries in the Hiss and Remington cases impelled me to take a
deeper look at this holiest of holies, first in "The FBI" in *The
Nation* in 1958 and later in the book *The FBI Nobody Knows*,
published in 1964. The title was more perspicacious than I realized
at the time; for, though I shredded many popular myths about
Hoover and his bureau, official investigations in the early 1970s
further demolished the untouchable image.

At the time I was investigating the FBI, J. Edgar Hoover was perceived as a law enforcement genius, a man of impeccable rectitude and impartiality, the supreme crime-fighter who had molded his agency into the super-perfect nemesis of crime.

The FBI, boasting (incorrectly) a 97 percent conviction record, had compiled seemingly impressive statistics by pursuing the stumblebums of crime, not the dark rulers of the underworld. It rode to glory by shooting down bank robbers like John Dillinger, and tracking down kidnappers and car thieves. Hoover annually snowed Congressional committees (composed almost exclusively of his partisans willing to be snowed) with figures showing the immense amounts of stolen goods the FBI had recovered. These statistics were always inflated by a factor that Hoover consistently omitted—that a lot of this recovered loot for which he took full credit had really been located by local or private forces working in conjunction with the FBI.

Hoover and his Bureau ignored the menace of organized crime, virtually denying that it even existed. He kept insisting that there was no such organization as the Mafia. And, if there was, it didn't fall in his interstate province but was a matter for local and state police departments.

Even after the great Appalachian conclave of more than one hundred underworld chieftains in 1957, Hoover hewed to the same obstinate line. He had the Bureau re-examine its position, a study which produced a huge, two-volume analysis. One high federal prosecutor who by mischance got a peep at it had it snatched out of his hands before he could determine whether Hoover and the Bureau had finally recognized reality. The evidence seemed to indicate that they had not, because, even in the early 1960s, Hoover used all of his prestige and exerted all of his pressure to discredit leaders of the International Association of Police Chiefs, who were calling for an all-out attack on organized crime.*

---

* The FBI did not change its attitude until after the Kennedy Administration took office. Attorney General Robert F. Kennedy made organized crime a topmost priority and forced Hoover to get into the battle. Hoover perforce began widescale bugging and tapping of mobsters in a hurried effort to catch up, but his heart was not wholly in the battle. When the FBI launched a massive drive against the five major families in New York in summer 1983, Kenneth P. Walton, deputy assistant director of the New York Bureau, told the New York *Times* (August 31, 1983): "We realized that we had to take a different approach [by infiltrating the crime families] because of the enormous strength of organized crime in this area. I candidly believe the end result will be devastating for the five families, but it also raises questions about what the FBI had been doing for sixty years. I don't have an answer to that."

Hoover's record on civil rights was equally bad. His FBI was composed almost exclusively of white Anglo-Saxon conservatives, many of them agents from the South; and its policy for years had been to milk local police forces for all the information it could get—a practice that necessitated adherence to the good-old-boy buddy system. Consequently, many FBI agents were bosom pals of some of the most racist police forces in the nation, and although the FBI investigated 461 cases of police brutality against blacks in the South between January 1, 1958, and June 30, 1960, not one resulted in a conviction. There had been forty bombings of Birmingham, Alabama, homes and churches since 1947, but not a single arrest had been made until the final atrocity on September 15, 1963, killed four little girls who had just attended Sunday school in a Birmingham church.

This racial bias accorded perfectly with Hoover's police-state mentality. He kept dossiers on everyone. A newspaper colleague of mine told me of a friend of his who had been interviewing one of Hoover's top aides. The FBI official asked the reporter whether he knew anyone in the newspaper business in the South who might be able to give the Bureau a line on what was happening. The newsman recalled the name of a reporter on a small weekly newspaper in a Podunk town in Georgia; and to his astonishment, Hoover's aide pressed a button and asked for the file of the man in question. The shocked newsman told my friend, "My God, if they've got a file on that fellow, they must have dossiers on *all of us!*"

All evidence indicated that they did. Every liberal senator or congressman felt certain that Hoover had compiled a file on him or her; and the fear of how the wild gossip in those files might be leaked served as a chilling deterrent to any legislator reckless enough to challenge the FBI. The record showed that the few who had ventured on such a course had had their political careers terminated by scurrilous leaks from those FBI files.

When I wrote *The FBI Nobody Knows*, I got a rare inside look from Jack Levine, a young New Yorker who had gone through FBI training and worked as an agent—and then quit in disgust. Levine said that new agents were brainwashed from the beginning of their training by FBI instructors peddling the most arrant Radical Right propaganda. Harvard and Yale "pseudo-intellects" were derided; the trainees were told that "they have more Communists in Harvard Yard than you can shake a stick at." One Bureau official commented that it was fortunate Adlai Stevenson did not get the 1960 Democratic presidential nomination because his close supporters and advisers were Communists. Communists were everywhere: the National Association for the Advancement of Colored People was a Communist front; so was the American Civil Liberties Union; so were many of the nation's leading newspapers— the Washington *Post*, the New York *Times*, the Denver *Post*, and the St. Louis *Post-Dispatch*: even the U.S. Supreme Court was Communist-tainted. Rabid rightists were trying to impeach Chief Justice Earl Warren, and a Bureau official told the new trainees that "the Director is very much in favor of this movement and that the Director feels that this country would be a lot better off without Communist sympathizers on the Court."

The picture that I developed was of a ruthless man wielding such overwhelming power that he reigned unchecked by Congresses and presidents. He was as irresponsible as Joe McCarthy, whom he publicly admitted he liked and defended, but he was more secretive. He popularized phrases like "pseudo-liberal" and "fellow traveler" and "parlor pinko." His faith in informers was complete and unalterable. He testified before one Congressional committee that the FBI had always found Elizabeth Bentley completely reliable. Yet some of Bentley's tales of espionage and subversion had been so wild that they had been demonstrably false at first glance—for instance, her assertion that she had given the Russians well in advance the exact date of the D-Day invasion of Normandy. Not even General Eisenhower could have done that, for the invasion date depended on the weather; and, as Eisenhower revealed in *Crusade in Europe*, the originally scheduled date had had to be postponed for twenty-four hours because of storms over the Atlantic. Yet no brain on any Congressional committee was alert enough, or conscientious enough, to question either Elizabeth Bentley or Hoover about her preposterous claim. The result was the wholesale brainwashing of the public mind with horrifying tales of espionage and subversion, all under the imprimatur of the one infallible man who was pictured as the guardian of all American liberties.

A society cannot be free when debate about vital issues is inhibited, as it was, by the dark shadow of police-state intimidation. Fortunately, since Hoover's death and the devastating exposures of the conduct of our super-secret agencies in the official probes of the 1970s, important changes have been made in the administration of the FBI. The Bureau's current drive against powerful crime families, for instance, is just one illustration of the change for the better.

During 1961, I compounded all of my previous offenses by writing for *The Nation* two full-issue articles that exposed the other grim complexes of our time: the CIA and the military-industrial complex. I had no personal insights into the structure and maneuvers of the CIA, but George Kirstein, the publisher of *The Nation*, filled this gap. On a trip to the South Pacific in winter 1961, George had encountered a number of foreign correspondents who had had close contact with CIA agents; and over some elbow-bending exercises at various bars, they had filled him in about some of our devious maneuvers in Southeast Asia. George came back convinced that we should devote a full issue of *The Nation* to an exposé of the CIA.

Carey McWilliams was just as enthusiastic, but he was cautious. He set rigid guidelines for me: I was not to conduct any interviews of my own; I was not to try to dig up anything new about the Agency. I was merely to collate everything that had been published, everything already in the public domain, pull it all together and present a focused picture, something no one had done up to that time.

It says a lot about the climate that Carey McWilliams, courageous editor that he was, had to be deathly afraid that if I should inadvertently disclose some CIA "secret," the power complex would be only too happy to try to put *The Nation* out of business.

Fortunately, a mass of material was available from scattered sources about the workings of our super-secret cloak-and-dagger agency. A great boon to the researcher was CIA Director Allen Dulles, who had not been able to resist bragging, and the medium he had chosen (though, of course, he had not been quoted directly) had usually been a multi-part series of articles in *The Saturday Evening Post*. Foreign correspondents on the scene in Laos, Iran and other trouble spots had written some detailed accounts of what they had observed and learned; and Senate and House committees had poked sporadically and gingerly into some CIA activities.

Carey had carefully preserved a letter to *The Nation* dated December 5, 1957, from an intelligence officer, who wrote: "As an American intelligence officer, I feel duty bound to state my apprehensions as to the future of my country." The writer was, he said, concerned about the mortal damage America was inflicting upon itself via the interlocking power and misconceptions of two men: John Foster Dulles, then Eisenhower's secretary of state, and his younger brother, Allen Welsh Dulles, director of the CIA. America was being pushed along the road to foreign policy disaster, he wrote, by the closed minds of the Dulles brothers and their insistence on torturing facts to fit the requirements of predetermined policies. This four-year-old letter read like the most perceptive of prophecies at the time, for this was the spring of the Bay of Pigs, that misconceived and ineptly executed adventure into which the CIA had dragged the new Kennedy Administration.

Quotes from this 1957 letter struck me with special force:

The following circumstances are cause for deep concern:
1. United States foreign policy is not formulated on the basis of an objective study of facts, particularly those made available by the Intelligence Service, but is being determined by John Foster Dulles' personal rash conceptions.
2. The fact that Allen Dulles is in charge of collection and evaluation of all information makes it possible for the Secretary of State to distort the information received as he sees fit. Facts thus presented disorientate not only the President and Congress but also the people of the United States.
3. As a consequence, our foreign policy is not based on the real interests of the United States. It has suffered one defeat after another and may eventually draw us into a nuclear war.

The Central Intelligence Agency was created in 1947, its assigned task to upgrade United States foreign intelligence activities. But it quickly developed a "dirty tricks" side in which intelligence gathering became subordinated to aggressive activism, all shrouded in the utmost secrecy. The CIA had a colossal budget, but no one knew the exact amount because its funds were concealed in a number of appropriations for different departments. The so-called oversight committees of Congress were snoozing watchdogs, told only as much as the CIA wanted them to know; and even within the Agency itself, secrecy was carried to such an extreme that one project worker could be ignorant of what was going on in the next office—even at the next desk. In other words, the Agency became a cloak-and-dagger bureaucracy, a beehive with secret cells. The danger that such cells could run amok was implicit in such a structure.*

My research soon uncovered some gems of foreign policy idiocy along the lines described by the intelligence officer who wrote to *The Nation.* Such as:

• Laos—This peaceful interior section of Indochina, 99 percent agricultural, was damaged when the CIA smothered a barter economy with $310 million in "aid," which led to ruinous inflation and such corruption that the Communists won control of the government. The CIA's answer was an attempted military coup, but its figurehead general was more interested in dipping his hands in the till than fighting—resulting in a takeover by the Communist Pathet Lao of a nation that could otherwise have remained neutral.

• Burma—The Dulles brothers' favorite fantasy was that Chiang Kai-shek, who hadn't been able to hold China despite billions of dollars in American aid and military equipment, would somehow lead a successful invasion of the mainland from his island base of Formosa (now called Taiwan). When a contingent of Chiang's soldiers fled to Burma, the CIA supplied them with arms and other aid in the hope they would fight the Communists; but all these noble warriors wanted to do was to hunker down in the poppy fields and grow opium. These hopheads became such a nuisance that Burmese troops had to drive them out.

• Iran—This was one of Allen Dulles's proudest achievements. Mohammed Mossadegh, himself a wealthy landowner, became premier and capitalized on a strong nationalistic sentiment to appropriate the holdings of British-owned Anglo-Iranian Oil Co. Western financial interests boycotted Iran, a move that threatened

---

* This did indeed happen later in the 1960s, when the CIA formed a partnership with the Mafia in an attempt to liquidate Fidel Castro, plots that were first unknown to the FBI and to Attorney General Robert F. Kennedy. Considerable testimony in the investigations of the 1970s indicated that the CIA persisted in some of this activity even after it was supposed to have been halted.

to wreck the Iranian economy. Mossadegh indicated he might
have to turn to Russia for help. Allen Dulles reacted by master-
minding an intricate 1953 plot that overthrew Mossadegh and
placed Shah Mohammed Reza Pahlavi on the throne of Iran. The
U.S. thought the Shah would be "our" strong man in the Mid
East, but his lavish personal expenditures, the brutalities of his
secret police force, the corruption of his government and the
unrelieved poverty of his people combined to foster a growing
anti-American sentiment in Iran that led eventually to the Shah's
downfall.
• Guatemala—In 1954, the electorate chose Jacobo Arbenz Guz-
mán, whom the Dulles brothers saw as a Communist. In fact he
was sufficiently leftist to threaten the holdings of large landowners
as well as the imperial interests of United Fruit and other large
American corporations. Dulles initiated a coup, toppling Arbenz
and imposing a brutal militaristic regime on Guatemala.
• The U-2 Disaster—The spy plane that could take crystal-clear
pictures from fifteen miles up in the sky was a CIA triumph.
U-2s had been overflying Russian territory with great regularity,
but by 1960 the Russians were tracking the planes and shell bursts
were coming alarmingly close. Despite this, the CIA ordered
another risky U-2 flight on the eve of a crucial Paris summit
conference, after which President Eisenhower was to fly to Moscow to visit Premier Nikita Khrushchev. When the plane and its
pilot, Francis Gary Powers, were shot down deep inside Russia,
the CIA put out a ridiculous cover story denouncing the Russians
for shooting down a weather plane that had wandered off course.
Eisenhower and his administration waxed righteously indignant.
In a stormy scene Khrushchev exposed the deceit: he exhibited
photographs of the wrecked plane—and of Powers himself, captured alive deep inside Russia. The Eisenhower-Khrushchev love
feast never took place and détente was placed on a back burner.
The CIA had managed to wreck any possibility of easing Cold
War tensions.

All of this served as a prelude to the most humiliating CIA-
engineered disaster, the Bay of Pigs invasion. The Agency had
trained a clandestine force of Cuban exiles in Guatemala, which
had been made safe for such activities by the 1954 coup. Allen
Dulles seemed convinced that Cuba could become another Gua-

temala. He envisioned a population panting to revolt against Fidel Castro, but Cuba's poor had been so oppressed by the previous Batista dictatorship that they were in no mood to revolt. Independent pulse-takings of the popular mood had affirmed this, but these were ignored.

No invasion was ever planned more foolishly. The CIA hierarchy seemed to believe that the invasion would spark a spontaneous popular uprising, but no effort was made to stimulate such an outburst. The Agency deliberately sidestepped Cuban exile leaders in this country, some of whom might have been helpful, but who were regarded as "too leftist." On top of this, the CIA masterminds sent the Cuban exile brigade ashore in a swamp from which only two narrow routes exited on the Cuban plain. All Castro had to do was to cap these exiting bottlenecks and pound the invaders to pieces, which was precisely what he did.

Our nation's losses did not end with that defeat. When one of the airplanes that raided Castro's landing fields was damaged and had to come down in Florida, the CIA put out the story that the pilot was a defector from Castro's Air Force—and that the fighting going on in Cuba was the result of a domestic uprising. UN Ambassador Adlai Stevenson, a man with considerable international prestige, was fed this sleazy tale and made a passionate speech, ridiculing the idea that the United States had any involvement in the Cuban fighting. Then Castro paraded some 1200 prisoners for all the world to see.

In summing up my critique of the CIA for *The Nation*, I wrote that the Congress-created agency had achieved such power that it could embark on projects that predetermined national policy. "This is an issue that goes to the very guts of the democratic process," I wrote. "Involved here is the question of whether the 'black arts' (sabotage, revolution, invasion) are to dominate all American democratic functions and determine for our people willynilly, without debate, without knowledge even of what is at stake, the course their nation is to take in the world. No lesser issue amounts to a tinker's damn here."

And, I added, "Our people do not understand that, even as our Presidents speak, the actions of CIA frequently invest their words with every appearance of the most arrant hypocrisy. The Presidents speak of peace; but the CIA overthrows regimes, plots internal sabotage and revolution, foists opium-growers on friendly nations, directs military invasions, backs right-wing militarists. These are not the actions of a democratic, peace-loving nation devoted to the high ideals we profess. These are the actions of the Comintern in right-wing robes."

My next attack on the power structures of the period, an exposé of the military-industrial complex, was inspired by a chance remark at a business luncheon. I was to see a publisher, a millionaire who had taken control of one of New York's large book publishing houses, and I was waiting with two of his editors in a New York restaurant. The magnate was late, and when he finally arrived, he was in a tearing hurry and obviously furious.

"Do you know what I think?" he demanded. Before any of us could even ask, "What?" he rushed on: "I think there are people in this country who want another world war. And you know something else? I think they are going to get it."

The publisher dropped the subject. Although I never discovered the cause of his outburst, I knew he traveled in powerful circles, and I could only assume his fury was based on fact. I couldn't get my mind off that chance, revealing outburst.

I knew that Carey McWilliams was casting around for another blockbuster fall feature; and I felt the thrill that comes with the certainty, "This is *it!*" I hurried back to the magazine and talked to Carey. He said, "Great! Let's do it. And I'll tell you just how to begin. Take Eisenhower's farewell address in which he warned about the dangers of the military-industrial complex and go on from there."

Carey had instantly put his finger on exactly the right focus for the article; and—marvelous compiler that he was—he pulled out a carton full of material on the subject. I began the research that would produce a feature issue of *The Nation,* consisting entirely of my article "Juggernaut: the Warfare State." This project culminated in a book, *The Warfare State,* published by Macmillan in September 1962.

In his last address President Eisenhower warned the people of the nation about new dangers arising from what he had called "the military-industrial complex." The general who had seen it all told Americans, "We annually spend on military security alone more than the net income of all United States corporations." This enormous spending had created a business establishment whose welfare and profits were wedded to the cause of an ever larger military. "The total influence—economic, political, even spiritual—is felt in every city, every state house, every office of the Federal Government," he said.

My research showed just how perceptive he had been: the prosperity of entire states depended on military contracts and installations and their ripple effect throughout the economy. For instance, when airplane and aerospace contracts were cut back in California, the entire southern part of the state was plunged into an economic abyss.

The turning point had come on March 12, 1947, when President Truman proclaimed to Congress what became known as "the Truman doctrine." The Truman Administration was alarmed at Soviet encroachments in Eastern Europe and the threat that Communist guerrillas posed to Greece and Turkey. Egged on by military advisers, the administration adopted a Rome vs. Carthage attitude, dividing the entire world into "theirs" and "ours." Common sense would dictate that the world had always been splintered with a number of different ideologies; but the Truman Administration subscribed to a simpler interpretation. There was plenty of evidence that the Communist world was divided, even as the free world was, by economic and nationalistic interests, and diplomats like George F. Kennan understood this. But the brass who influenced so much of Truman's thinking viewed the world in military terms; theirs was a philosophy of combatting political threats on the battlefield. And so Truman proclaimed: "Nearly every nation must choose between alternative ways of life, and it *must* be [he himself had deleted the State Department's softer 'should' and had insisted on the uncompromising 'must'] the policy of the United States to support free peoples who resist subjugation by armed minorities or outside pressure." We would not permit, Truman said, "such subterfuge as political infiltration."

The meaning was clear: Americans were going to defend our own version of the status quo, and we proclaimed for ourselves the right to intervene anywhere in the world. This struck me as a self-defeating policy that had the United States opposing change under all circumstances and put our nation in the corner of every militaristic dictator who used the most brutal methods of terror and suppression to subjugate peoples seeking a better life. Iran and Guatemala were just two examples (the ruin of a democratic Chile was still in the future). The effect of this rigid Truman Doctrine was to put Americans in opposition to all populations seeking freedom, and so to drive popular revolutionary movements into the "other" camp.

Common sense seemed to say that this was an irrational policy, and I coined the phrase Pax Americana in a mood of derision, pointing out that imperial Rome had exhausted itself trying to maintain its Pax Romana. Common sense said that no nation could run the world on its own terms. Accommodation rather than confrontation seemed even more essential in a world harboring a nuclear arsenal.

There seemed to be little public understanding of the developments that had escalated the scale of potential nuclear disaster. Hard-liners mounted a national campaign to convince the American people that the great majority of them could survive a nuclear war if they built their own bomb shelters. Similar types are attempting to brainwash the American people along the same lines today. The idea of survival in a nuclear war is preposterous. But in 1962—and I fear still today—there was inadequate understanding of one simple fact: the development of the H-bomb made the atomic bombs of Hiroshima and Nagasaki the mere peashooters of the nuclear age. Even a simple, standard 10-megaton H-bomb has *500 times* the destructive power of the weapon dropped on Hiroshima. And a 10-megaton bomb is an infant in today's nuclear arsenals containing 40- and 50-megaton bombs. A second insufficiently appreciated development was the harnessing of the A-bomb to field artillery. Any armed clash of major armies would almost certainly result in nuclear battlefield exchanges and the escalation to strategic heavy-megaton exchanges would be almost inevitable. This is the specter that continues to haunt the peoples of Western Europe and leads to massive demonstrations against nuclear power.

As I finished writing The Warfare State in April 1962, Vietnam was hardly a mote in the public eye, but I had a dread foreboding and wrote: "We are committed in South Vietnam to a dictator named Diem whom we persist in trying to picture as the George Washington of Southeast Asia. There is a limit to our money, to the burdens the American taxpayer can be expected to bear, to the drain on our gold resources and our manpower. If we engage in many more Koreas, if we are dragged into another 'limited war' in Southeast Asia, we shall bleed ourselves of our finest youth and our future leadership in a blind endeavor to halt and contain an ideology we detest. The battle, if it is fought on these terms, can only succeed in bleeding us white in endless 'police actions.' "

My crystal ball must have been working overtime when I wrote that passage years in advance of the calamity of the Vietnam War: but, unfortunately, this was not a time for the exercise of common sense. *The Warfare State* had hardly been published when the Cuban missile crisis brought the Soviet Union and the United States to the brink of nuclear war. In the panic of the moment, common sense was overwhelmed by passion, and the outcry was for more and better weaponry. It was a period made to order for the flag-waving patriotism and the passion peddlings of the Radical Right.

21

"Christians, to Arms!"

I N JANUARY 1963 AL SILVERMAN SENT ME TO BOSTON TO GET for *Saga* the first-person story of Laurence T. May, Jr., a former neo-Nazi who, while still a youth in high school, had worked his way through the jungle of the Radical Right.

I found May a slender, intellectually inquisitive youth, one so adventurously alive that he had not just joined the fanatics of the right but had hitchhiked all over the East to meet personally the leaders of the movement. His education had been a slow process. He had started afire with enthusiasm to fight a perceived menace—a Jewish-Communist conspiracy to rule the world—and he had ended up convinced that the greater danger lay in the heavily financed, secretly powerful, widely proliferated movements of the fascist right.

"You must understand," he said to me during one of our discussions, "that the radical left and the radical right are really blood brothers. They think alike. They have the same motivation; they want power. And so they can switch from one extreme to the other as easily as you can put on a coat."

I wondered how a youth as intellectually alive as May had become so deluded by Radical Right propaganda in the beginning, and his story explained much about the insidious workings of a fanaticism that subordinates intellect to passion.

May was born in 1941 in Waltham, about eight miles from Boston. His father was an electronics designer; he had three sisters and a younger brother—what he described as an average, happy American family, with no trace of racial or religious prejudice. No one should have been a less likely candidate for far-right fanaticism. But other influences were at work on young May's mind.

He had been brought up in a predominantly Catholic neighborhood, in an area where Joe McCarthy and the virus of hate and suspicion that he cultivated had found some of the most impassioned followers. A couple of May's teachers in grade school spread anti-Semitic dogma subtly in class, using well-understood catch phrases, and in private they often intimated to their students that they thought "Hitler was right." May was surrounded by classmates who were openly anti-Semitic. "Enlightenment" came when he was fourteen and a student in junior high school. One flagrantly anti-Semitic teacher kept talking about "hidden forces" and "world rulers," and she kept urging "political awareness" on her students. She urged May to read Hitler's *Mein Kampf*, where, she assured him, he would find all the answers.

He was exhilarated by *Mein Kampf*. He accepted it whole, disregarding history; for him, Buchenwald and Auschwitz hadn't existed. He had been brainwashed into accepting the conspiracy theory of history: we in America had not been told *the truth* about Hitler.

Already a convert, young May became a zealot when he watched the Army-McCarthy hearings on television. McCarthy, as a crusader against Communism, had become a great hero of his—and he was not alone: the Boston area's "Friends of Senator McCarthy" claimed some 1600 dedicated members. Young May viewed the hearings and eclipse of McCarthy as a Jewish-Communist plot to destroy this mighty crusader. Convinced he was "doing God's work," he hitchhiked all around the East, seeking out the most prominent leaders of the movement. He described them all for me: Conde McGinley, of Union, New Jersey, a courteous, soft-spoken Texan who published *Common Sense*, a periodical with 100,000 circulation that pictured the Kennedy Administration as perverted by Jews; James H. Madole, of New York, head of the National Renaissance Party, a man who could not look you straight in the eye; Robert Welch, the one-time candy manufacturer who had founded the John Birch Society and had the habit of scratching himself as though he had fleas; and George Lincoln Rockwell, then the most blatant Nazi in the nation and the head of the American Nazi Party.

Two things finally opened May's eyes. He became disturbed when he found that some of his comrades on the far right had anti-Catholic as well as anti-Jewish biases. At first he dismissed Catholic-haters as persons who were wrong on this one issue, but were "right" on the larger things that mattered. But the more he heard anti-Catholic slurs, the harder it became for him to dismiss them. May was still rationalizing his faith when something happened to shatter that faith forever.

Gordon D. Hall, of Boston, was conducting his own crusade against hate groups that he felt endangered the nation. May heard one of Hall's radio addresses in 1958 and was incensed. Conde McGinley told him, "Hall's record is really too foul to reveal, but he deserted his Negro wife and two children in order to live with his homosexual friends."

Determined to challenge such a human monster, May telephoned Hall and to his surprise found him a very reasonable man. Hall offered to show him documentation for every charge he had made and invited May to visit him. May accepted—and got the shock of his young life: Hall was living a normal domestic life with his white wife and their two sons. May realized that he had been the victim of colossal deception, and it made him sick.

Laurence May's experience with the Radical Right struck me as a vivid illustration of the brainwashing that was sweeping the nation. I had studied the effects of this movement for *The Warfare State*, in which I had devoted a chapter to the links between the Radical Right and the military.

Stephen M. Young, then a Democratic U.S. senator from Ohio, recounted that at a Washington dinner party one of the guests, "a well-known, ultraconservative congressman," had burst out in a tirade, virtually frothing over "homegrown Communists who chew away at the foundations of the republic." As Senator Young turned away in disgust, a veteran diplomat from an European country leaned toward him and said: "One thing has always puzzled me about you Americans. You have nightmares about Communist demons burrowing from within. Yet for years American fascists have grown increasingly dangerous and nobody seems disturbed—least of all your congressman."

This incident and others like it seemed to indicate that astute foreign observers had a clearer picture of America than Americans did. My studies showed that for years many of the nation's most powerful industrialists and their corporations had financed and promoted a passion-peddling campaign equating liberalism with socialism and Communism. This right-wing propaganda, as young May had discovered, was riddled with exaggeration, misrepresentation and lies, and all to one purpose: to taint innovators with suspicion; to halt all further reforms; and to block further New Deal legislation.

The propaganda campaign was stepped up the instant John F. Kennedy was elected president. Kennedy was viewed by ultraconservative, big money men as a dangerous "liberal" who posed a threat to the status quo. Conservative minds feared his New Frontier would become as obnoxious to business as Roosevelt's New Deal.

This paranoia in the executive suites of Big Business resulted in a wedding of the Respectables and the Kooks. The passion peddlers were the front men, waving the flag, cloaking the wildest charges in the trappings of religion, arousing passion in a manner that recalled the technique of Hitler. Behind them, financing their rallies, putting up millions of dollars for radio and television exposure, were some of the largest business interests in America.

The link between the Respectables and the Kooks shows most plainly in California, where in 1961 and 1962 circuit riders of the radical evangelism whipped up prejudice and hate in a rash of anti-Communism "schools"—so-called project alerts and survival seminars. These perfervid extravaganzas united religious fanaticism, the military in the persons of admirals and generals, and heavy business financing.

The Radical Right circus in California revolved in these early Kennedy years about the unlikely person of Dr. Fred C. Schwarz, a medical doctor and part-time psychiatrist from Australia, a Jew turned Baptist and lay preacher, an immigrant who had arrived in this country in 1953 with just $10 in his pockets. Schwarz founded the Christian Anti-Communism Crusade, a quasi-religious, quasi-political organization he built into a million-dollar-a-year business.

Schwarz contended that he was merely "a teacher" giving his audiences "the truth" about Communism. Here is a typical Schwarz exhortation:

> Christians, to arms! The enemy is at the gate. Buckle on the armor of the Christian and go forth to battle.
> With education, evangelism and dedication let us smite the Communist foe and if necessary give up our lives in this noble Cause! . . .
> We cry, "We shall not yield! Lift high the blood-stained banner of the Cross and on to Victory!" . . .
> Co-existence is impossible . . . Communism is total evil . . . its methods are evil and its ends are evil. . . . We must hurl this thing back into the pit from which it came!

Californians by the thousands responded to Schwarz's rabble-rousing outcries. At some of his larger rallies, he toned down the rhetoric in an attempt to appear more reasonable, such as when he presided over the five-day Southern California School of Anti-Communism held in Los Angeles in August 1962. Schwarz denounced foreign aid and called for "dedicated individuals" to repel the Communist threat; we must rely, he told his audiences, on dedicated, determined, highly trained persons "with a practical program for the seizure of power."

Military brass attended Schwarz's rallies. At this Southern California "school," retired Rear Admiral Chester Ward called for Cold War victory, not accommodation. We must let it be known, he said, "that we are at all times ready for war to keep the peace"; we should arm a hundred merchant ships with Polaris missiles; we must "get rid of the architects of accommodation, the foreign-policy advisers who gave President Kennedy bad advice."

W. Cleon Skousen, a former FBI agent and a member of Schwarz's "faculty," called for the severance of all diplomatic relations with the Soviet Union; a ban on all trade with the Soviet Union and China; withdrawal from the United Nations unless the Charter could be rewritten to our liking; and a thoroughgoing Congressional investigation to root out the "small left-wing group in the State Department" that had caused all our troubles.

An actor named Ronald Reagan took the stage and added a vital ingredient to these themes: a denunciation of the Welfare State, which, he said, represented a centralization of government as dangerous for Americans as Communism.

The five-day Southern California Seminar was a great triumph for Schwarz, and he used it as a springboard for a larger and more colorful production billed as "Hollywood's Answer to Communism," held in the Hollywood Bowl on October 16, 1962, with bands playing, flags waving, and prominent Hollywood stars like Linda Darnell, Dale Evans, John Wayne, Cesar Romero, Pat O'Brien, Jimmy Stewart, Robert Stack and Roy Rogers blessing the performance with their presence. Some 15,000 persons crowded into the Hollywood Bowl to listen to three hours of impassioned denunciations of the Menace. It was a grand occasion for the Radical Right.

But some observers despaired. For one, the novelist and screenwriter Guy Endore, who watched the rally intending to write an article about it for *The Nation*. Yet when the last ranting voice had died away, he found himself incapable of putting words on paper. In a letter to Carey McWilliams, he explained: "I swear I meant to write an article for you. But have you any idea of the state of despair that I was thrown into as I listened to speaker after speaker and noted how not one of them uttered the word war, but every one of whom hammered home ideas that made the outcome absolutely inevitable? And then saw fifteen thousand youths rising again and again to cheer these ideas, deliberately boxing themselves in with death? And boxing us in, too?"

This reality that haunted Endore was the same as the one Albert Einstein was writing about in his last letter when death stilled his pen. "In essence," Einstein wrote, "the conflict that exists today is no more than the old-style struggle for power, once again presented to mankind in semi-religious trappings. The difference is that, this time, the development of atomic power has imbued the struggle with a ghostly character; for both parties know and admit that, should the quarrel deteriorate into actual war, mankind is doomed. . . . Political passions, once they have been fanned into flames, exact their victims."

Dr. Fred Schwarz continued to rave, averring in a San Francisco *Chronicle* interview that Premier Khrushchev had a timetable for the conquest of the United States by 1973. "I believe he has chosen San Francisco as the headquarters of the world Communist dictatorship," said Schwarz. "The Mark Hopkins Hotel will make splendid offices for him." Schwarz thought Khrushchev had had San Francisco in mind for his future capital ever since he visited the United States during a brief period of détente in 1959. What would happen to the people of San Francisco by the time of Khrushchev's triumph in 1973? "The people of San Francisco—those they don't dump in the Bay—can be put in the Nevada desert, which is quite handy," Schwarz said.

One of Schwarz's foremost supporters was the Allen-Bradley Company of Milwaukee, Wisconsin, manufacturers of "quality motor controls and quality electronic equipment."

Ironically, Allen-Bradley had been an associate of General Electric in the price-rigging consortium that had conspired to fix the price of Tennessee Valley Authority generators a few years before. The company had been fined $40,000 in that scandal, but it exhibited its opinions about the American free enterprise system by distributing hundreds of thousands of copies of a huge handbill reproducing Schwarz's testimony before the House Un-American Activities Committee.

This spread was headlined in boldface capitals: **WILL YOU BE FREE TO CELEBRATE CHRISTMAS IN THE FUTURE?** In a series of answers, the flier proclaimed: *not unless* Americans began "to understand and appreciate the benefits provided by God under the American free enterprise system"; *not unless* Americans woke up to the menace of Communism; *not unless* Americans began to understand "that 'academic freedom' without morality leads to national suicide." In black type, boxed with black borders, the flier wound up by proclaiming: COMMUNISM IS OUT TO DESTROY YOU!

Allen-Bradley offered twenty-five copies of this flier to anyone who wanted them. To schools and churches, it offered copies "free in any quantity," a bargain that was snapped up so avidly that Schwarz later boasted: "This document, I understand, has had wider distribution than any government document in the history of the United States, with the exception of the Bill of Rights, the Declaration of Independence and the Constitution."

Allen-Bradley was only one of Schwarz's big-business sponsors. The evangelist's principal angel for his series of Southern California seminars was Patrick J. Frawley, then the chief executive officer of Technicolor Inc., the head of Schick Safety Razor Company (not to be confused with the manufacturers of the Schick electric razor), and chairman of the board of Eversharp. Frawley, at the tender age of thirty-one, had been hailed as one of the nation's foremost young industrialists when he developed the Papermate pen.

When Schwarz held his five-day Los Angeles "school," Frawley contributed $10,000 and his Schick razor company sponsored the local telecast. When Schwarz staged his huge Hollywood Bowl rally, Respectables ensured that television coverage would blanket the entire West Coast. Frawley's Schick company underwrote the costs in the Los Angeles area, and Richfield Oil bore the burden of the network telecast. Leading the applause for these patriotic sponsors was Joe Crail, president of the huge Coast Federal Savings & Loan Association of Los Angeles—then the third-largest enterprise of its kind in the nation. Crail set up what he called the Free Enterprise Bureau in Coast Federal, allocating 4 percent of the institution's net revenue before taxes to the project. In 1962, Coast Federal mailed out 2 million pieces of propaganda to depositors, borrowers and business concerns. According to Crail, 5000 American companies inquired about his program, and 2000 established similar Free Enterprise bureaus.

Crail's propaganda bureau put out what it called a "Myths and Truth" kit, which asserted that cultural exchanges amount to nothing more than "weapons of espionage, propaganda and sources of income for the Communist Conspiracy"; "America is declining as the 'majority'-mob reaches for divine right to rule over the individual"; and that the assumption that "Human rights are above property rights" is a dangerous myth.

Joe Crail chortled that the telecast of the Hollywood Bowl performance had been seen by 7 million viewers; and in a speech to fellow businessmen, he urged them to get in on the action. "Anti-Communism builds sales and raises employee performance," he declared. Evidence of the effect of this Radical Right propagandizing was visible on the streets all over Southern California as car bumpers broke out in a rash of stickers proclaiming "Americanism—The Only Ism for Me," "Socialism Is Communism," "No on Red China" and "Goldwater for Me."

Schwarz and his Respectable backers did not escape unscathed. California Attorney General Stanley Mosk in a televised address declared that verified figures showed that within ninety days Schwarz had grossed $311,253 in Los Angeles alone, with a net profit of $214,737. The attorney general added: "This is indeed big business—nearly a quarter of a million dollars in ninety days! At that rate there would be a million dollars a year—in just one city. No one is told, except in generalities, what is happening to the Oakland profits—or to the $100,000 taken out of Philadelphia, the $40,000 out of Phoenix, and so on in city after city. No wonder this whole movement has been called 'Patriotism for Profit.' "

Frawley rushed to Schwarz's defense. He declared that Schwarz was a thoroughly responsible man who had been "completely cleared" in a journalistic investigation masterminded by Norman Chandler, the conservative publisher of the powerful Los Angeles *Times*. Frawley placed other leading Respectables in Schwarz's corner. Schwarz's show had been approved by Sears Roebuck's head office in Chicago, he said; it had been backed by the American Security Council, a lofty, militaristic, right-wing braintrust that Sears and General Electric reportedly had helped to finance.

Encouraged by such backing, Frawley brought "Hollywood's Answer" to New York. A videotape had been made of the Hollywood Bowl frenzy, and Frawley's Schick and Technicolor paid the costs for a three-hour rerun over WPIX. This was coast-to-coast brainwashing on a colossal scale—made possible only because the bankrolls of the Respectables had been put at the service of the Radical Right. In a letter after the presentation Frawley exulted to a correspondent that he had received "6,000 letters, of which only fifteen were critical of our public service sponsorship."

Dr. Schwarz may have been the most colorful purveyor of Radical Right dogma in 1961–62, but he had numerous and well-financed rivals. H. L. Hunt, the Texas oil billionaire, once admitted that he "guessed" he spent $1 million a year sponsoring what he called "pro-Freedom" programs. Hunt's money was poured into a television series called *Life Line*, which featured an anti-liberal, anti-Communist evangelist named Wayne Poucher, whose views were aired daily over 212 radio stations in twenty-eight states. Poucher saw the UN as "one of the most dangerous threats the United States has ever faced"; and he warmed the cockles of H. L. Hunt's heart by a diatribe against "the *police* Welfare State." With one hundred million professed Christians in America, there shouldn't be any need for welfare from local, state or federal governments, Poucher proclaimed—an attitude that disregarded the nation's disastrous experience with Christian charity in the debacle of 1929–30.

Hunt's millions spawned another preacher of far-right faith, Dan Smoot, originally a spokesman on Hunt's unsuccessful television show, "Facts Forum." After "Facts Forum" failed, Smoot struck out on his own with "Dan Smoot Reports," and became one of the favorite oracles of the Radical Right. His radio and television programs blanketed the West, Southwest and Midwest: the radio program was sponsored on seventy stations in twelve states; the television act was beamed to forty stations in twelve states. Smoot, who had served in the FBI during World War II, proclaimed: "I equate the growth of the Welfare State with socialism and socialism with Communism. . . . The Communist conspiracy in Washington is even worse than it was in the days of Alger Hiss and Harry Dexter White." Smoot wanted the U.S. to invade Cuba and oust Fidel Castro; he advocated the impeachment of Chief Justice Earl Warren; he wanted to scuttle Social Security and the Welfare State.

These views brought him another wealthy sponsor, D. B. Lewis, an ardent Los Angeles right-winger who ran the Lewis Food Co., purveyors of Dr. Ross Dog Food, Skippy and other pet products. Lewis was also president of the Organization to Repeal Federal Income Taxes, Inc.—the income tax, he claimed, was "one of the most vicious laws ever passed." Lewis backed Smoot with strong-arm measures, using the bludgeon of economic power to force networks to put Smoot's programs on the air. The results enchanted Lewis. He told Fletcher Knebel of *Look* that his firm had sponsored "Hopalong Cassidy" and "Tarzan," "but Dan is far and away the best seller. I'm getting more for my advertising dollar than any business in America."

The basic themes that united the Radical Right with many plain conservatives become clear: abolish Social Security, abolish welfare, wreck unions, abolish the progressive income tax; and spend billions for armaments.

The irrationality of this program became obvious in the doctrines of the John Birch Society, the most powerful conservative movement of the period. The society was founded in Indianapolis in December 1958 by Robert Henry Winborne Welch, Jr. Welch had spent most of his life as a salesman and executive of the James O. Welch Candy Co., run by his brother in Belmont, Massachu-

setts. In the business world, he had become prominent enough
to serve for seven years as a director of the National Association
of Manufacturers and for three years as an NAM regional vice
president. When he decided to abandon candy for anti-
Communism, he called together some kindred spirits for a two-
day conference in Indianapolis.

Welch had committed his views to what he later was to insist
was "just a private letter," although it had the bulk of a book.
Entitled *The Politician*, it was an argument against President
Eisenhower, who, although he had finally driven the detested
Democrats from the White House in 1952, had not turned the
clock back to the era of William McKinley, as Welch and other
representatives of big business would have preferred. Social security, welfare, the progressive income tax were still with us. The
ultraconservatives who had rallied to Welch's call were prepared
to back a new movement—but they weren't prepared for what
they heard when Welch sprang *The Politician* on them.

This Indianapolis conclave heard what would not become public
knowledge for several years. The group heard Welch describe
President Eisenhower as "a dedicated conscious agent of the Communist conspiracy." George Catlett Marshall, Army chief of staff
during World War II and later, as secretary of state, author of
the Marshall Plan that was to save Western Europe from Communism, was also to Welch "a conscious, deliberate, dedicated
agent of the Soviet conspiracy." John Foster Dulles was "a Communist agent"; Franklin D. Roosevelt had been guilty "of plain
unadulterated treason"; Nelson Rockefeller was planning "to make
the United States a part of a one-world Socialist government";
and Chief Justice Warren should be impeached because "he has
taken the lead in . . . converting this republic into a democracy"
and because democracy "is a weapon of demagoguery and perpetual fraud."

Such was the nightmare world of Robert Welch. Men in their
right minds should have shunned such a person like the plague.
But not these Respectables. They simply told Welch that *The
Politician* wouldn't do, but then they listened to him while he
held forth in a tape-recorded monologue that became *The Blue
Book* of the John Birch Society.

This one wasn't much more rational than *The Politician*, but it
did avoid such idiocies as calling Dwight Eisenhower and George
Marshall Communists. Welch charged that World War II was

"largely brought on through the world-wide conniving of Stalin's agents"—not by Hitler's aggressions. The Communists had "the full cooperation of our government" both during the war and the postwar period, and this explained their success everywhere in the world. For Welch, there was no distinction between a democratic-Socialist government and an authoritarian-Communist one. For him, Norway, Iceland and Finland were Communist countries; even Hawaii was Communist-controlled; and the Communist design was to convert the United States "into a Socialist nation, quite similar to Russia itself in its economy and political outlook."

The Respectables bought this ideological package and backed Welch in the formation of the John Birch Society, an activist organization named after an obscure foreign agent who had been killed by Chinese guerrillas ten days after the end of World War II. Welch proposed to establish reading rooms to promote the wider dissemination of right-wing literature and to form "front" organizations for specific purposes—to break up liberal rallies by the use of hecklers and to use the same "mean and dirty" tactics the Communists employed to fight the society's perceived political foes. The John Birch Society was organized as a monolithic body, with Welch himself in a Führer-like role, dictating all policy. His goal was the acquisition of one million members who would stop at nothing to "save America."

The eleven Respectables who were present at the birth have never been identified, but there is every reason to believe they were among the men who comprised the first governing council of the society. According to the 1959 *Blue Book*, they included three former presidents of the National Association of Manufacturers; a former U.S. commissioner of internal revenue; a former assistant secretary of state and ambassador to Latin American countries; a one-time personal aide to General Douglas MacArthur; a former head of the notorious "China Lobby" that had supported Chiang Kai-shek; and powerful industrialists whose influence was supreme in their own communities.

Though the ultimate disclosure of Welch's crackpot views in *The Politician* discredited him and the society for a time, the damage was confined largely to Welch himself. Conservative politicians like U.S. Senator Barry Goldwater, who had close ties to the Birchers, were compelled to disown Welch more in sorrow than in anger. Goldwater wouldn't utter a word against the society or its aims because, he said, he knew many Birchers who were "mighty fine people." So the secret, radical society lived on, promulgating its perverted view of the world; and it has succeeded periodically right down to the present day in electing some of its members to Congress.*

Another enterprise that had the blessing of such behemoths of American industry as General Motors, General Electric, Boeing and Lockheed was Harding College in Searcy, Arkansas, which had been established as an idea factory for the Radical Right. The college was operated by the Church of Christ, a fundamentalist sect, and its president, Dr. George Stuart Benson, was a former missionary in China and an ardent advocate of union-curbing legislation. This activity moved Alfred P. Sloan, then president of General Motors, to donate $300,000 to the college in 1949. Charles R. Hook, then chairman of the board of Armco Steel, followed his lead; so did the Falk Foundation of Pittsburgh and many others. By spring 1961, when Cabell Phillips, of the New York *Times*, visited the Searcy campus, he found that Harding College was being bankrolled with a $6-million endowment fund, "virtually all of it from industrial donors."

The kind of propaganda that a $6-million bankroll buys is illustrated by what happened at Harding. Dr. Benson created an adjunct to the college, the National Education Program, to produce films and organize Freedom Forums, which distributed Dr. Benson's messages on a massive scale. All parroted the favorite themes of the Radical Right: opposition to all welfare legislation, attacks on unions as "monopolistic," championing of right-to-work laws, and denunciation of anything that smacked of liberalism— and so could be magnified and equated with Communism. A weekly column by Dr. Benson was distributed free to 3000 weekly newspapers; a monthly reprint of these columns, titled "Listen, Americans!", was sent in bulk to one thousand business organ-

---

* When Soviet fighter planes shot down Korean Airlines passenger jet 007 in September 1983, one of the 269 victims was Representative Lawrence Patton McDonald, a Georgia Democrat and national chairman of the John Birch Society. McDonald had been criticized in 1979 for spearheading a successful effort in Congress to help his fellow John Bircher, Nelson Bunker Hunt, son of the billionaire H. L. Hunt. Nelson Bunker Hunt had been trying to corner the silver market in a manipulation that threatened the stability of the stock market, and McDonald successfully blocked sales of silver from the government's military stockpile that would have depressed prices and ruined Hunt's bullish investment ploy. In the end, Hunt's attempt to drive silver prices through the stratosphere collapsed disastrously anyhow. (The New York *Times*, September 2, 1983)

izations; a series of high-school study outlines was dispatched free
to any school requesting them; and some thirty motion pictures
of high professional quality were produced.

One of the films, *Communism on the Map*, produced under
the supervision of John Green, a member of the John Birch Society, expressed Welch's alarmist view of Communism gobbling
the globe. The film colored the entire world Red with few exceptions: West Germany, Formosa, Switzerland and the United
States. Even Great Britain, our free world ally, was tainted pink;
even Canada was left in an equivocal "white" status, not quite
pink but decidedly not pure because the film alleged that many
Communists occupied high positions in Canadian government.
Communism on the Map presented such a phony, inaccurate picture of the world we live in that even Dr. Schwarz, the brains of
the Christian Anti-Communist Crusade, disowned it. But not the
Respectables.

Boeing Aircraft (holder then of $1 billion in war contracts) ad-
mitted that it had shown the film, together with an equally distorted House Un-American Activities Committee film, to thousands
of its employees in captive audiences because the films "serve as
an alarm clock alerting the country and the people to the dangers
around us." Lockheed Aircraft (then the holder of another $1
billion in war contracts) had similarly shown the film to its employees. So had Sandia Corp., a wholly owned subsidiary of West-
inghouse Electric, and Space General, a subsidiary of Aerojet,
maker of the Polaris missile. General Electric, according to an
executive who was one of Dr. Benson's vice presidents, "uses
NEP films extensively in their many plants." Queried directly,
an official of GE, for whom Ronald Reagan was shilling on nationwide speaking tours, confirmed the use of NEP films, writing:
"It is a pleasure to endorse without reservation the National Education Program."

Truth, facts, did not matter to the all-powerful Respectables of
American big business, intent on wedding a nonexistent domestic
devil to a highly visible foreign one in an effort to drive the
American people into the arms of the Radical Right.

Laurence May had been amazed at the flood of propaganda
turned out by these proliferating organizations on the far right.
Once your name got on a mailing list, he told me, you were

deluged with the outpourings of far-right fanatics from all over the nation. In the article I wrote for him, May described it: "It is amazing—and this perhaps is a danger symptom to evaluate with some care—how the agitation on the right mushrooms. You join just one group, and the next thing you know, your name is on mailing lists everywhere. You quickly discover that there are so many organizations you cannot keep track of them. Some have only five or six members; others 75 to 100. The individual membership roles by themselves are not impressive, but the number of these stewing, milling, unaffiliated groups certainly is."

A theme of violence ran throughout this frenzy on the right. It was obvious in organizations like the Minutemen, whose members armed themselves and underwent combat drills, but it was usually expressed in catchphrases and emotional harangues designed to incite violence. For example, I had never heard of James H. Madole, the Bronx neo-Nazi leader, until May mentioned him to me; but by the time *Saga* got around to publishing May's story some months later, Madole's neo-Nazi toughs had battled police in the Bronx and Madole himself had been arrested. Police had found a variety of knives, guns and erotica in his clubhouse.

Laurence May, his curiosity ever impelling him, had discovered traces of a ghostly, faceless leader who had "a practical program for the seizure of power" such as Dr. Schwarz had advocated. May first learned of this shadowy figure from George Andrews Moriarity, of Ogunquit, Maine, the veteran patriarch of New England right-wing movements. Moriarity was the epitome of white, Anglo-Saxon Protestantism, his anti-Semitic prejudices strong, his anti-Catholic prejudices only slightly less so. Moriarity had weighted May down with bundles of Gerald L. K. Smith's literature, including copies of his virulently anti-Semitic magazine, *The Cross and the Flag*. Through Moriarity, May had also learned about a widespread, loosely knit organization run by a hidden Führer known only as the Patriot. May had heard rumors about a super-secret group before he met Moriarity; but when Moriarity started to talk mysteriously about "the real fighters," May's ever lively interest had been piqued. He kept after Moriarity until Moriarity had finally confided that he meant the Patriot.

The young—and at this point the completely committed—Laurence May had been thrilled to be let in on this secret and

to have the chance to make contact with this secret source of
power. He wanted to join the Patriot's organization; and Moriarity, who wouldn't reveal the name of the leader, told him he
would have to be investigated. Apparently he was, for soon he
began to receive instructions by mail from this secret source.
There was no visible organization; there were no meetings; no
speeches. But from time to time, May would receive instructions
by mail about recruiting or other duties he was asked to perform.
When he had carried out his orders, he had to notify the Patriot
by writing to designated post office boxes in either Memphis,
Tennessee, or Dallas, Texas.

The Patriot's literature repeated the favorite themes of the
Radical Right with emphasis on the "Jewish plot" for world dom-
ination. But the Patriot added some terrifying, almost incredible
nuances. He charged that the Jews already were literally de-
vouring the nation and that the time was near when good Americans would have to take control by force. When this last desperate
hour arrived—and the Patriot warned it might be very close—
the members of his organization would be armed and given the
task of assassinating government officials.

This plan for extreme action had made May even more avid to
learn the identity of the Patriot. Conde McGinley, he felt certain,
knew who the Patriot was, but McGinley, like Moriarity, would
never tell him. All that May could learn was that the Patriot was
a young family man from Dallas with plenty of money and no
obvious connection with any Radical Right group. Vague traces
of the Patriot showed up, however, across the spectrum of the
Radical Right; May recognized phrases from his literature in the
literature of a number of organizations—an indication of his far-
reaching influence.

This was as much as May could learn about the ghostly, sinister
Dallas figure who operated only through designated post-office-
box numbers. More and more disturbed by the increasingly violent tone of the Patriot's communications, he consulted with
Gordon Hall; and, with Hall's help, he turned all the information
he had been able to collect about the Patriot and his sinister
program over to the FBI.

And there the story ended. The assassination in Dallas was still
months in the future.

22

November 1963:
The Lone-Killer Theory
Demolished

L IKE MILLIONS OF AMERICANS, I SHALL NEVER FORGET
 where I was and what I was doing that afternoon of November 22, 1963, when a burst of gunfire in Dallas ended
an era of optimism and hope.

I was in my study typing a manuscript. My wife left to visit a
friend, and I went downstairs to make my lunch. The new issue
of *Life* magazine had just arrived with a big cover display on the
Quorum Club in the Carroll Arms Hotel on Capitol Hill, a water-
ing place graced by seductively shaped and clad waitresses, favorite scenery for senators, congressmen and big lobbyists. I began
to read this exposé when the television channel my wife had left
on suddenly broke into its regular program and an announcer,
his voice shaking, gasped out the news: President Kennedy had
been shot in Dallas. The wound was believed to be in the head.

I jumped up from the table and started to pound my fist against
the wall of the archway between our dining and sitting rooms,
my eyes still fixed on the television set. "Those Goddamned sons
of bitches!" I shouted. I had little hope Kennedy would survive;
a head wound was almost certainly fatal.

Everyone who lived through those next three hectic days, glued
to their television set, will recall the pell-mell rush of events: the
president was proclaimed dead; Lyndon Baines Johnson was sworn

in; Lee Harvey Oswald, arrested for shooting and killing Police Officer J. D. Tippit, was then charged with having shot the president.

In a wild few hours, with the Dallas police headquarters a madhouse of reporters and cameramen, details linking Oswald to the assassination emerged. A former Marine, he was a Communist who had once defected to Russia but had returned; he had been employed in the Texas School Book Depository where, hidden on the sixth floor, an Italian-manufactured Mannlicher Carcano rifle he had purchased from a mail order house had been found; three shells discharged from the gun that had fired the fatal shots had been found on the sixth floor near the window. In less than twenty-four hours, the whole case appeared wrapped up and the official verdict given: Oswald, a psychopathic Communist nut, was the lone killer; there was no sign of conspiracy; the hate groups of Dallas were not only absolved, they were hardly ever mentioned.

I watched and listened to all this with a residue of skepticism. The evidence as it flowed to me in television sequences seemed convincing—and yet I wondered. I wished I were in Dallas to do some investigative reporting myself. But I had no organization behind me to finance such a trip; the task was far beyond the resources of *The Nation*, even if it had been willing, so I sat and watched like millions of others as the drama unfolded.

Sunday morning came, and Lee Harvey Oswald was to be transferred from Dallas Police Headquarters to a secure prison. The most elaborate security measures were put into effect to guarantee his safety. My son was so sure that nothing else could possibly happen that he went out into the yard to rake leaves while I stayed behind, mesmerized in front of that TV set. I saw Oswald being led forward between two police officers; I saw a squat, bulky man suddenly lunge forward, heard a shot go off, saw Oswald gasp and slump, his arms over his stomach.

I saw, but couldn't believe. My first reaction was: "What the hell are those kooks in Dallas doing? Are they trying to put on a show or something?" I had to see the reruns before I became convinced that this was not just some crazy staged act but an actual assassination carried out in the full view of millions of television watchers.

Once I grasped the incredible act I had just seen, I began to wonder. My long experience with police work, my knowledge of the way contract murder is ordered and carried out, told me that Ruby's slaying of Oswald fit the pattern. The hit man, especially in a sensational case that will cause intensive investigation, becomes dispensable the minute he has pulled the trigger. He represents too great a danger to those who ordered the hit—so he has to be eliminated. But officials didn't seem to be even considering this possibility. They were still asking us to believe that Oswald was a lone irrational nut who killed the president—and that then he was killed by Jack Ruby, another lone irrational nut.

It seemed too incredible. But as I read the newspapers and watched television, I saw that it *was* being believed. There seemed to be virtually no hard, on-the-spot investigative reporting; the news reports merely mirrored the official versions. (My friend from *World-Telegram and Sun* days, Bud Nossiter, later told me that the Washington *Post* had been ready to send him to Dallas and he had been eager to go when the lightning arrest of Oswald, the "quick" solution, killed off all interest. "We'll just let the wire services handle it," he was told.)

Since so much has been written about the Kennedy assassination, I shall tell here only about my own involvement in efforts to bring about a thorough investigation. Early in December 1963 I went to Washington on a magazine assignment, and I learned from a number of sources that many veteran newsmen were as concerned as I about the lightning-fast wrap-up of the case.

One of my contacts, who had been talking to a CBS news executive, told me that the executive was deeply disturbed and frustrated. His team in Dallas, he said, had uncovered leads that seemed to require further digging, but had run into the stonewall of network indifference. No one was pursuing obvious leads, and the official investigations seemed concerned with proving the official version without looking into any discrepancies.

Two of the best national reporters on the scene, Richard Dudman and Ronnie Dugger, had expressed doubts about the lone-assassin verdict. They were suspicious, for example, about the unbelievable speed with which the Dallas police had radioed an almost perfect description of Oswald just ten minutes after the lethal shots had been fired. Unless there was a setup, this seemed miraculous in the midst of so much turmoil and confusion.

Also while I was in Washington, a friend of mine who was working as an investigator for a Senate committee and had close ties to the National Rifle Association, led me to stumble upon another unexplained angle:

The Mannlicher Carcano that Oswald allegedly used to kill the president was one of the crankiest rifles ever invented; its bolt action most peculiar (as I later found out the one time I handled it). The old World War I Springfield, with which I had had a passing association in ROTC in college, had a smooth bolt action— you pulled the bolt straight back to eject the spent cartridge, then slammed it straight forward to seat a new charge. With the Mann- licher Carcano, which had been the principal weapon of the Italian infantry, the bolt had a squirreling action that slowed its rate of fire and sometimes got stuck, to the frustration of the marksman. This was later established during test firing that the Warren Com- mission conducted. Although only championship marksmen were used, one of them, even after practicing with Oswald's rifle, be- came so entangled with the squirreling bolt action that he could not get a shot off at all during one round.

This squirreling bolt was not the only defect of the weapon: the ammunition was equally recalcitrant. Bullets tended to swerve and swoop instead of speeding unerringly to their target. When Italian resistance collapsed at the end of World War II, hundreds of thousands of these balky guns fell into American hands, and we had an immediate use for them if they could ever be made to work properly. Communist guerrillas were threatening to overrun Greece; the Greeks opposing them, whom we supported, needed arms. If the Mannlicher Carcano could be turned into an effective weapon, the vast numbers we had captured would be invaluable in the Greek civil war.

Nothing could be done about that awkward bolt action, but experts from the National Rifle Association and an Army ordnance team conducted extensive experiments at the Aberdeen proving grounds in Maryland, "And they came up with one of the most perfect bullets ever designed," my source said. "It could be fired from the Carcano, and it would go straight to its target every time. That had a lot to do with chasing those Communist guerrillas out of Greece."

And with the killing of our own president?

One skeptical marksman had written an article about his experiments with the Mannlicher Carcano. He had purchased a rifle just like Oswald's, had bought the right ammunition for it, and then on the firing range, he had found that shot after shot turned out to be duds; hardly any went straight to the target. When I returned to New York, I visited several Lower Manhattan gunshops and asked about ammunition for the Mannlicher Carcano. All I could find was the old Italian-made ammunition, deteriorated from age and unreliable at best; none of the shops had the American-perfected cartridges.

Carey McWilliams was not enthusiastic about the trend of my researches. He checked out the bullet angle with the district attorney's office in Dallas and was told (falsely, as it turned out) that Oswald had been using the original Italian-made ammunition. That was as far as Carey was willing to go just then.

President Johnson, the calculating political manipulator, had twisted the arm of Chief Justice Warren, persuading him to head a special commission to investigate the assassination. Norman Redlich, with whom Carey had been allied in civil-rights causes, was one of the senior counsels, as was Joseph A. Ball, whom Carey had known in California from law school days and for whom he had great respect.

"With Earl Warren heading the commission, this is going to be a thorough investigation," Carey told me. "Nothing is going to be covered up. Let's just wait until the commission has time to make its investigation and file its report."

I was still more skeptical and more impatient. FBI Director J. Edgar Hoover was using every stratagem at his disposal to determine what the verdict of the commission would be. In a memorandum to Carey on December 3, 1963, I spelled out my doubts about the kind of report that would be produced. I was especially disenchanted with the composition of the commission, all solid Establishment types who could be almost guaranteed to uphold the Establishment view. Gerald Ford had long been noted in Washington as a strong FBI partisan; and as for Allen Dulles, I wrote: "Naming Allen Dulles to the commission was about as suspect a thing as could be done." (Long after the commission's work was finished, it would be disclosed that Dulles sat there silently, not letting any of his fellow commissioners know that his CIA had already entered into partnership with the Mafia in plots intended to kill Fidel Castro, certainly a vital bit of information.)

As for Hoover, referring to articles that had appeared in the press, I wrote that "the old authoritative leak system at which the FBI is especially adept was used. Day after day we were treated to stories that contained only a smidgen of new information in their leads—stories that went on to point out that the FBI report, whose details nobody was permitted to know, concluded definitely and positively that Oswald was the killer; that he acted alone; that there was no conspiracy. By the time the public is permitted to get a peep at the FBI details that justify this conclusion, the conclusion will have been so drummed into us, so thoroughly accepted, that it will be a bold man indeed—and where the hell does one find them today—who questions the details."

This turned out to be an uncannily accurate forecast, for once the Warren Commission got organized it found its case—a case it was expected to accept—had already been made by the FBI. Some members of the staff resented the way in which they had been boxed in. But Carey's faith in Earl Warren and the commission was unshakeable. I could not move him. And since I had contracts for two major books that had to be finished not too many months down the road, I had to shelve my concern with the Kennedy assassination and get on with my work.

I have never seen an official report greeted with such universal praise as that accorded the Warren Commission's findings when they were made public on September 24, 1964. All the major television networks devoted special programs and analyses to the report; the next day the newspapers ran long columns detailing its findings, accompanied by special news analyses and editorials. The verdict was unanimous. The report answered all questions, left no room for doubt. Lee Harvey Oswald, alone and unaided, had assassinated the president of the United States.

The chorus of acclaim impressed me. I watched television program after program; I waded through the massive columns of the New York *Times*—and even I was finally convinced. My earlier conviction that there must have been a conspiracy obviously had been wrong. The Warren Commission after months of investigation had found no trace of conspiracy, and all of the best news and editorial brains in the nation were hailing its conclusions. I accepted the verdict and turned to other things.

Two months later, left alone one evening with nothing else to do, I decided to take a closer look at the report. I had purchased the Doubleday Edition, with an impressive foreword by the eminent attorney Louis Nizer. The television programs I had seen at the time the report was issued had left two vague, nagging questions in my mind.

The first stemmed from what I had heard in Washington the year before about the suspiciously fast description of the gunman. According to the report, these details had come apparently from Howard L. Brennan, a forty-five-year-old steamfitter, who had been sitting on a concrete retaining wall opposite the Texas School Book Depository at the corner of Elm and Houston Streets, where the presidential motorcade made a slow left-hand turn into Elm. Brennan told police that he had seen a man in the sixth-floor southeast window of the depository before the motorcade arrived and that he had seen him in the act of discharging his final shot.

The initial shot had been fired at 12:30 P.M.; the Dallas police radio had carried a description that fitted Oswald at 12:45. This description, according to the Warren Report, had apparently been based on Brennan's almost instantaneous account to police. Brennan had described the gunman as white, slender, about 165 pounds, 5 feet 10 inches tall, in his early thirties. Oswald was white, slender, about 150 pounds, 5 feet 9, twenty-four years old. It was a fantastic match. I wondered whether it was possible.

The sixth-floor window of the sniper's nest had been only partially open; the room behind it was dark, unlighted; cartons had been piled up behind the window as a screen, and one had been placed on the window ledge as a gun rest. Was it possible that, from 120 feet away, gazing up at what must have been a shadowy figure against this dark background, Brennan could have come up with a nearly letter-perfect description of Oswald?

I had doubted Brennan's ability and had tested my doubts. I walked around New York streets, looking up at lighted fifth- and sixth-floor windows in which men were working. Even in these circumstances, only a portion of a man's body would be visible; and I found I couldn't tell how tall the men were or what they looked like. Yet the commission had accepted Brennan's description, despite the physical difficulties involved. Brennan's accuracy was difficult to explain, unless Oswald had been pointed out to Brennan in advance—but that is something we will never know.

Next, I turned my attention to a second question that had been nagging me. Texas Governor John Bowden Connally, Jr., who had been riding on the jump seat in front of the president, had been struck by a bullet that entered his back, passed downward through his chest, exiting below his right nipple; then passing through his right wrist, which had been in his lap, and finally inflicting a wound in his left thigh. The Warren Commission had concluded that the first shot fired by the sniper had entered "the base of the back of his [the president's] neck, had passed through his neck and had continued downward," wounding Connally. In other words, both the president and Connally had been wounded by this same bullet.

Connally told a clear, cogent, convincing story. He said he had been familiar with guns all his life, and he had instantly recognized the first shot as a rifle shot. He knew it had come from behind him; he had turned his head to the right in the direction of the book depository; then he had started to turn to his left, trying to get a look at the president, when he himself was hit and collapsed in his wife's arms. In shock, he never heard the final, fatal shot that tore off the top of the president's head; but he was positive that he had been wounded not by the first shot that had hit Kennedy but by a second, separate shot.

Connally's calm, step-by-step, explicit recital had the ring of complete truth. Why, then, I wondered, had the Warren Commission discounted this best possible eyewitness evidence? Why had it insisted so strongly that Governor Connally *had* to be mistaken? To answer these questions, I hunted in the report's index and went directly to the sections dealing with Connally and the commission's interpretation of the shot sequence. It took me perhaps an hour, and I found the Warren Commission Report— so wholly accepted—falling to pieces in my hands.

The key, I quickly discovered, was the film of the assassination taken as it was happening by amateur photographer Abraham Zapruder with his 8mm movie camera. Zapruder's camera took 18.3 frames a second; so, by numbering the frames, it could be determined just how many seconds elapsed between shots. The sequence seemed to show that the president could not have been hit before frame 210, when he disappeared momentarily behind a Stemmons Freeway sign. When he emerged into view again at frame 225, his hands were just beginning to jerk upward toward his throat, a movement that was completed by frame 227. Yet at this time, the film showed, Governor Connally was facing forward, face serene; it was simply impossible to believe that his whole body had already been furrowed by a nearly lethal bullet.

Connally showed no visible reaction until frames 231–234; expert testimony before the Warren Commission held that he could not have been hit after frame 240. Now another factor, firing speed, had to be added to the equation. The commission had determined that the fastest trigger finger in the FBI could not get off shots from Oswald's Mannlicher Carcano in less than 2.3 seconds between shots. On the basis of no evidence whatsoever, the commission had rationalized that Oswald, no champion marksman, could match the fastest gun in the FBI; but even this did not solve its problems with the lone-assassin thesis. Even assuming that the president had been hit at the earliest possible instant, at frame 210, there would have had to be another 42 frames before the lone gunman could have gotten off the second shot at frame 252. But the Zapruder film showed that Connally had been wounded much earlier, no later than frame 240—and so not even the fastest gun in the FBI could have gotten another shot off by that time. The whole lone-assassin theory foundered on this time rock; and the only way of resurrecting it was to theorize, as the Warren Commission had, that the first shot that hit the president must also have wounded Governor Connally.

But this was theory; this was rationalization; this was not hard judgment based on solid facts as everyone had supposed. As soon as I found this flaw, I saw that the report throughout was a tissue of rationalizations in which the most credible testimony (as in the case of Connally) had been discarded because it did not fit the lone-assassin hypothesis, and the most suspect word was accepted as valid and ultimate truth because it did.

I felt the hair prickle on the back of my neck with excitement at this discovery, and I hurried upstairs to my typewriter to start writing a memorandum tearing at the guts of the Warren Report. And that was the beginning of all my trouble.

Knowing that I was challenging a verdict that was considered almost as holy as the Bible, I spelled out the firing sequence and the evidence of the Zapruder film in great detail. My memorandum ran some seven pages. Once it was finished, I was confronted with the problem of what to do with it. I knew Carey McWilliams's views, but I also felt that *The Nation* was the only magazine with sufficient independence and nerve to print the kind of article I wanted to write. In hopes that my reasoned analysis would persuade Carey, I sent him the memorandum.

There followed three weeks of silence. Then Carey rejected the idea, telling me that he and others could find no flaw in my reasoning, but *The Nation* didn't want to criticize the Warren Report. I gathered that he was influenced by one overriding fear: if the assassination proved to be the work of a conspiracy, it might start another irresponsible witch-hunt comparable to that of the detested McCarthy era.

I didn't agree. The most credible evidence seemed to me to point to a conspiracy; and if conspirators could get away with murdering a president as popular as Kennedy, there was no guarantee that they would not repeat the deed any time a leading politician's program posed a threat to their interests. Still, everywhere I encountered opposition. My literary agent, Barthold Fles, shuddered when he read the memorandum. Like Carey, he could find no flaw in it, but he had difficulty believing it. "You may be right, Fred," he told me, "but I wish you wouldn't do this." I told him I felt I had to, and I wanted him to try for publication. Reluctantly, he raised the issue with Peter Rittner, then my editor at Macmillan. "Oh, my God," Bart reported Peter's saying. "Fred has exposed the CIA, the FBI and the military-industrial complex. All he needs now is to attack the Warren Report!"

On the domestic front, I was also getting a lot of flak. Julia had never questioned my writing decisions, but she did now. "Why don't you just forget it?" she asked. "Kennedy is dead, and nothing can be done about it." I explained my fear that an evil, dangerous precedent might have been set. "Well, who are *you* to challenge the Warren Commission?" she demanded. "Who are *you* to criticize some of the most famous men in the country who heard the evidence and made the report?" Exasperated, I snapped, "Well, God gave me a brain to reason with, and just plain common sense says they were wrong. It's like adding two and two and getting six. It *just doesn't make sense, Goddamn it!*"

We never agreed, and I continued to press Bart Fles. He showed the memorandum to *Esquire*, but *Esquire* had already assigned

Dwight Macdonald to write an assassination feature—an article, as it turned out, that was filled with philosophical words adding up to nothing. *True* magazine had run articles on the controversy arising from Abraham Lincoln's assassination, so I'd hoped it would prove receptive for my story. *True* weighed my little bombshell for almost a month, but finally decided it wouldn't go ahead because, well, who knew what might happen by the time the magazine got out? An editor at *Playboy* had expressed some interest in my writing, so my suggestion went there. There was another month's delay, and back it came with an excuse similar to *True's*. No one could find anything wrong with my analysis, but no one was going to publish an article based on it either.

I took the memorandum back from Bart and decided to see if I could do something with it on my own. Finally, in summer 1965, I sent it off to Edward J. Keating, then the editor of *Ramparts*. Silence. Then, about 10:30 on an August night, just as my wife and I were about to set out on a three-week vacation we'd planned for some time, the telephone rang. Keating had studied my memorandum, he said; he had shown it to others; everybody agreed the analysis was solid. Could I turn out a blockbuster article for *Ramparts* for the December issue? There went our vacation.

Little did I know I was about to get the worst double-cross I have ever had from a publisher. *Ramparts* agreed in a letter to Bart Fles to pay $1000 for my article; Keating sent me a number of sensible editorial suggestions, which I accepted. The December 1965 *Ramparts* did not include my piece. We queried. When January and February came and passed, we protested. Then in March 1966 *Ramparts* made the incredible claim that it had never agreed to publish the article in the first place—this despite the fact that I had in my files a flier the magazine had sent out in the fall soliciting new subscribers and promising it would have among its upcoming exposés "Fred J. Cook's massive reevaluation of the Warren Commission Report on President Kennedy's assassination." Finally, in April 1966, after holding the article in cold storage for six months, *Ramparts* made me a token payment of $500 and returned the manuscript.

After over a year of struggle, I was more angry and frustrated than I had ever been. In desperation, I sent the article off to Carey McWilliams. Though I knew his views, I hoped that once he saw the finished product he might have a change of heart.

Another month-long silence ensued. Then I read in one of the gossip columns that Edward J. Epstein had written a book, *Inquest*, a critical look at the Warren Report that was about to be published. I called Carey's attention to the item, warned him that time was running out and that if he ever intended to do anything with my article, he had to get a move on. So finally he did. *The Nation* published the article in two installments, June 13 and June 20, 1966, more than a year and a half after I had first proposed it. The editors prefaced it with a disclaimer that this was just my view.

I have never really recovered from my disillusionment with the Warren Commission. The twisting of evidence began with the commission's effort to establish that Oswald was an excellent shot. Marine records showed he was "a rather poor shot." The last time he had been tested on a firing range, in 1959, he made "the lowest of low marksman's" rating by a single point. The commission got around this difficulty by giving weight to the testimony of a Marine marksmanship expert who said that Oswald, as a result of his Marine training, could be considered "a good to excellent shot" compared to a civilian who had not had such intensive training. The "rather poor shot" record was ignored.

Rationalization verged on deliberate deception in the commission's treatment of Kennedy's first wound. The report's description of this first shot as having hit "at the base of the back" of the neck fudged the fact. Even worse, the schematic drawing which it presented falsified the picture. These drawings moved the wound from the "base of the back" of the neck well up on to the neck, with an arrow drawn through showing a downward trajectory of more than 17 degrees. But the pathologist's report (supported by the evidence of the bullet holes in Kennedy's jacket and shirt) showed that this first shot had not hit Kennedy in the neck, but in *the back*. The entrance wound was located specifically 5½ inches below the point of the mastoid bone and the same distance in from the shoulder—almost in the middle of the upper back. During my research, I consulted doctors and pathologists. All agreed that the path through Kennedy's back from this entrance point to the exit wound just below his Adam's apple indicated an almost flat trajectory. "The only way you can reconcile these wounds with the projected downward trajectory would be if the president had been leaning forward at an angle of almost twenty degrees when he was struck," one pathologist said. The Zapruder film showed, however, that he had been sitting bolt upright, one hand raised in greeting to the crowd. The commission's emphasis on a neck wound, its use of inaccurate schematic drawings to create a false impression, condemned it as irresponsible—at least. I believed its actions were worse than that. During my research, I mentioned the inaccurate trajectory to my National Rifle Association source, and before I could say anything else, he responded, "Yes, but that wouldn't be so if the president was leaning forward at an angle of twenty degrees"—word for word what the pathologist I quoted had told me. So I think I am justified in believing that some of those on the inside of the investigation knew the reality that the official report ignored.

Rationalization piled upon rationalization when the commission discounted a whole series of reports in which Oswald, or an Oswald look-alike, had gone out of his way to attract attention in the weeks before the assassination. One gunshop employee had written the name "Oswald" on a tag for some work he had done on a rifle; several witnesses noticed that a man who looked like Oswald had called attention to himself by his actions on a Dallas firing range. A car salesman, his testimony supported by several others in the agency, told how a man who looked like Oswald and used the name "Oswald" had inquired about purchasing a new car; he had driven a test car wildly at sixty to seventy miles an hour and, when terms of payment were discussed, mentioned that he expected to come into quite a sum of money shortly. The commission disregarded all of this on the basis that the real Oswald wasn't in Dallas, or was somewhere else in Dallas, at the times the various incidents allegedly took place. In the case of the car salesman's story, the commission cited an additional reason: Oswald did not know how to drive.

In every criminal case, there are always publicity hounds who want to get into the act. Some of the alleged sightings of Oswald could have fallen into that category; but it is difficult to dismiss the account of the car salesman, supported as it was by associates in the agency. And two other incidents were even more significant.

The first involved Jack Ruby, the mystery-man killer of Oswald. Seth Kantor, an experienced reporter who had been stationed in

Dallas and knew Ruby personally, had followed the president and Governor Connally to Parkland Hospital after the shooting. He was dashing up a stairway to a briefing room to find out whether the president was alive or dead when he felt a tug at his coattails. Kantor turned and found himself face to face with Jack Ruby, who was anxious for information about the outcome of the shooting. Kantor noted the encounter by writing Ruby's name in his notebook at the time. But Ruby swore he had never been near Parkland Hospital. The commission decided that Kantor, who could not possibly have been mistaken about a man he knew so well, simply must have been mistaken—and that Ruby, this character with a shady past and the proprietor of a sleazy nightclub, was the soul of veracity. I take Kantor's word over Ruby's. Later, when Ruby was questioned in his jail cell by Chief Justice Warren himself, he indicated there were things he could tell if Warren could get him out of Texas, where he felt his life was in danger. But Warren, incredible as it seems, ignored Ruby's obvious offer to talk.

The second incident also had decidedly sinister implications. Sylvia Odio was a wealthy Cuban exile living in Dallas; her mother and father had both been thrown into prison by Castro. Odio told the FBI—and later the Warren Commission—that on the night of either September 25 or 26, 1963, three men visited her apartment to ask for help in raising funds for the anti-Castro cause. Two of the men looked like "Latins" and gave their undercover names as "Leopoldo" and "Angelo." Their companion, an American, was introduced to Mrs. Odio as "Leon Oswald." Sylvia Odio said that the men had the correct code names for her mother and father and seemed familiar with her family background; but she was still distrustful and she didn't let the men into her apartment.

This unusual visit was followed the next day by something even more strange, a weird phone call. "Leopoldo" called Mrs. Odio merely to explain, unnecessarily it would seem, that he was bringing the American, "Leon Oswald," into the underground movement "because he is great; he is kind of *loco*." He then volunteered the information that Oswald had served in the Marines and was an excellent shot. "Leopoldo" further quoted "Oswald" as saying: "Cubans don't have any guts. . . . President Kennedy should have been assassinated after the Bay of Pigs."

When Kennedy was assassinated barely two months later, Mrs.

Odio saw Oswald's picture on television, recognized him instantly—and fainted. Her account, both of the September meeting and her reaction after the assassination, was corroborated by her sister, who had been present both times and who had herself instantly recognized Oswald as the "Leon Oswald" of the September meeting.

This Odio encounter was crucial in two respects: If "Leon Oswald" had actually been Lee Harvey Oswald, it showed that he was not acting alone, but had confederates; if "Leon Oswald" was, on the other hand, just an Oswald look-alike, it would indicate the existence of a deep-laid plot prior to the assassination to draw attention to the real Oswald. The commission asked the FBI to check the Odio story.

The FBI, lackadaisical throughout (it knew about Oswald prior to the assassination, but it hadn't mentioned him to the Secret Service), seemed to be in no hurry to investigate the Odio incident. Warren Commission attorneys first jogged the Bureau in July; they got no answer. In late August, with its work nearing an end, the commission sent the FBI a more urgent request. The FBI then came up with an excuse for ignoring the whole matter. It reported that it had interviewed Loran Eugene Hall, an anti-Castroite with underworld connections, who said *he* had visited Mrs. Odio in September, accompanied by Lawrence Howard and William Seymour. No "Oswald" was present; no "Latins" either. The Warren Commission concluded, "Lee Harvey Oswald was not at Mrs. Odio's apartment in September 1963."

Hardly had the commission's report been issued when the FBI whitewash was exposed. Howard and Seymour, interviewed just a week after Hall, denied ever having been at Mrs. Odio's apartment. Then Hall retracted his statement. This left Mrs. Odio and her sister vindicated, their account unchallenged. But the commission seems never to have taken their testimony or any of the other incidents seriously; it dismissed each on one ground or another without any recognition that, tied together, they might indicate a sinister pattern.

Soon after the publication of my Warren Commission articles, there came a series of strange events in startling succession. I reported on the first of these in a letter to Carey on July 13, 1966. Bart Fles had received a cablegram just the previous Friday from a Japanese magazine that wanted to purchase rights to my Warren Commission articles; the matter was "urgent," the cablegram said, and an immediate reply was necessary. We accepted the offer in a cablegram that same night. The next day, Saturday, Fles received a second cablegram: the magazine called the deal off without explanation of any kind. "I'd like to be able to read the State Department cables on that one," I wrote Carey.

Next a devious attack was made on me in my own favorite publication, *The Nation*. A concerned Carey telephoned me one afternoon, saying he had an article written by a professor who reported that the Warren Commission had never seen the X rays and photographs taken of the president's body at the autopsy because the Kennedy family had prohibited the use of this basic evidence. Carey wanted to know if it was all right with me if he ran the piece. I said I had no objection; I certainly didn't have any exclusive rights to everything about the Warren Commission; and if he had a good legitimate article from someone else, he should run it.

When I saw the article in the July 11, 1966, issue of *The Nation*, I blew my stack at Carey for the first time ever. The legitimate point of the article that Carey had mentioned to me was there, buried deep in the body of the piece. The whole approach, the whole tone, however, was slanted to ridicule critics of the Warren Report. The article was filled with snide references to me and to Vincent Salandria, a Philadelphia lawyer for the American Civil Liberties Union and one of the first critics of the report, and it was speckled with lines like: "Has it come to this, then—the doctors' word against the word of Cook, Epstein, Salandria, et al.?"

The rapidity with which the attack had been made—only twenty-one days had elapsed after my second *Nation* article—indicated to me that it must have been hatched almost the instant my articles appeared, and I began to smell a rat. Why Carey hadn't caught the odor, why he hadn't exercised rudimentary editorial judgment, I'll never know; but I was so furious I wrote a reply and delivered an ultimatum: unless Carey printed my answer to this academic character word for word, I would never write again for *The Nation*. The author of the back-stabbing exercise that so infuriated me had announced that he was going to withdraw from the ivy halls, become a full-time free-lance writer, and produce a book that would silence all critics and vindicate the Warren Commission. In my reply, I pointed out that I knew how extremely difficult it was to make a living by free-lance writing; I didn't believe it could be done by someone who hadn't established a broad reputation in the field, and I was convinced that the man who had done the job on me must be privately financed by some government agency like the CIA.*

There was never a rebuttal to this accusation. A couple of reactions came from other sources: from Tom Caton, who had been a professor at Monmouth College, in West Long Branch, New Jersey, and Vince Salandria. Their feeling was that, once the report was exposed and the assassination issue raised, agencies were going to have to take out after *somebody*. They had both met the back-stabbing author of *The Nation* article and asked him why he had gone out of his way to take such vicious potshots at me. He told them that he had done it "for that very reason"—because he wanted to discredit me in my own forum.

Caton and Salandria also told me about the reaction of Allen Dulles during a tape-recorded session with students at a California university. The students had copies of *The Nation* exposé and asked Dulles about it. *"The Nation"*? Dulles exclaimed—and then he went off into a fit of hyena-like laughter. The students, grim-faced, began to press him about aspects of the assassination, and Dulles abruptly broke off the exchange, remarking that if they didn't have anything better to discuss, he was going to bed.

Sometime later in that summer of 1966, I got a late-night telephone call from Vince Salandria. He was in Boston, where he had just had a debate with my *Nation* back-stabber. Salandria was excited. "Fred, I told him that you had accused him of being a CIA front—and he did not deny it. He did not deny it!"

After the debate, Salandria said, he and his opponent had a

---

* It was just some kind of intuition. I did not know at the time, none of us did, that the CIA was financing and sponsoring the publication of somewhere in the neighborhood of 1000 books that were being brought out in the United States as if they were the products of independent scholarship. This activity—totally illegal since the CIA had been specifically barred in its charter from domestic activities—did not become public knowledge until the mid-1970s investigations of our secret intelligence agencies. Even then, the CIA refused to identify any of the writers, books or publishers it had helped finance; and efforts since that time to obtain such vital information under Freedom of Information actions have been barred in the courts. The result is that we do not know to this day the full extent and insidiousness of the CIA's brainwashing endeavors.

long, private bull-session. "He's a very disturbed person," Salandria told me, "and I wound up feeling sorry for him. He has a
lot of conflicts within himself, and he finally admitted that he
knows we are right, but he said: 'The truth is too terrible. The
American people would never be able to stand it.' In the end,
however, he said he was not going to write his book." And he
never did.

I got another strong, personal indication from inside the Warren
Commission itself that there were those who thought the critics
could be right. In late July 1966, over a telephone hookup, I did
battle with Burt W. Griffin, who had been an assistant counsel
to the commission and is now a judge, on Harv Morgan's Cleveland "Contact" show.

Griffin did his best to defend the report. He ridiculed my
conclusion that a shot, or shots, had come from the grassy knoll
overlooking Dealey Plaza at the right front of the motorcade.
There was some exceptionally hard evidence, as well as the
wounding of a spectator by a bullet splinter, to indicate shots had
come from this direction. Griffin insisted that the first shot that
hit the president had followed the downward trajectory necessary
to wound Governor Connally; I told him what an expert pathologist had told me; and he conceded that if the one-shot, multiple-
wound theory was invalid, the commission's whole lone-assassin
case had to fall by the wayside.

Interestingly, it seemed to me, he admitted that there might
have been too much haste in closing out the conspiracy angle.
Warren had been impatient, he said; the commission was being
pressured to get out a fast report; proof of conspiracy wasn't easy;
and if anything had been overlooked, Griffin thought that it was
due to this impatience.

We discussed the very real possibility that Oswald had been
an FBI informer. A Dallas deputy sheriff had told a reporter that
he knew this was so; the Warren Commission had been thrown
into a flap by what Warren called "this very disturbing" rumor—
but the whole matter had been dropped on J. Edgar Hoover's
word that Oswald hadn't been on the FBI payroll. Harv Morgan
asked Griffin the direct question: Did he think Oswald had been
connected with the FBI? Griffin replied that he thought no one
was ever going to know. I asked him if this wasn't a pretty horrible
admission: here we had a very popular president assassinated—

and we weren't going to be permitted to know about such an important link if it existed? "I am just stating a fact of life," Griffin said. He added that he was certain that if anyone from any of our great federal agencies had been involved, the record would have been covered up so thoroughly that no one could ever find out.

After the radio program was over, Griffin asked to speak to me personally. "I admire what you people are trying to do," he told me, "but I have to tell you that you're not going to get anywhere." He thought, he said, that the critics were performing "a public service" because he hoped that if anything like this happened again—and he prayed it wouldn't—"it certainly never ought to be investigated in this way."

Harv Morgan was as surprised as I was. "Fred, did you hear that?" he exclaimed after Griffin had gone. "My God, did you hear *that!*"

I wrote some additional, minor articles about the assassination and the Warren Report during the next few years, and in 1968 I joined the Committee to Investigate Assassinations formed by Bernard Fensterwald, Jr., a Washington attorney who had served as a counsel to different Senate committees. I had met Bud when he was chief counsel for Senator Edward Long, of Missouri, in an investigation into official invasions of privacy, an inquiry that was aborted after some of the federal agencies being investigated leaked stories to the press about the senator's receipt of legal fees from his private law firm, which was connected with the Teamsters.

Leaving government service, Fensterwald decided to devote his time to probing assassinations—not just that of President Kennedy, but also the 1968 slayings of Dr. Martin Luther King, Jr., and Robert F. Kennedy. The "lone-gunman" solutions of each had raised just as many questions as the assassination of the president. Bud's convictions stemmed in part from a personal encounter with the rabid Radical Right in Dallas. As the principal aide and speechwriter for Senator Estes Kefauver, he had accompanied Kefauver to Dallas during the 1960 presidential campaign. Kefauver had made a rousing speech in support of John F. Kennedy's candidacy. Afterward, a high police spokesman told Bud, "You know we have some pretty fanatical people here, and I think it would be a good idea if you and the senator didn't stay in town overnight, but left right away."

Bud had relayed the warning to Kefauver, who inquired, "Do we have enough bourbon?" Bud assured him the liquor cabinet was well-stocked, and Kefauver agreed to the change of plans, saying, "All right, then, let's go."

Fensterwald's hope in forming the committee was that it would be able to keep the assassination issue alive, help to mold public opinion, and bring enough pressure on public officials to force a genuinely thorough investigation, and several members of the committee worked extremely hard toward this end. I remember especially Mary Ferrell, of Dallas, a legal secretary and one-time secretary to a governor of Texas. She collected and analyzed every scrap of material pertaining to the president's assassination; she even had a separate air-conditioned room built on her home to house the collection, which remains probably the most thorough in the nation. Yet an orchestrated campaign was mounted in books and magazine articles to label all who questioned the validity of the Warren Report mere "scavengers" who were out to make a fast buck by preying on the trauma of the American people. No propaganda campaign was ever more vicious or more untrue; some of those engaged in the research spent thousands of dollars of their own money, almost bankrupting themselves in the process.

Yet the door of the media remained firmly closed. The New York *Times*, with one of the best journalistic staffs in the nation, ran a month-long investigation into the bona fides of the Warren Report. When it was all over, the *Times* deep-sixed the whole project. The paper's attitude became obvious in 1971 when its op-ed page included an essay by David W. Belin, one of the Warren Commission counsels, upholding all the findings of the report—and, at the same time, it refused to print a responding letter from Fensterwald. The op-ed page is supposed to be a free forum in which opposing points of view can be discussed—but not where the Warren Report was concerned.

One of Fensterwald's arguments merited attention. He pointed out that Police Chief Jesse Curry, who had been in charge of the Dallas force when the president was assassinated, had developed serious doubts about the validity of the Oswald case. He had described these in a small book, *JFK Assassination File,* in which he had disclosed that scientific tests had not shown what they would have to have shown if Oswald had fired a rifle: after such a firing, powder residues are left on the cheek of the gunman.

These may be detected by analysis of a paraffin cast. The FBI had made such a test of the side of Oswald's face, but had failed to find any residues. The Bureau had argued ambiguously that such tests were not always infallible—so the Warren Commission had disregarded the evidence. There was, however, a more sophisticated and infallible test: neutron activation analysis. The FBI, as Fensterwald pointed out, had performed this test—and had failed to find any trace of residues that would show Oswald had fired a rifle. This negative finding, which seemed, as Fensterwald wrote, to show that "Oswald did not fire a rifle on November 22," was what had shaken the faith of Police Chief Curry in the Warren Commission verdict. But it did not make any difference to the *Times*.

The efforts of the committee continued for years. Gradually, I devoted less and less time to it, mainly because I had a free-lance living to make and couldn't make it if I didn't stick to the typewriter. Finally, in 1979, partly as a result of the committee's efforts, a Congressional committee was appointed to investigate the assassinations of President Kennedy and Dr. King. Unfortunately, the probe became snarled at the outset with personality conflicts, and it never did get itself on the track. The internal wrangling gave dubious members of Congress the only excuse they needed to scrimp on funds and cut the inquiry short. However, through acoustic tests the committee did establish that a fourth shot had been fired from the grassy knoll overlooking Dealey Plaza, as I and many other critics of the Warren Report had contended.

The findings of the Congressional committee were forwarded to the Department of Justice for further action; but, if the experience of the past is any criterion, they can be expected to rest in peace in Justice—forever.

23

The Evangelists of Hate

EARLY IN SPRING 1964 I WAS STRUCK BY AN IDEA THAT LED
to a magazine article, a book and eventually a legal action
that went all the way to the U.S. Supreme Court. And it
all started with my son.

Everyone knew that Lyndon Johnson would be the Democratic
candidate for president that fall, but the Republican nomination
was in doubt. Senator Barry Goldwater, of Arizona, seemed to
be the front runner, but many—including me—doubted that the
party would give its nomination to someone so far to the right.
However, my son, Fred, a great compiler of statistics, had been
charting the inroads that the Goldwater forces had been making
quietly in state caucuses, and his figures showed that Goldwater
had so many pledged delegates that, if he didn't already have the
nomination sewed up, he had such a commanding lead that it
would be virtually impossible to deny him the nomination.

My home-grown political expert had sparked my interest, and
I began to take closer notice of pro-Goldwater publications. Goldwater had written two books—*The Conscience of a Conservative*
and *What I Believe In*—and three powderpuff, man-on-the-white-
charger biographies had made their appearance. I had come across
no countervailing offering and felt that there should be at least
one critical analysis of Goldwater's philosophy.

I was acquainted with Wayne Phillips, former New York *Times* staffer who was then chairman of publicity for the Democratic National Committee. He, it turned out, had been thinking similar thoughts and he told me that nearly all the research material one would need to compile such a book could be supplied by the Democratic committee. The Democrats had filing cabinets full of Goldwater material that they had been gathering for years—texts of speeches and television appearances, entries from the Congressional Record and folders full of newspaper articles, profiles and magazine in-depth portraits. In effect, Wayne said, "Come on down, and we can give you virtually everything you need."

I had in mind to research, write and publish the book as swiftly as possible—probably in paperback because there just wouldn't be time for the slower hardcover process. Barthold Fles was enthusiastic. I made a date with Wayne Phillips, and I told Carey McWilliams about my project. He, of course, had a suggestion of his own. Radical Right broadcasts and television programs continued to blanket the nation as they had been doing for some three years, he said; and he understood that the Democrats were finally taping these broadcasts. "When you're in Washington," Carey said, "why don't you ask Wayne Phillips about this, too, and see if there's a story in it for *The Nation*." This is the idea that was to become history.

When I talked to Wayne, I found out that the Democrats had indeed been taping the extreme frothings of Radical Right evangelists who were doing their utmost to brainwash Americans. I culled a large collection of direct quotations from a number of these passion-arousing programs; and when I returned home, I wrote "Hate Clubs of the Air" for *The Nation*. The opening paragraph constituted something of a summary of what I had found: "Right-wing fanatics, casting doubt on the loyalty of every President of the United States since Herbert Hoover, are pounding the American people, this presidential election year, with an unprecedented flood of radio and television propaganda. The hate clubs of the air are spewing out a minimum of 6,000 broadcasts a week, carried by more than 1,300 radio and television stations— nearly one out of every five in the nation—in a blitz that saturates every one of the fifty states with the exception of Maine."

The Democrats had placed black dots on the map for every station airing this kind of Radical Right tripe, and it looked as if the entire nation had broken out in a virulent rash. By the best estimates, the propaganda cost nearly $20 million a year—a large percentage of it tax-exempt because the spouters of hate masqueraded behind religious or educational fronts.

On October 10, 1963, syndicated columnist Marquis Childs reported that President Kennedy (already scheduled for his fatal trip to Dallas) had "unburdened himself with considerable bitterness on the subject of top-bracket taxpayers and the tax-exemption they use to spread propaganda of the extreme Right." The tax-exempt Christian Beacon, Inc., carried the voice of Carl McIntire, of Collingswood, New Jersey, five days a week over 546 radio stations in forty-five states; H. L. Hunt's Life Line was a tax-exempt foundation with 325 radio stations and sixty-nine TV stations in forty-two states and the District of Columbia; the Christian Freedom Foundation, initially bankrolled by more than $800,000 of J. Howard Pew's oil money, had a program heard weekly on 362 stations in forty-eight states. The Christian Crusade of the Rev. Billy James Hargis, bankrolled by an estimated $1 million in tax-exempt income, and the Church League of America, joined the chorus of fanaticism.

Aides of the Democratic National Committee who had been monitoring these programs found that the Red-smear campaign against Kennedy had been transferred without a breathing pause to Lyndon Johnson. This despite the fact that Johnson's campaigns had been heftily financed by H. L. Hunt and other Texas oil tycoons like Sid Richardson. The fanatics charged that the Communists had been instrumental in getting President Johnson to appoint Chief Justice Warren to head the Kennedy assassination investigation.

Many of these programs had close ties with the John Birch Society through partially interchangeable directorships; and the common themes that ran through many of them were those of Robert Welch and his big-money backers: Get the U.S. out of the UN and the UN out of the U.S. Abolish all foreign aid. Abolish unemployment compensation. Promote right-to-work laws in the hope of crippling labor unions. Impeach Earl Warren and other justices of the Supreme Court. Abolish Social Security, a "socialistic" device; sell the Tennessee Valley Authority to private interests because it was "socialistic"; fight integration; oppose Medicare. A more subtle and insidious virus ran through some of these programs, though not through all: "take care" of the Jews and Catholics—and even that preponderance of the Protestant ministry that refused to heed the siren songs of the hate peddlers.

The Rev. Billy James Hargis had one of the highest batting averages in the against-everything league. In a single speech, he condemned Communism, liberalism, the National Council of Churches, federal aid to education, Jack Paar, federal medical care for the aged, Ed Sullivan, the Kennedy-Khrushchev meeting, Eleanor Roosevelt, disarmament, Steve Allen and the Freedom Riders then active in the civil rights movement in the South.

In *The Nation* article, I pointed out that the Federal Communication Commission's regulations should provide some recourse from such broadcast bigotry. The commission had ruled that stations must give free time for replies to persons attacked on such programs, and they also must notify those accused of such attacks. These rules were not very effective because the hate peddlers spread their venom with a broad brush; they did not make their attacks sufficiently specific for the aggrieved to have a chance to reply. A typical case was a Dan Smoot broadcast suggesting that "people should move away from closely organized churches." The statement brought a storm of protest from Smoot's Indianapolis audience, but he hadn't been specific enough to pinpoint any particular group. An Indianapolis *Times* writer noted: "Smoot has an evasive way of failing to name names or organizations in his sweeping attacks. For example, when he intimates that church leaders are Communist dupes, it is unlikely that any local minister is going to step forward and declare himself to be a Trotskyite, pinko, Comsymp, or such in order to qualify as the offended party entitled to rebuttal time."

After my "Hate Clubs of the Air" was published in *The Nation*, May 25, 1964, I went ahead with my Barry Goldwater book. I had sampled the material in the Democratic National Committee's files and had assured myself it was not just a partisan collection of anti-Goldwater material. On the contrary, it was a compilation of virtually everything Goldwater had said and done for years, along with all kinds of profiles of the man. Research was a simple matter—finding a willing publisher was far more difficult. Bart Fles had lunch one day with an editor at a major paperback house, outlined my proposition, and the enthusiastic editor suggested a $10,000 advance. But when the editor took the proposal back to his publisher, he got a flat rejection. The publisher couldn't believe that Goldwater would be nominated (he wasn't as astute as my son); the Eastern Republican Establishment would simply never let such a thing happen, he said. And if Goldwater wasn't nominated, the book would be worthless.

Bart encountered this attitude almost everywhere. New Yorkers seemed unable to imagine that Goldwater was really going to be nominated. And the two largest paperback houses had arranged to publish the Warren Report almost overnight when it came out in September—it was impossible to wedge another rush job into their already crowded schedules.

Bart and I were both stumped, but then Robert Hatch, managing editor of *The Nation*, suggested we take the idea to Barney Rosset, publisher of Grove Press, who jumped at the idea.

I plunged ahead. The title—*Barry Goldwater: Extremist of the Right*—expressed my considered judgment of Goldwater, based largely on his own utterances. But I never considered Goldwater a personal ogre. In fact, I saw him as a much nicer individual than the forces supporting him. He shot from the hip, and said everything bluntly and forcefully. The trouble was that his beliefs made little contact with the twentieth century. For example, he said that if he were elected he would just call in the Joint Chiefs of Staff and tell them the Vietnam War was theirs; they could do anything they wanted to win it. Many military men were itching to take the atom bomb and blast Vietnam, as the common expression of time had it, "back into the stone age"—an act, clearly, of utter irrationality. A joke that was making the rounds at the time illustrates my perception of the man: "The Russians are coming!" Goldwater cries. "Boys, draw the wagons in a circle."

Behind Goldwater's charming personal façade—his good looks, his winning manner, his ease on television—lurked the fanaticism of the Radical Right. Governor Nelson A. Rockefeller, of New York, had contested the nomination at the outset, and his supporters in California had been literally beaten down with Storm Trooper tactics. On Barry Gray's WMCA broadcast on July 5, 1964, Rockefeller described the California disaster:

> We had Rockefeller-for-President offices all throughout these counties. They received over 200 bomb threats. Every office got them. The women workers, particularly, would get calls at night—threats, vile language. One of our women delegates almost went to pieces under this kind of pressure. Her car was pushed off the road late at night. These tactics, in my opinion, are a very serious portent for the future.

We had a reception given by Leonard Firestone, who was my Southern California chairman. Some of these young Goldwater supporters tried to come in the front door, but were not able to get in because they were carrying these placards and so forth. So they came in the kitchen and up the back way, tore down all our posters. There were about 5,000 people there. They put stuff in the punch—it may have been acid—to spoil it. They went around with their hands and stamping on the sandwiches.

Then the leader of this group . . . got in a fight with a young businessman. They ended up on the floor. There was a big cigarette ashtray—the kind you see standing in hotels—made of porcelain. That was upset and the businessman was pushed over on it and had to have seven stitches in his arm! . . . This just doesn't seem like America.

Rockefeller came out of Northern California with a sizable lead, but the Birchite South, where the incidents he described occurred, gave Goldwater a 75,000-vote margin, enough for him to win the primary by a wafer-thin 1.8 percent of all the votes cast. Rockefeller was out of the race.

The Republican National Convention, held in the Cow Palace in San Francisco, was another exercise in neo-fascism. With Rockefeller gone, the Eastern Establishment tried to coalesce behind Governor William Scranton, of Pennsylvania; but Goldwater's hold on delegates was so strong that Scranton was in effect beaten before his drive could get started. With a certain victory, there was no need for Storm Trooper tactics.

It says much about the new, powerful, multimillionaires of the West and Southwest that even in these circumstances they could not persuade their followers to behave with common human decency.

Ugly incidents took place that were not seen in much of the East because of the time difference. I am again indebted to my son for sitting up so late and watching. Many Eastern viewers never saw the following events:

• One black delegate (there were precious few at the convention) who refused to join a Goldwater demonstration suddenly discovered, as the paraders passed him a second time, that his coat jacket had been set on fire.
• James Brophy and family bolted the Georgia delegation for

Scranton and were greeted with snarls: "You're nigger-lovers,
Communists!"
• One Southern California delegate (he later tried to deny he had
said it) was quoted as declaring: "Lee Oswald should have got the
Congressional Medal of Honor."
• Another Goldwater delegate told the columnist Stewart Alsop:
"If Scranton gets it, there'll be blood three feet deep on the Cow
Palace floor, and the nomination won't be worth the powder to
blow it to hell."

Hard-featured private eyes guarded Goldwater's suite and were
even stationed on the fire escape. When Mary Scranton tried to
descend the fire escape to reach her husband's offices below Goldwater's, they turned her back. After the Goldwater nomination,
when she left the Cow Palace and went down a ramp to join her
husband in a waiting trailer, the ramp suddenly burst into flames
behind her; she was lucky to escape, and police said they suspected arson.

The stench of fascism pervaded the air.

I was not immune. Word had gotten around my community
that I was writing an anti-Goldwater book, and I began to get
telephone calls in the night, denouncing me as a Comsymp. The
callers, of course, never had the guts to give their names, and I
finally raged at one of them: "Why don't you come over and show
your face, you cowardly son of a bitch?" My son tried to calm me
down; I was just playing into their hands by showing such anger,
he said. But I was fed up to the gills with Americans acting like
followers of Adolf Hitler.

I also began to get Radical Right literature in the mail. Some
thoughtful soul mailed me the July 1974 *Liberty Letter*, a Radical
Right tract produced in Washington, whose headline proclaimed
SECRET TREATY DANGEROUS RED PLOT. The "plot" referred to
was a proposed Consular Treaty; and the *Liberty Letter* contained
statements like "Johnson and his friends at the State Department
CANNOT establish this espionage network for the Soviet Union"
without the approval of the Senate. Thus, the Senate "must become the battleground again where patriots can resist." The envelope was decorated with Barry Goldwater trading stamps.

My anti-Goldwater book didn't begin to record the kind of sales
I had hoped for. It did not reach the stands until mid-September,

which gave it a very short selling season, and Goldwater did such a foot-in-mouth performance during his campaign that most voters didn't need to read a book to learn why they should vote against him. In addition, there may have been subtle Radical Right pressures at work. A bookstore owner in Peoria, Illinois, told Grove Press that he had been visited by a band of vigilantes who had warned him that if he wanted his store left intact he had better not display my book; in a panic, he sent the carton of books back unopened.

After Goldwater's defeat, I became the target of a vicious smear campaign. William F. Buckley, Jr., then editor of *The National Review,* started it, and he was joined by the Rev. Billy James Hargis, one of the most raucous voices of the Radical Right. They claimed I was a thoroughly despicable character who had been fired in disgrace by the *World-Telegram and Sun* in 1959 for making a false charge on a television program. Sifting the truth from the falsehoods takes a bit of backtracking.

In the late 1950s, Gene Gleason and I, the paper's top investigative reporters, teamed up. We won a New York Newspaper Guild Page One Award for exposing the way police were bugging the headquarters of Transit Authority motormen during contract negotiations. Gleason is one of the best and toughest reporters I have ever met, possessed of an insatiable passion to take on the world in the cause of justice. He was described by Robert A. Caro in his massive work, *The Power Broker: Robert Moses and the Fall of New York,* "Gleason was *Front Page.* Big, brawny and boisterous, with a crooked Irish grin and a nose that must have been broken at least once in his thirty-two years, he looked the part—complete to the collar of his trench coat, which was invariably turned up . . . the sacred profession of journalism was to him the newspaper game, and he played it with a swagger."

In summer 1957, the front office decided to launch us on an investigation of the empire of Robert Moses, the builder of massive bridges and parkways, the autocrat of public authorities that kept their books closed even to the public legislatures that created them. Moses was the czar of the city's slum clearance program, run with Title I funds supplied by the federal government, supposedly to stimulate private investment in middle-class housing.

But Title I as Moses ran it was a bonanza for unscrupulous real-estate operators who, without risking a dime of their own money, acquired title to large blocks of city property, bulldozed housing and ran parking lots on the vacated land, collected rents from the buildings left without providing heat or other services—and finally walked away with huge profits, not even bothering to pay city taxes. Under Moses, Title I was a disaster and a disgrace; instead of building housing, it destroyed more than it created; it tore up and scattered to the winds entire ethnic neighborhoods; and when some projects were actually completed after years of delay, they contained penthouses renting for $8000 and tiny, one-and-a-half-room apartments priced at $325 a month—hardly middle-class housing in the 1950s.

Gleason and I hacked away at this monumental scandal, but the hotter our disclosures, the more tepid became their reception by the news desk. Robert Moses was to New York as J. Edgar Hoover was to the nation. The New York *Times* and other large newspapers had virtually worshiped at his feet for years; and no matter what Gleason and I uncovered, the remainder of the press ignored the scandal. This general lack of interest in the rest of the fourth estate had its effect in our newsroom. Some of the toughest shots I took at Moses were deleted; and when Gleason and I broke what we thought should be an important page-one story, we often found it cut and buried on an inside page. "Nobody understands this stuff," the news editor growled.

We became so frustrated that we decided to tip off some of our rivals to get some competition going—and so force our own newspaper to use our story. Gleason was friendly with William Haddad, of the New York *Post*, and he fed Haddad enough information to get him interested. Haddad began digging—and writing; the *Post* began beating us on our own story—and our own news desk began screaming at us to catch up. We were back in business.

Some of our exposés had Mayor Robert F. Wagner's administration squirming. In fact, the City Hall gang was gored so badly that one day Gene Gleason came bouncing into the newsroom, practically walking on the balls of his feet, a broad grin on his round, Irish face. He seated himself on the edge of my rewrite desk and announced, "They want to buy us."

He had just come back from a meeting with an administration official who was so disgusted that he had become one of our valuable news sources. The official, Gene told me, paced nervously around his office, then finally came to the point: If Gene and I would lay off, the administration would put both our wives on the city payroll under their maiden names for $5000 a year.

They wouldn't have to work; they wouldn't have to show: we would just have to stop turning up new scandals. "I wouldn't touch it with a ten-foot pole," I told Gene. "Okay, neither would I," he said. "And since we've turned it down, let's not say anything about it to them" (nodding in the direction of the city desk). I gathered he still wanted to protect his friendly source.

But soon I became worried about Gene. I was in the office, relatively safe at my typewriter, but he was out on the street, alone and exposed. The play began to get rough after we broke one of our biggest stories, a story that we wangled out of the City Comptroller's office; a story that showed how the city had been gulled for delinquent taxes by shyster promoters who pocketed the cash from condemned properties and then moved on. Suddenly Gene was followed everywhere he went; his contacts wouldn't even be seen with him; and a letter from an administration source was sent to the front office accusing Gene of seeking a payoff. I worried about what kind of insidious damage this kind of innuendo might cause and asked my city editor for a private lunch. I told him the whole story of the bribe offer.

By late summer 1959, the unrelenting pressure had dried up most of our sources, and at this point I suggested to Carey McWilliams that the entire Wagner–Moses–Title I mess would make a good blockbuster issue for *The Nation* in the fall. *The Nation* published "The Shame of New York" on October 31, 1959. Aided by Gene's research, it was probably the most powerful magazine article I had ever written. It became the talk of New York, and the Wagner Administration reacted angrily. One of District Attorney Frank S. Hogan's deputies began making a series of denigrating speeches to Democratic clubs, saying that Gene and I were a couple of cheap hacks who would write anything for money. The truth was that Gene had received just $500 for his research, and I had been paid $1000 to write the article—and I'd had to take a month's leave of absence without pay to do it. My only reward had been liberation from Roy Howard's zoo for a month to work at home on a project that I felt was important.

At this juncture, a young assistant editor of *Esquire* telephoned me. Would Gene and I be willing to do a full-length profile on Robert Moses for the magazine? Would we! The editor joined us for a drink at a bar near our office, and we discussed the project. Near the end of our talk, he asked, "Weren't you ever threatened

or didn't they ever try to bribe you?" We told him the story of
the bribe offer.

"Well, why didn't you use it?" he asked me.

"Because I can't prove it," I said.

The editor shook his head. "That doesn't make any difference.
You don't have to prove it. Everybody knows that's the way things
are done in this town, and everybody will believe you."

Thus the seed was planted. Later, when we were asked to
appear on David Susskind's late-night television show, I told the
story of the bribe offer that we had rejected. All hell broke loose.
The next morning District Attorney Hogan's office summoned
Gene and me for questioning. Before we left the office, Roy
Howard and Lee Wood talked to us. Howard indicated he didn't
like my writing for *The Nation.* "I guess we all know what *that*
is," he said with a sneer. "I want to talk to you later about that,"
he told me. "But we are all in it now, so go over and tell your
story." That was the last time I saw Roy Howard.

As Gene and I were leaving the building, a newsboy came
running after me with a message: Lee Wood wanted the Scripps-
Howard lawyer who was to be present at the questioning to telephone him before the session began. The lawyer talked to the
office, then put Gene on the phone. Gene seemed nervous. "We
have to be very careful about the way we put this," he said to
me afterward. I replied, "There's only one way to tell it. Just like
it is."

Chief Assistant District Attorney Alfred J. Scotti, head of Hogan's rackets bureau, handled the interrogation. Gene still seemed
nervous, unlike his usual cocky self; and the questioning finally
reached a climax when Scotti slapped his hand on his desk and
said to Gene, "Here's the point. Did this man say to you, 'We'll
put your wives on the payroll for $5000 a year if you keep quiet?'
Did he say that?" And Gene, squirming, replied, "Well, I couldn't
put it quite that way."

I blew up. I jumped out of my chair, paced around the room
and demanded to know what the devil was going on. Gene looked
at me with a helpless, blank-eyed stare. Scotti said he wanted to
take a statement from Gene; but before he did, he called a recess.
We went out into the hallway.

I was furious. Gene said that he would go back and tell Scotti
the original story. But how could he? I shrugged helplessly. You

tell it right the first time or not at all. The Scripps-Howard attorney listened and offered no advice.

Long years later, Gene gave me his version of the telephone conversation before we went into Scotti's office. Both Roy Howard and Lee Wood were on the phone. Gene said, "And they kept asking me questions like: 'Well, you didn't take anything, did you?' 'No.' 'The man didn't actually have money in his hands that he offered you, did he?' 'No.' 'Then you can't say it was actually a bribe, can you?' 'Well, I only know what I was offered.' 'But isn't it possible that you were mistaken, that you misunderstood?' 'Well, I suppose anything is possible, but I know what I was told.' This went on and on. They kept urging me to go a little easy; they kept telling me that if I did, 'Nothing will happen.' They said that over and over: 'Nothing will happen.' "

Back in Scotti's office, Gene asked what would happen if he made a statement. I can see Scotti slapping his hand on his desk and saying, "It will rest right here. We'll tell the press we questioned you and have gotten your story. Then, in a day or two, we'll call in the man you've named and get his side of it."

In retrospect, this seems to bear out Gene's version that some kind of understanding had been reached in advance. The matter could have been handled the way Scotti had promised, but it wasn't. Gene's statement said that he had "exaggerated" the story he had told me; and this was blown up almost instantly. Before I got back to the office, the press wires were humming, and some radio and TV announcers were shrieking almost hysterically: "He lied! He lied!"

There was no question about what would happen to Gene after he confessed that he "exaggerated" the bribe offer. But my status depended on another issue. My city editor suddenly insisted I had never told him about the bribe offer. As the story got hotter, he made a public statement in which he recalled details of our luncheon conversation (even some I had forgotten)—everything except the bribe, the only reason I had asked to talk to him in the first place. I was fired along with Gene.

I shall never forget the turmoil of those days. My phone rang almost constantly. There were several job offers, some from the most surprising sources. I told the callers that I had two book contracts to fulfill and had already arranged for a year's leave of absence from the paper—only the *World-Telegram and Sun* couldn't wait an extra month to get rid of me. One persistent caller was Jack Olsen, then with *Time* magazine, who insisted on seeing me. I wasn't in any mood to talk, but Jack wouldn't be put off. "Fred, that story you told on television is the classic version of the typical New York fix," he said, "and I want to talk to you and Gene about it."

Jack came down to the Jersey shore, saw us both, identified and interviewed "Mr. X," the city official in the drama—and so developed what should have been a top-notch article for *Time*. But on a Sunday afternoon, a *Time* researcher called and began asking me questions about how old I was, how long I had worked for the paper, etc., etc. It was obvious that Olsen's article had been scrapped, and *Time* wasn't relying on it for even the most basic details. Some weeks later, Jack told me that he had encountered a senior editor who said, "Jack, I know we blew a good story, but I could never trust anything that man Cook said after what he wrote about Alger Hiss."

A couple of days after the firings, Bill Peer, Mayor Wagner's press secretary, telephoned me. He said that he had found the boys in Room 7, the press room at City Hall, were quite disturbed about what had happened to me; and he said that Roy Howard, after the administration had been helpful in settling a newspaper strike, had said that anytime anyone in the administration wanted to talk to him he would be available. "So I took advantage of the offer on your behalf," Peer told me, "and I had lunch today with Roy Howard. He said it was a blow to the paper to lose someone like you, but he intimated that there was something else involved. What can you tell me about it?" I told Peer that the only thing that had been mentioned to me as the reason for my dismissal was the flap over the television program. (I knew that Roy Howard hated my writing for *The Nation* and that I had been close to being fired after I first wrote about the Alger Hiss case, but I couldn't tell Peer that. I was chary about making another charge I couldn't prove.) All I could do was to thank Peer for his effort, which came as a total surprise to me.

To all of this, I shall add just one more note. Several years later, in a study of the borough president's offices, *Newsday*, the large Long Island daily, came across the maiden name of the wife of one of its former reporters on a borough president's payroll for $5000 a year. The reporter had left *Newsday* and set up his own public relations firm before this discovery was made, so the incident was quickly forgotten.

Five years later, William Buckley and the Rev. Billy James Hargis seized on the Gleason-Cook incident in an effort to ruin my reputation. I never pay much attention to Buckley, but Carey McWilliams called his attack to my notice. And I might not have known about Hargis's diatribe if Radio Station KXEN in St. Louis had not sent me a transcript of his November 25, 1964 broadcast.

Hargis said I had tried to smear and destroy Barry Goldwater and claimed that I had been fired for making a false charge on television; he cited *Newsweek* of December 7, 1959, as showing that "Fred Cook and his pal Eugene Gleason had made up the whole story and this confession was made to New York District Attorney Frank Hogan." (*Newsweek* had said no such thing, but had reported I was "a sympathetic figure to many of [my] colleagues.") Hargis continued by attacking my long association with *The Nation*, "one of the most scurrilous publications of the Left which has championed many Communist causes over many years." Hardly had I finished reading this diatribe when Bill Buckley struck again, quoting Hargis.

I had already gone to my long-time lawyer, Joseph N. Dempsey, of Asbury Park, who had written Buckley seeking a retraction. Buckley had given us the back of his aristocratic hand—and then compounded his offense by quoting Hargis. Since *The Nation* had been traduced in the Hargis broadcast, I asked Carey McWilliams whether the magazine would join me in taking some counteraction. Carey's advice was to ignore the whole thing. "I never pay any attention to kooks like Hargis anyway," he said. "The best way is just to ignore them and treat them with the contempt they deserve."*

---

* At the time, neither Carey nor I had any idea of the true character of the Rev. Billy James Hargis. In February 1976 *Time* magazine reported that Hargis had severed his ties with the Crusade for Christian Morality and its American Christian College in Tulsa, Oklahoma, after four male students and one coed charged that he had had sexual relations with them. According to *Time*, "Hargis's sexual troubles surfaced" in October 1974, when the first of the five students complained to the then vice president, David Noebel. *Time* wrote: "Noebel's account: Not long before, Hargis had conducted a wedding for the student: on the honeymoon, the groom and his bride discovered that both of them had slept with Hargis." According to two persons who attended a meeting between Hargis and college officials, *Time* reported, Hargis admitted his behavior and blamed it on "genes and chromosomes."

This may have been sound strategy from *The Nation's* stand-point, but I felt I was being batted back and forth like a shuttle-cock. Since there was no chance of getting a fair deal from Buckley, I considered suing him for libel. Joe Dempsey wasn't an expert in libel law, but another lawyer in our area, Harry Green, was. Green told me he wouldn't touch the case without a $2500 retainer up front; and he warned that his final fee would be a lot higher because libel cases drag on interminably, with depositions and counterdepositions. And, in the end, even if you get a verdict, how do you collect? *The National Review* was hardly a cash-rich enterprise—it had to appeal frequently for donations.

There had to be some way, I thought, of dealing with Hargis even if I couldn't sue Buckley. Ever since that blow-up with the *World-Telegram and Sun,* I had been treated most cordially by Hogan's office when I was writing articles about crime; and my friend Joe Alvarez told me that Hogan's staff was shocked at the way I had been dismissed. I suggested to Dempsey that we might write a letter to Hogan asking him to clear me; but Joe was scornful. "No politician is going to stick his neck out to help you," he said. "Why should he?"

I disregarded Joe's advice and wrote a personal letter to Frank Hogan, describing the Hargis and Buckley attacks, pointing out that it was impossible to go around the country suing everybody, and asking if he would be willing to give me a letter clearing my reputation. I mailed my letter to Hogan on a Saturday. In Tuesday's mail, I had his answer. "I wish to state," Hogan wrote, "that this office did not make any statement reflecting on your integrity at a press conference on November 23, 1959, . . . nor, for that matter, have we made such a statement at anytime." He pointed out that my reporting partner had "completely exonerated" me and added, "I shall hope that this brief statement will dispel any doubts that may have arisen as to what this office has said in connection with this matter."

Armed with Hogan's letter, I decided that I was ready to take on Billy James Hargis. The Federal Communication Commission's rules were specific about the handling of personal attacks: any station airing them was obligated to send the accused party a full transcript of the remarks and to offer him or her free air time to reply. But only one station, in St. Louis, had sent me a transcript of his accusation.

I telephoned Wayne Phillips because I had to find out how many stations Hargis had in his network, and I knew that the Democrats would have a full list of Radical Right broadcasts. Wayne sent me the information, and I saw at once that I had a huge project on my hands. Hargis's broadcasts were being carried by more than 300 radio stations across the nation, and I would have to contact all of them.

My daughter helped me with the mailing—addressing hundreds of envelopes, and stuffing, stamping and sealing them. We sent off the request for free time to reply to Hargis in daily batches.

When the replies began to come in, I found myself caught in a veritable maelstrom of confusion. Some stations pointed out that Hargis had two programs, one aired during the week, one just on Sunday; they had used one of his programs, not the other. Could I tell them on which of his programs the attack on me had occurred? Perhaps then they could tell if they had aired it. I was disgusted. It was evident that many stations hadn't given a damn about FCC regulations; they wanted *me* to tell them what they were putting on the air.

Fortunately, there were a few responsable broadcasters. Some fifty stations replied at once that they would give me free time if I would send them a tape. I pointed out that Hargis had every right to criticize my book if he wished; everyone had a right to express legitimate criticism, and I would never quarrel with that. But, I said, Hargis had indulged in a personal, vindictive attack which was not supported by the facts, as anyone who had taken the trouble to check with District Attorney Hogan's office could have found out. And then I quoted from Hogan's letter exonerating me. The only help I received from the Democrats (contrary to later rumors) came when I mailed the tape to Wayne Phillips, who had a half-dozen copies run off for me. I began mailing out the tapes to the stations that had offered me free time, with the request that they let me know when they had aired my reply and return the tape. As the tapes came back, I mailed them out again.

But fifteen stations made a fatal mistake. They had the effrontery to tell me that I could have time on the air as Hargis had—and they enclosed their rate schedules. Ha, I said to myself, this is like blackmail; and I composed the letter which, I am convinced, did more than anything else to send this case to the U.S. Supreme Court.

In a letter to Ben F. Waple, secretary of the Federal Communications Commission, on February 7, 1965, I pointed out that the broadcasting industry was ignoring the commission's basic rule that stations must notify victims of personal attacks. After I started the battle with Hargis, I managed to find out, through correspondence with some of the stations involved, that the Rev. Carl McIntyre had leveled a similar blast at me. McIntyre had an even larger audience than ᴵᵛ ⸱ᵍis, yet not a single station had notified me of his attack. Here I was, apparently the target of a well-organized Radical Right cabal, and I had learned about it only by accident and too late to protest. My letter said: "They are insisting that they are not obligated to permit me to reply to Hargis unless I pay for the time. In correspondence with several of these stations, I have pointed out to them that such an interpretation could result in virtually an air-wave blackmail racket. A station, if this were permitted, could air a scurrilous and unfounded charge against an individual—and then make money by insisting that he pay to clear his name. I am certain from my own reading of the 'fairness doctrine' that this is not at all what the FCC intended, and therefore I am filing this formal complaint against stations that have taken this attitude."

I closed by naming the fifteen stations, and the FCC took the case from there.

When some stations refused point-blank to honor an FCC order to grant me free time, the FCC went into the U.S. District Court in the District of Columbia. The court ruled unanimously for the FCC's Fairness Doctrine. But one station, WGCB, in Red Lion, Pennsylvania, owned by the Rev. John M. Norris, refused to yield and carried the case to the U.S. Supreme Court. On June 9, 1969, the court in a unanimous 7 to 0 decision upheld the FCC. Justice Byron R. White, usually quite conservative, wrote that the FCC fairness rules "enhance rather than abridge freedoms of speech and press protected by the First Amendment." He added: "It is the right of viewers and listeners, not the right of the broadcasters, that is paramount."

My fight had been purely personal, but the obduracy of WGCB had escalated the issue and resulted in a Supreme Court ruling that made Red Lion a benchmark case with tremendous impact on the broadcasting industry.

Robert Louis Shayon wrote in *The Saturday Review* that the

case was "one of the most important opinions of the century." He added: "Broadcasters generally were aggrieved and surprised by the sweeping nature of the Red Lion decision. They had pressed the assault on the Fairness Doctrine with deliberate power and at great expense in legal fees. . . . The broadcasters, anticipating a victory over regulatory powers that they have sought for forty years, have been stunned by what they consider the Court's over-kill. The Red Lion case is a historic assertion of the public's stake in the effective use of the broadcast media for the ends of self-government."

After the decision, Rev. Norris wrote me from Red Lion on June 19, 1968, offering me fifteen minutes of free air time. I weighed his offer, but I was afraid I couldn't talk about Hargis for fifteen minutes without saying something that would give *him* the right to demand free time to reply to *me*. In addition, four and a half years had passed, and no one would know what the devil it was all about—or care. So I declined Norris's offer, pointing out that I had wanted only five minutes *at the time* to reply to Hargis and that I hoped the Supreme Court's decision would induce stations in the future to give free time for replies when they mattered.

That should have ended the case, but it didn't. In summer 1974, I received a telephone call from Fred W. Friendly, the Edward R. Murrow Professor of Journalism at the Columbia Graduate School of Journalism and an adviser to the Ford Foundation, who said he was researching a book on the Fairness Doctrine and the Red Lion case and why I started it. Friendly was so cordial that I came to think of him as Friendly Fred Friendly. And he was terribly flattering to me, once saying, "I think history is going to be very good to you, Fred. You've been proven right on so much that you have done—the pieces on the CIA, the FBI, the military-industrial complex, even perhaps in the end on the Alger Hiss case. Yes, I think history will be good to you."

I am not enough of an egotist to believe that history will even take note that I have existed, but such honeyed words are disarming, even to an old cynical reporter. So it was with utter shock that on Sunday, March 30, 1975, I picked up *The New York Times Magazine*, a publication I had written for over the years, and found the cover devoted to a montage of me, Wayne Phillips, the

Goldwater book, Jack Kennedy and Lyndon Johnson. The lead article was "What's Fair on the Air?" by Friendly Fred Friendly.

Friendly's theme was that I had been part of a conspiracy hatched in the catacombs of the Johnson Administration. He insinuated (a slur that was immediately picked up in an analytical news account in the *Times*) that the Democrats had gotten me (the implied message was that I had been paid) to palm off on *The Nation* the "Hate Clubs of the Air" article. He charged that the Democrats had actually written my FCC letters for me (apparently I had suddenly lost the facility to express myself in English) and that my whole "campaign" had been made possible by a Democratic cabal. He concluded that I had not brought my action against Red Lion "simply as an offended private citizen" but that I had been part of "a carefully orchestrated campaign initiated by politicians to inhibit views they believed to be harmful to the country, as well as to their own political fortunes."*

I was stunned. So much for Friendliness. I had sat in my living room and told this man the whole story in detail: how I had consulted and paid my own lawyer; how I had drawn up and had printed at my own expense the letter requesting time to answer Hargis; how I had handled the expense of mailing the envelopes and tapes. I had told him that my contact with Wayne Phillips

---

* The Fairness Doctrine remains a controversial issue. On June 19, 1983, *The New York Times Magazine* ran an article by Judge Irving R. Kaufman, of the U.S. Court of Appeals for the Second Circuit, advocating the repeal or modification of the doctrine. Judge Kaufman pointed out that Mark Fowler, chairman of the FCC, and Arthur Ochs Sulzberger, publisher of the *Times*, had called for "partial or total abolition of content-based broadcast regulations." He noted that the FCC had "given notice of its plan to consider rescinding in large measure its rules affording individuals the right to answer personal attacks and the right of political candidates to respond to critics and challengers." The article, like Friendly's before it, made a spurious equation between print and broadcast journalism. It argued that, since the government under the First Amendment cannot interfere with the printed word, why should it have the right to interfere with broadcast journalism? It is like comparing the four-horse shay with the modern Concorde. Print journalism does not rely on any rights in the public domain for its existence; broadcasts exist only through licenses permitting them to use the public's airwaves. Print journalism, if it errs, had its own words in black and white to confront it, and the newspaper can be brought quickly to account. Broadcasts, as I had demonstrated, can slander one on programs scattered throughout the nation, and the person attacked might never know what was happening. Judge Kaufman cited my Red Lion case as if Red Lion were a lone, isolated example; it was not. Red Lion was the only remaining, obstinate survivor out of a broadcasting hookup of more than 300 stations. The Red Lion case was symptomatic of a wave of vicious Radical Right brainwashing, and the only protection lies in the enforcement of the Fairness Doctrine. Removal of all restraints would simply give heavily financed fanatics carte blanche to spread their poisons throughout the nation.

was limited to his getting me a list of Hargis's stations and duplicating some tapes for me. I wrote immediately to the *Times Magazine* that Friendly Fred's charges were "all demonstrably untrue: and what saddens me is that Mr. Friendly must have known it because I went over these specific points with him."

Carey McWilliams and Wayne Phillips were as furious as I was because Friendly had also distorted what they had told him. The *Times* printed our letters, and Friendly's only comment was that, well, it was good to have a discussion and exchange of ideas. What a pity that the man couldn't recognize the truth when it was told to him in the first place.

At times like this I remind myself of a bit of earthy wisdom passed on to me by the woman behind the counter in the drugstore where I picked up my evening papers: "Mr. Cook," she said, "haven't you learned yet that you can't trust nobody about nothing?"

24

The Summing Up:
Julia II

ALL OF US MUST DEAL WITH THE DEATH OF A LOVED ONE and whatever the circumstances, the experience is traumatic. It is hard enough to get over a loss when death was inevitable, but when it could have been averted through elementary caution and care, the despair is compounded by bitterness and frustration. My special cross was to deal with such a death: one that should not have happened.

Here is the story of my bleak, Stygian year. Life for me all but ended: for months I could not work; I could not think; I could not care.

Julia and I had been married for thirty-eight years when she died in the summer of 1974. I had been in love with her for forty years; without her, life stretched before me like a vast and endless waste.

We had lived for seventeen years—and had coped as best we could—with the knowledge that Julia had a defective mitral valve in her heart. When we were young, it hadn't mattered. She could swim longer than I could; she could play Ping-Pong longer; she had more stamina. But then, one bitter night early in the winter of 1957, she staggered through the front door after choir practice and leaned against the wall. "I can't breathe," she said.

That was the scary beginning. Years of examinations, consultations with different doctors, and stays in different hospitals followed. The toll on her spirits was devastating; I have often wondered how I would have lived with the specter of death hovering over me every day. I only know that this burden greatly changed the cheerful, optimistic girl I had fallen in love with. As the years passed, as she found that she could do less and less—she even had to give up what she loved most: singing in the choir—a feeling of doom settled upon her, a conviction that nothing could be done to save her.

We knew that open-heart surgery with a valve replacement was a possibility, but a succession of doctors had shied from recommending the procedure unless it became absolutely necessary. Julia's age and weight deterred them. The slim young woman I had married had put on a lot of pounds after the birth of our children; and, though she tried to control her eating, she had a thyroid problem that made it difficult for her to shed weight unless she was on a starvation diet.

By 1974 the dreaded decision could be put off no longer; Julia went into New York Hospital for open-heart surgery. She came through the ordeal remarkably well; our family experienced a feeling of relief bordering on euphoria. We had lived in such fear of the surgery that it seemed as if the most dangerous hurdle had been passed; Julia would be fine; she would live a good, a better, life for years to come. Or so we believed.

After a mitral valve replacement, a heart patient has to be put on a blood thinner, Coumadin, to keep blood clots from forming. No one told us that Coumadin can be deadly. Unless the blood is kept in perfect balance, this drug, which acts erratically on some patients, thins the blood so excessively that cerebral hemorrhages occur. This is why the blood should be constantly and carefully monitored. According to the *Physicians Desk Reference*, blood tests should be made a couple of times a week at the beginning. But our doctors disregarded the warning in this Bible of the profession. They evidently thought that once every two weeks would be sufficient. Ten days after we brought Julia home, the Coumadin did its deadly work; blood flooded her brain, and in thirty-six hours she was dead.

I blamed the hospital that hadn't warned us of the Coumadin hazard and the local heart specialist who hadn't bothered to make certain that blood tests were taken on time. And I blamed myself.

I was an investigative reporter; I had written a book in 1966 about hospitals and patients' financial problems. Yet I hadn't taken the time to research my wife's case; I had put blind faith in a hospital considered one of New York's finest and in the cardiologist who had one of the best reputations in our local area. Even when there were signs that Julia was not recovering as rapidly as she should have, even when there were indications that she was in some kind of distress, I put my faith in the Great Doctor, who assured me that she was just undergoing a psychological trauma. I could have done what I had advised others to do: I could have called in another doctor; I could have gotten a second opinion. I could have done almost anything but what I did: I sat and waited like a dumb bunny in the happy faith that all was well and only time was needed for the cure.

The medical profession was in a panic at the thought that I might hit the hospital and the doctor with huge malpractice suits. But I never seriously considered this. I didn't want money for my wife's death. I wanted to do something to help others avoid such needless tragedies. I decided to track down exactly what had happened: where and why everything had gone so disastrously wrong. I became convinced that one of the medical profession's greatest and most dangerous flaws lies in the superior attitude of doctors. So many of them seem to consider themselves gods, possessors of esoteric knowledge that poor common boobs cannot be expected to understand. Leave everything to us, they say; *we* know what we are doing—*you* don't have to know and wouldn't understand it anyhow.

Calling this a lack of communication is a grave understatement. Had I known about the dangers of Coumadin, had I known about some of the most obvious warning signs—like the acute tenderness of the skin about which Julia complained—I would have known enough to see that remedial measures were taken in time. It doesn't take any genius to follow such simple instructions.

I pulled myself together enough after Julia's death to write an account of her ordeal for *New York* magazine, which ran it as the cover story on November 18, 1974. The article led to a book, *Julia's Story, the Tragedy of an Unnecessary Death*, a year later. Nothing else that I have ever written has brought such a response. My files bulged with the accounts of heartbreaking cases, descriptions of comparable tragedies. Many of those who wrote had felt as I had: they had not wanted to collect blood money—no money could possibly compensate them for their loss—and they wrote out of a need to share their grief with someone who understood. This experience convinced me that, though the medical profession may be harassed by unjustified malpractice suits, it is lucky that it is not sued even more for its mistakes and omissions.

I did get some satisfaction in writing the *New York* magazine article about Julia. Shortly after it appeared, a man in my neighborhood who had had the same kind of mitral valve operation began exhibiting some of the same symptoms. Someone in his family had read the article, became alarmed and called in the doctor. This patient was taken to a hospital before it was too late.

A second case ended more tragically. Only about five weeks after Julia died, one of our life-long friends who worked in a doctor's office asked me to dinner. I had no sooner entered the house than she said to me: "Fred, a man died today who shouldn't have." When I pressed her for more details, professional secrecy took over. "It was exactly the same thing as in Julia's case," she said. "You mean it was a cerebral hemorrhage resulting from Coumadin?" She said, "No names. No names. But, yes, it was the very same thing. My doctor is wild about it. He keeps saying, 'How can they let such things happen?' "

As the result of my writing about Julia's case, I was asked to serve briefly on the Advisory Council on Medical Licensure and Professional Conduct of the New York State Legislature, which was composed largely of doctors and hospital administrators. A highly qualified nursing supervisor and I were among the few outsiders in the group. The council's staff exposed a couple of glaring instances of medical misconduct, but as the meetings dragged on, I became more and more incensed at the prevailing attitude of the medical professionals. When we discussed the need for more community representation on hospital boards, to ensure that the interests of the people the hospital served were honored rather than simply the profession, one of the most arrogant doctors on the panel exclaimed: "We don't care who you put on the boards. You can put on Ralph Nader himself! *We* are still going to run the hospitals."

Except for these efforts, the year after Julia's death was psychologically destructive for me. All during that summer, except for my medical research, I literally stewed, unable to concentrate on anything, unable to stay in the house for more than minutes at a time, unable to stay away from it. I had two contracts for

juvenile nonfiction books that had to be delivered, but I could
not keep my mind on the research. I couldn't keep my mind on
anything. I glanced at the headlines in the newspapers; I never
read the stories. I couldn't even concentrate my attention on the
Watergate hearings that drove Nixon out of office—a spectacle
that under normal circumstances would have had me happily
mesmerized. I would pick up a novel, then put it down; I had no
will to read. I would take my prize collie, Taffy, for a walk, return
home and try to settle down; then jump up in a few minutes, go
to the boardwalk, and pace restlessly up and down. Many nights
I couldn't sleep. I remember one night in late August, about a
month after Julia died, that I took two sleeping pills, and—still
wide awake—tried every bed in the house, never closing my eyes
until I napped for a brief hour just as the sun was coming up.
Periodically, without warning, a great wave of despair would over-
whelm me and I would find myself clutching at the railing of the
boardwalk for support, tears streaming down my face, while my
body heaved with uncontrollable sobs.

Finally, a friend of Julia's and mine, sensitive to my suffering,
offered to introduce me to a widow whom she thought I would
like. "Fred," she said, "you've got to get out of that house. You
can't just sit there with the dog staring at four walls. You have to
have someone you can talk to, or take out to dinner, or go to a
movie with." I shook her off. At sixty-three, I thought, the chances
were one in a million that I could ever adjust to someone else,
or that someone else could ever adjust to me. This went on for
a year. I do not know how much longer I could have stood it.
Fortunately, the bleakest and loneliest day depressed me so much
that it made me desperate to change my life. It was July 4, 1975,
one of the sunniest, most beautiful summer days anyone could
imagine. I took Taffy for her late-afternoon walk through Interlaken; and it was as though the neutron bomb had wiped out all
living things and only she and I had been left. My neighbors next
door, who were usually splashing in their pool, had departed for
the day; my friends across the street were boating on Sandy Hook
Bay; everybody, literally *everybody,* in our whole town seemed
to have vanished. I took Taffy home after our walk, and I said to
myself, "My God, I can't take any more of this." I telephoned
my friend. "Bring on your lovely widow." That was how I came
to meet Irene Line—the best thing that has ever happened to
me.

Irene, who had taught school for forty years, had suffered through more than her share of tragedies: she had been twice widowed. When I came to know her, I marveled at how courageously she had survived the first one. Her husband, David Bryant, was superintendent of a crew working on the construction of a large federal building in Cleveland. On one of those oppressively hot Ohio days, with the temperature somewhere around 110 degrees, David Bryant was supervising a large concrete pour from a high scaffold. No one knew whether he slipped or was overcome by the heat, but he fell to his death. He was to have been on the construction project for two years, and Irene had given up her teaching job in East Orange, New Jersey, to be with him. So suddenly and tragically widowed, with their young son to support, she returned to East Orange and got back into teaching. She resolved, as she later told me, never to marry again until her son, David, was fully grown, and she adhered to that resolution until she had put him through college and saw him launched in business. Only then had she married a friend of long standing, Larry Line, of Interlaken, a man several years older than she. When he died in 1972, she was alone again.

It did not take me long to discover that Irene was a strong and lovable woman. Like Julia, she possessed one of the warmest and most generous of hearts; and with it went a strength of character that I admired. We soon found that we were so much in tune that, when one of us started to say something, we would have to laugh because the other was starting to express the same thought in almost the same words. Almost before I knew how it happened, I realized that I was deeply in love. Irene and I were married in June 1976. With her help, I have been able to rebuild my life and resume the kind of crusading reporting for which I was noted in the past.

This time I undertook to expose the most powerful private complex in America: the consortium of gigantic oil companies that dominates nearly every aspect of American life. I followed the trail of this monopolistic monster for more than three years in articles for *The Nation* (which won me my fourth Newspaper Guild of New York award for crusading reporting); and, after this, I brought all my discoveries together in a book: *The Great Energy Scam: Private Billions vs. Public Good.* The book told the story of the enormous concentration of power held in ever fewer, interlocking hands—an amalgamation of incredible wealth that threatens democracy in America and leaves the great majority of the American people utterly helpless to take any actions affecting their own destiny.

What worries me most as I look back on the power complexes I have exposed is that while huge, secret bureaucracies like the CIA and FBI trample on the rights of a free people with impunity, they are only the excrescences of the real forces at work. The official agencies have been supported in their excesses by an imperial financial empire so powerful that it could bring the whole economy of the nation down in shambles. The phony oil crisis of 1979 illustrated both the power and the ruthlessness of a cabal wedded to one ethic: making profits.

In 1978 a group of collusive oil companies, interlocked with some of the largest banks in the nation through directors sitting on boards of both, began a campaign to drive gasoline prices to more than $1 a gallon, a price unimaginable at that time. This first effort at manipulation failed because it was clear that oil supplies were abundant; then came the Iranian revolution. It gave Big Oil the smokescreen it needed to achieve its long-held objective; and almost before the people of the nation were aware, we had a "crisis" on our hands, with cars stacked up for blocks waiting to get a few gallons of gasoline at the pumps. Almost overnight the whole economy of the nation was disrupted—and, as abundant evidence shows, there was absolutely no necessity for it. The "great Iranian oil crisis" was a ploy to drive both gasoline and No. 2 fuel oil prices to stratospheric levels.

The truth, as numerous but largely suppressed analyses showed, was simple. This country imported only about 4 percent of our crude oil from Iran; this "Iranian shortfall" as it was described by the media was more than compensated for by increased supplies from Saudia Arabia, the North Sea, the North Slope of Alaska, Liberia and Nigeria. One carefully documented U.S. Treasury analysis showed that the big oil companies were actually better off because much of the crude they received from these sources was better than Iranian oil; it contained less sulfur, fewer impurities; it was cheaper to refine; and it yielded more gallons per barrel.

But with the aid of media that took the Establishment's words almost without question, and the support of a supine Carter

Administration, the oil companies promoted the "crisis" to create panic. Allocations to gas stations were cut back, technically by the Department of Energy, actually by the companies themselves, because DOE acted only on what the oil companies told it. When such a panic is created, drivers will pay almost any price to get the fuel they must have; and this is precisely what happened. Gasoline soared high above $1 a gallon; and No. 2 fuel oil, for half a century one of the cheapest products of the refineries, became one of the costliest, tracking right along after gasoline until in one bitter winter it reached $1.30 a gallon.

The whole economy went into a steep decline. Industries, hard-hit like the homeowner, tried to cut their costs, and unemployment became a problem as thousands of workers were fired. The American automobile industry was a casualty. *Technology Review*, the publication of the Massachusetts Institute of Technology, later pointed out that there was a months-long inventory of Japanese cars for which there was little market at the end of 1978; six months later, Japanese cars were at a premium and American automobile plants, with billions of dollars' worth of machinery, were almost obsolete. Airlines that had been paying 10 cents a gallon for jet fuel suddenly had to pay more than $1; and multimillion-dollar deficits began to appear.

Only Big Oil benefited. In one quarter, Exxon posted an incredible net profit of $1.9 billion; and ever since the phony 1979 Iranian oil crisis, its quarterly profits have averaged $1 billion or more. Others in the Big Oil consortium, though smaller, profited in proportion; and they began to buy up America. Major oils gained control of most of the nation's coal and natural gas reserves; they bought the two largest copper companies in the nation; they became huge agribusiness concerns and went into meatpacking. As S. David Freeman, chairman of the Tennessee Valley Authority, told Brian Ross of NBC: "The question is, Are we going to wake up in 1990 and find half a dozen or so major oil companies own all of this nation's energy resources and are charging Arab-style prices for these resources? If we do we will find that they own America."

This was the power complex that I exposed in *The Great Energy Scam* in 1983. By the time the book was published, the phony crisis of 1979 had dissipated; the world was awash in a glut of oil;

and prices had fallen back from their 1979–80 highs. This "fall-back," so comfortingly reported by the major media, ignored a cardinal fact: the 1979 panic had forced prices to a new high plateau, and American consumers would never again see gasoline and heating oil priced below $1 a gallon, a level incredible before the mythical "Iranian shortfall."

Then came the bitterly cold early winter of 1983–84—and another demonstration of the oil cartel's muscle. In one month, from mid-December to mid-January, prices for No. 2 home-heating oil leaped 20 cents a gallon. This at a time when there was no shortage, at a time when there was still an oil glut in the world. The Northeastern states were the prime victims. Energy Commissioner Leonard Coleman, Jr., of New Jersey, reported that retail prices for home-heating oil had leaped to an all-time state high of $1.28 a gallon, and he estimated the extra cost to consumers would be $70 million. Representative Matthew J. Rinaldo, an Elizabeth, New Jersey, Republican, denounced the situation as "outrageous," and he and other congressmen joined with Coleman in calling for investigations by the Federal Trade Commission and the Department of Energy.

I had heard it all before; I had sat through endless hearings productive of much angry rhetoric and no results; and if the federal government ever acts to curb the greed of the all-powerful oil combine, I will be the most amazed man in the world.

I come now to the end of my story. I don't know how much I have accomplished in my years of lonely crusading, but at least I have tried. I have dealt with issues that seemed to me important; issues that I felt *had* to be investigated and exposed. I have told the truth as I found it as honestly and uncompromisingly as I could. This has made me enemies at times; sometimes I have been maligned. It does not matter. I have enjoyed my life. I have relished the hunt, the ferreting out of hidden truths, the challenge of writing about them. I have been, I suppose, much like the seeker of sunken treasure; and many of the satisfactions I have had have been as rewarding, psychologically at least, as the discovery of bullion in a long-lost Spanish galleon. What more can one ask of life?